NEXT TIME ROUND IN PROVENCE

Also by Ian Norrie

A Celebration of London (photographs by Dorothy Bohm)
Hampstead: London Hill Town (photographs by Dorothy Bohm)
The Book of Hampstead (ed. with Mavis Norrie)
The Book of the City (ed)
The Heathside Book of Hampstead and Highgate (ed)
The Book of Westminster (ed)
Writers and Hampstead (compiler)
Hampstead, Highgate and Kenwood: A Short Guide
Sabbatical: Doing Europe for Pleasure

Publishing and Bookselling (with Frank A Mumby)
Publishing and Bookselling in the Twentieth Century
Sixty Precarious Years: A Short History of the National Book
League, 1925-1985
A Hampstead memoir: High Hill Bookshop, 1957-1988

Novels:

Hackles Rise and Fall
Quentin and the Bogomils
Plum's Grand Tour

NEXT TIME ROUND IN PROVENCE

The Vaucluse and Bouches-du-Rhône

IAN NORRIE

with drawings by Michael Floyd

AURUM PRESS   London

A High Hill Book

First published in Great Britain 1993
by Aurum Press Limited, 25 Bedford Avenue
London WC1B 3AT

A High Hill Book

A catalogue record for this book is
available from the British Library.

ISBN 1 85410 239 7

Designed by Ken Garland and Associates

Maps drawn by Colin Bailey

Typeset in Palatino by Dataserve Associates

Printed in Great Britain by
Hartnoll's Limited, Bodmin

For Min with love;
it was her idea that we should
live for a spell in Europe.

The author is deeply grateful to friends and family who read parts of the typescript and made helpful suggestions for its improvement; to Rainer Esslen who read it all and commented in depth, and particularly to Min, who lived through it all, accompanying him on most of his journeys, researching, copy editing and occasionally putting in phrases and sentences of her own which she thought he wouldn't detect.

List of drawings

Contents

VAUCLUSE &
BOUCHES-DU-RHÔNE

FRANCE

Grignan

Valréas • Nyons

Vaison-
la-Romaine

Orange

Sault

Carpentras

Pont du Gard • Avignon

V A U C L U S E

Apt

Nîmes

Cavaillon

B O U C H E S - D U - R H Ô N E

Arles

Salon-
de-Provence

Aigues-
Mortes

ETANG
DE
VACCARES

Aix-
en-Provence

ETANG
DE
BERRE

Marseille

Cassis

M E D I T E R R A N E A N

10   20   30   40   km

'My' Provence

It is early afternoon in February. I am enjoying a picnic in the town of Cadenet whilst watching local lads playing boules on a sloping pitch in front of a bar. Beyond, across the river Durance, are the Trévaresse hills. The sun pours down out of a pure, deep blue sky. I am wearing only slacks and a shirt with sleeves rolled up, and I am pleasantly warm, almost hot. This is the bliss of Provence in winter and my only regret is that Min, who joined me on most of the journeys recorded here, is not sharing the bottle of white Château la Canorgue which I have just uncorked. But she is at work in the garden of the house we have bought in another town some forty kilometres away.

Soon the sun will be obscured by the great steeple of the scaffolded church beside me and I shall climb the hill, honeycombed with once inhabited caves, to the ruins of a château. Cadenet, with its medieval street pattern of precipitous alleys and terraces, its church built and rebuilt over several centuries, its one item of Roman heritage, a sarcophagus now used as a font, its vestigial castle on an eminence, has typical Provençal features. It has also a unique personality but is not so famous that the reader will necessarily have encountered it on a first visit to these parts.

First-time visitors to Provence will concentrate, as we did in 1962, on the major sights and sites. At Avignon they will climb the Rocher des Doms and gaze down at the broken bridge on the Rhône; they will tour the Palace of the Popes. At Arles, Nîmes and Orange they will see splendid Roman remains; at the Pont du Gard, they will look upon the finest of them all. They will journey to the Camargue in search of wild horses, flamingoes and cowboys (there called *gardians*). They will stroll about the small walled town of Aigues-Mortes and perhaps stop at the once tiny fishing village of Stes-Maries-de-la-Mer. At Aix they will stroll beneath the great avenue of trees in the Cours Mirabeau before driving to the Barrage de Bimont to gaze upon the face of Montagne Ste-Victoire. It is unlikely that they will climb that peak on foot but, almost certainly, they will motor over Mont Ventoux before descending to the excavations at Vaison-la-Romaine. They will go to

Fontaine-de-Vaucluse to observe the river Sorgue gushing (or trickling) mysteriously from the foot of the mountain and pay homage, hazily, to a poet they have probably not read. If they achieve all this, plus windswept moments on Les Baux, if they drive in the Dentelles de Montmirail, clamber about a couple of *villages perchés* in the Luberon, and pant their way up to the ruined palace at Châteauneuf-du-Pape, they will have done well. They will also be on, or even over, the verge of cultural indigestion.

This account does not ignore star attractions. I love all of them, even the interior of the papal palace now that a guided tour is no longer obligatory, but I have proportionately less to say about them than about other places. My theme is Next Time Round. It may be the second, third, fourth time. That is why I devote more space to St-Michel-de-Frigolet than to the lovely church of St-Trophime at Arles; why I concentrate more on the castle at Ansouis than on the grim Château d'If, where the 'Count of Monte-Cristo' was imprisoned, and give greater length to Fabre's house and garden at Sérignan and to Cadenet, than to the arena at Nîmes, or to that windmill at Fontvieille known as Daudet's. Also why I draw attention to the exceptionally well presented Félix Ziem museum at Martigues, yet all but ignore Cézanne's atelier at Aix.

The first night of my life spent outside Britain was at Marseille where the recorded history of Provence began about six hundred years before the birth of Christ. It was 1946. I was eighteen. By the time my daughters had attained that age they had travelled far and wide in Europe but my parents did not take continental holidays – to which World War Two anyhow put a stop.

The earliest known traders came over the water to Marseille; I arrived by air in a Sunderland flying boat which must have touched down on the Etang de Berre, the inland sea now so heavily industrialised and polluted. The Royal Air Force had posted me to Bombay where it was intended that I should take shorthand notes at a court martial. I, a recent conscript, flew with middle-ranking officers of two services, which led to a droll encounter at the BOAC terminal at Victoria.

'Your name please, sir,' asked a clerk without looking up.

'Norrie.'

'Yes sir. Air Commodore Norrie?'

'No. Air*craftman.*'

However, the officers were democrats and treated me civilly, one of them including me in the party he took to dinner in Marseille, where we all stayed at the Hôtel Splendide. It was situated in a typically rowdy street where people shouted slogans and banged shutters for most of the night. I became convinced that actual riots were occurring on the balcony of my room and cowered under the blankets. Would 'abroad' be all like this, I wondered.

I never took notes at that court martial because the RAF 'lost' me on a transit camp near Karachi – but that is another story. Its relevance to this one is that on those drives to and from the flying boat I saw, for the first time, part of the enchanted Provençal landscape which I have loved ever since. I was not to see it again until 1962 but, after that, it became so familiar that it was natural, when looking for a second home, to seek it there, although not close to the huge conurbation that Marseille had become by 1988.

Min and I had stayed several times at a friend's house in the town of Bédarrides which is rapidly becoming part of extended Avignon. From there, to reach Fontaine-de-Vaucluse, we had to pass through L'Isle-sur-la-Sorgue, an attractive place built beside several strands of the river on which there are many weed-bedecked water wheels. Some instinct suggested we should stop for lunch. The town made an instant appeal, so we visited an

L'Isle-sur-la-Sorgue

11

estate agent who showed us a compact villa on a small estate close to the centre. We bought it the following year. The formalities were few, the bureaucracy surprisingly streamlined. We congratulated ourselves on purchasing a modern property in which we could start living straightaway. Several friends had fallen for old farmhouses in advanced states of decay. 'No running water,' one of them shrieked, 'no electricity. It's bliss!'. We looked smug, and said ours was fit for instant occupation.

It wasn't. In the first instance, the agent, as an act of *gentillesse* on our behalf, had given permission for the elderly vendors to remain in residence for ten days after completion because the flat to which they were moving was not immediately available. So we paid £40 per day to stay in an excellent nearby hotel. Had my command of French been better I would have asked the notary conducting the deal if the vendors would be meeting the bill. Min could have done so but she doesn't make scenes. Thus, although the house was ours on June 2, the keys were not until the 12th. Nor did we move in then because whilst there was running water and electricity, the latter was represented by bare wires dangling from the ceilings and walls, and both bathroom and loo are interior rooms in the French style. It is apparently the custom to dismantle all shelving, remove all fitments and to leave a veritable shell for the new occupant. Our net gains were a broken lawnmower, a television aerial allowing for restricted viewing, a large frying pan with holes in it for roasting chestnuts, the base for a sun umbrella and the vendors' modest picnic lunch which they left by mistake. We did not move in for a further eight days by which time half the work force of L'Isle had been engaged to make our house habitable.

Neighbours firmly advised us to have a well sunk which was how we came to employ – in addition to a mason, electrician, painter, decorator, carpenter, locksmith, plumber, gardener and curtain-maker – a waterdiviner.

But we did not endure such tribulations as Peter Mayle describes in *A Year in Provence*, his amusing account of moving into an older property in the nearly Luberon. Our workmen were reliable and punctual and, unlike their British counterparts, they did not request interim payments every second day or expect mugs of hot, sweet tea at hourly intervals. Thanks to them, 'instant occupation' became reality within a short while.

Thus L'Isle-sur-la-Sorgue became the base for most of the journeys to places here described, although sometimes we went on safari, staying in comfortable hôtels in the Bouches-du-Rhône, or northern parts of the Vaucluse, the two departments which I believe encompass the greater part of essential Provence.

To the enquiry *where* is Provence, the simple answer is that it is an area bordering the Mediterranean in south-east France. There is no simple way, however, of defining its precise borders unless we are prepared to accept the official designation of its present regional status, clumsily labelled Provence-Alpes-Côte-D'Azur. This comprises the two departments mentioned above plus the Var and three others with Alpine names.

If we look at the map of the Roman province on the wall of the museum at Vaison we see that its extent far outstripped the present administrative region of France. It stretched northwards to Vienne and Geneva and beyond Toulouse to the west. In medieval times, during the Renaissance and long after, the boundaries and identity of Provence changed as the result of conquest, marriage and death. Quite recently, Corsica was improbably added to it until, under Mitterrand, that island became a region in its own right.

So I don't have to feel inhibited by ancient frontiers which were never constant for long, or by more recent boundaries formed by the eighteenth-century decree that no department should be so large that its prefect could not visit any part of it on horseback within a day. 'My' Provence, then, is limited to the Vaucluse and the Bouches-du-Rhône but takes in small areas of the Gard, the Drôme, Alpes-de-Haute Provence, and once makes a brief sally into the Var. If it did not include the Gard, for instance, Nîmes would be omitted along with part of the Camargue, Beaucaire (though not Tarascon on the opposite bank of the Rhône) and Villeneuve-lès-Avignon. Also, the Pont du Gard. So that will not do.

My method is personal. There are no catalogues of church furnishings, no brick-by-brick examinations of west fronts, no canvas-by-canvas countdowns of famous collections. Nor do I mention every ruined castle or church of twelfth-century origin. Some of the one are hauntingly impressive, some of the other surpassingly beautiful, but it is not so in every instance. By and large, fonts and altar-pieces do not have much to say to me. I prefer the architecture of churches to the ornament, the outside to the inside. I am repelled by gaudy baroquerie. As for secular buildings whose remains are scant, the rewards of contemplating them are, to non-specialists, minimal. One should not pretend otherwise.

Almost everywhere in 'my' Provence signs of ancient life have been found, neolithic, perhaps mesolithic, occasionally palaeolithic. Until we get to the Greeks and Romans and the tribes they disturbed not much remains to be seen. Only the practised eye will perceive an earthwork four or five thousand years old. Small artefacts – tools, cooking utensils, shards – such as are to be found under the glass cases in the museum at Vaison are not exciting to most of us but we must respect them for what they tell the experts to tell us about the past. We can relate more easily to the evidence of Roman existence of which there is much. Inevitably there is even more of Romanesque, and that has the stamp of a lifetime's familiarity because a twelfth-century church is as instantly recognisable for its function as one built in our own time. Most have suffered depredation, alteration, decay, as well as from changes in the social pattern; most have continued as places of worship almost uninterruptedly for seven hundred years or more. They have been rebuilt, restored, enlarged, according to the needs of the moment. Many underwent temporary secularisation, many were merged with other buildings, so that it is common for shops and houses to be part of them.

The object of travel, for me, is to experience the quality of life in another land. It is not to 'do' Provence, or anywhere else, with the urgency of one who must have six churches, three châteaux and a cloister under his belt by lunchtime. Better the enchantment which comes from strolling around in an unfamiliar landscape and learning about it gradually. In France, given the obsession with closing almost everything from midday until mid-afternoon, plus shutting museums and galleries on Tuesdays and holidays, blocking roads in order to resurface the entire width in one prolonged operation, and boarding-up ancient monuments for months, or even years of total rehabilitation, you are fortunate to see a quarter of what is on your itinerary. It doesn't matter. There is so much on offer that you can look at something else instead.

In that spirit, drive with me, mostly on secondary roads (deviations allowing), often down veritable lanes, seldom, if ever, on motorways, and walk with me in villages and cities, on foothills and mountains, to savour 'my' Provence and agree or disagree with my prejudices. All travel should be undertaken in a state of joyous anticipation of the marvels to come, and of readiness to be indignant about what 'they' have caused to happen, and of what 'he' has had the audacity to write.

To understand the present it helps to take at least a brief look at the past.

The known chronology begins about 600BC when Phocaean traders (Greeks from Asia Minor) landed near present-day Marseille. They were not the first to step ashore – there had been Carthaginians, and other Greeks from Rhodes – but they were the first about whom something particular is known. They were greeted by friendly indigenous Ligurian tribesmen whose welcome was exceptionally cordial because the local chief's daughter was about to be wed, though to whom was yet to be decided. It was her right to choose the man who most attracted her; when she selected a Phocaean Greek Massalia was effectively founded. There is no way of authenticating this romantic episode, but that Marseille was a Greek city is fact and the writer, Freda White, insisted that in the features of its citizens Greek characteristics could be detected two-and-a-half millennia later.

The Ligurians also welcomed Celtic tribes from the north and inter-married. One result of the union was the emergence of the Salyans who settled at Entremont, a hill to the north of what is now Aix-en-Provence. Theirs was an advanced culture as is evident from artefacts in the Granet Museum at Aix, but they did not inherit the overall geniality of the Ligurians. They indulged an unpleasant cult of decapitation which some historians attribute to their Celtic origins.

The Carthaginians continued to visit, both as traders and raiders, and wrested control of Massalia from the Greeks for more than sixty years, during the fifth to fourth centuries BC. About two hundred years later, Hannibal, their most famous general, made his extraordinary invasion of Italy by leading his army and elephants over the Pyrénées and the Alps, passing through Provence en route. Meanwhile Rome had superseded Greece as the dominant power in the Mediterranean and Massalia had become its ally so, when the Salyans became hostile, it was the Romans who were called upon to vanquish them. The tribesmen were duly defeated at Entremont and Rome won a foothold in the region.

The Salyans having been suppressed and Aix founded, there was an even more impressive encounter with invading hordes of Teutons twenty years later. The barbarians swept in from northern Europe looking for an entry into Italy but marching, at first, towards Spain. When they reached the Rhône, in the vicinity of Arles, they changed direction eastwards. The Roman general Marius laid a trap, allowing them to pass his encampment near present-day St-Rémy, and head for the rest of his army which lay in wait beyond Aix. There, under the shadow of Montagne Ste-Victoire, the Teutons were massacred.

Fifty years later the Greeks unwisely backed Pompey in the civil war against Marius' nephew, Julius Caesar, who besieged and conquered Massalia. Its importance thereafter diminished, because Caesar's favoured city in what was soon to be declared the first Roman province outside Italy was Arles which, with Nîmes, was at the height of its glory in the first centuries AD. Before the golden age of indirect Roman rule blossomed, further tribesmen, mostly in the Alpine regions, were repelled by Augustus, the first emperor. It was he who granted something like autonomy to Provence ten years before the birth of Christ.

The Christian presence in Provence came early with the arrival of Trophime whom St Peter sent to spread the word in Gaul. He was in advance of a boatload of saints said to have landed on the shores of the Camargue where the resort of Stes-Maries-de-la-Mer now spreads into the hinterland. Two of the Marys (Salomé and Jacobé) remained there, another, Mary Magdalene, took Lazarus, brother of Martha, to Ste-Baume. Martha went to Tarascon where she rid the citizens of a terrifying beast by confronting it with a cross. (The subduing of monsters by brave Christians is a feature of Provençal history at this time.) It is not known if any of them met

Trophime who was busy proselytising in the region. His most notable convert was a senior Roman official at Arles, the city where he is best remembered. In the fourth century a more eminent convert, the Emperor Constantine, had his headquarters there before selecting Byzantium as his capital.

The Roman province was first based on Narbonne (today in the Aude) but in 284AD it was split into two, divided by the Rhône. That part to the west of the river retained the name of Narbonensis; the territory to the east was called Viennoise.

Roman domination ended in the fifth century. Then Provence entered a long period of invasion by Visigoths, Burgundians, Saxons, Franks and Saracens until Charlemagne became Holy Roman Emperor in 800AD. His grandsons eventually split the Carolingian domain into three. The middle section went to Lothair who created the kingdom of Provence. This lasted precariously into the eleventh century when it was again absorbed into the Holy Roman Empire, wherein it stayed for about one hundred years. There was, however, still a high degree of autonomy allowed to the counts of Provence who prospered because their territory lay on routes of both pilgrimage and trade.

From the mid-twelfth century the counts of Toulouse ruled one part of Provence and the counts of Barcelona the other, but there were constant boundary changes thanks to marriage contracts and plunder. Confusingly many of these counts bore the same name – Raymond. The Barcelona ones had a Bérenger added, or sometimes prefixed, and the last of them, Raymond Bérenger V, drove the Toulousians out of their local lands. He also reformed the laws and the administration but died young.

Against this background the troubadours flourished at the so-called courts of love, and western lyric poetry was born. Strangely, although they came from many parts of France, Italy and Spain, they wrote and sang in the Provençal language. Less pleasingly the Albigensian crusade was waged when the Roman church became fearful of the Cathars, pious heretics whose behaviour had been mild enough for them to be left in peace until dogmatists became assertive. Their barbarous extermination brought back the authority of the church with a vengeance and provoked a long-lasting schism in which the lands of the Comtat Venaissin were wrested from the counts as retribution for having sided with the Albigensians. (The area included much of modern Vaucluse.)

In the early fourteenth century Pope Clement (a Frenchman), finding life in Rome dangerous, was permitted by King Philip IV (who had been excommunicated by an earlier pontiff) to transfer his throne to Avignon. There the popes remained, through the horrors of the Black Death, for most of the century but, even after their return to Rome in 1376, there were alternative princes of the church, known as anti-popes, who clung to office for another thirty-five years.

The last count of Provence to remain independent of France was Good King René. After the terrible fourteenth century, with its plagues and papal quarrels, there could only be an improvement. This was symbolised by the foundation of a university at Aix in 1409. René, who was Duke of Anjou and King of Sicily (the latter only in name) became Count of Provence in 1434 and lived from 1470 in Aix where he was admired as a scholar and a painter, a linguist and musician, and also as poet and peasant, it being his custom to join the workers in the vineyards. After his death in 1480, his nephew ceded both Provence and Anjou to France. This left the Comtat and Avignon still in papal hands while Nice, plus parts of eastern Provence, was under the house of Savoy. The whole, difficult as ever to define, remained fragmented.

Fifty years on the Holy Roman Empire returned temporarily under Charles V. Further religious persecution soon followed, directed against adherents of the protestant Vaudois sect which, although declared heretic centuries before, had remained undisturbed in several villages of the Luberon. In 1545 one of them, Mérindol, was destroyed by a decree of the Aix parliament after the Vaudois had sacked Sénanque abbey. Inevitably this provoked a wholesale massacre of the sect in several centres and heralded the appalling Wars of Religion (not confined to Provence) lasting from 1560 until the Edict of Nantes was proclaimed in 1598, by Henri of Navarre. That admirable monarch tactfully allowed himself to be 'converted' to Rome before giving Protestants the right to worship freely. In Provence both factions waged war intermittently for nearly forty years leaving a trail of blood and butchery. After the Edict Protestants as well as Catholics could attend to praising their Lord instead of murdering each other. That is until Louis XIV revoked it, almost a century later, driving hundreds of thousands of Huguenots into exile.

During the fourteenth Louis' last years, the anomaly of the Principality of Orange was tidied up by its absorption into France. Orange had been independent since the eleventh century, although its territory had been reduced from time to time. It belonged to the Dutch house of Nassau and provided England with a king, William III. Even by Provençal standards this item of history is bizarre.

Following the Revolution of 1789 the Comtat and Avignon at last became part of a France in which Christianity, but not murder, was outlawed. The boundaries of 83 departments were drawn, or re-drawn, to make most of them of equal size. The Comtat was integrated into Vaucluse, including the separate territory of Valréas which was entirely surrounded by the Drôme.

After the Revolution came the Terror which was succeeded by

Napoléon as Emperor, a brief return of the monarchy and then, in 1848, the Second Republic. This quickly gave way to the Second Empire under Napoléon III, since whose defeat in the Prussian War of 1870 France has remained a republic.

Despite the unsettled conditions of France during most of the nineteenth century this was the time in which Provence, and especially the south-eastern part of it, including the Côte d'Azur, attracted tourists, particularly from Britain. The coast from Cannes to Menton was colonised. Avignon, too, became popular whilst the antiquities attracted increasing numbers. In 1882 Henry James wrote:

> It was a pleasure to feel oneself in Provence again – the land where the silver-grey earth is impregnated with the light of the sky. To celebrate the event, as soon as I arrived at Nîmes I engaged a *calèche*. to convey me to the Pont du Gard.

In 1830 Frédéric Mistral was born, the poet who devoted his life to reviving the Provençal language which had ceased to be officially recognised in 1539. He led a group of writers and others, known as the *Félibrige*, who did more than invest an old tongue with new life. They re-established Provence as a region proud of its heritage and did so peaceably. Thus their nationalism was tolerable and has its innocent fruit today in the dual signposts which, for instance, show in French, AVIGNON, and in Provençal, AVIGNOUN. Slightly more interestingly, FONTAINE-DE-VAUCLUSE becomes VAU-CLUSO LA FONT.

James's enthusiasm for Provence was echoed by countless foreign writers over the next hundred years. Many settled in the land which in 1939 Ford Madox Ford heavily romanticised, in a volume simply entitled *Provence;* although much of the book is about London or any other subject which sprang to his mind. It was to be the last evocation for several years.

World War One did not reach these parts though thousands of Provençal men were needlessly slaughtered in the trenches of Picardie and the Marne. When the Germans invaded France in 1940 Provence was, for a while, in unoccupied territory but, in November 1942, such neutrality as it had enjoyed, ended. Two years later the Allies made landings on the Mediterranean coast and once again the area experienced conflict. Memorials to the Resistance fighters, and to one outstanding leader, Jean Moulin, who harried the enemy from within before the Liberation, are to be seen in many towns and villages.

Since 1945 the south of France remains as popular as ever and Provence shares with the Dordogne and the Roussillon an attraction for foreigners in search of second, or even permanent, homes. The telephone directories of Vaucluse and Bouches-du-Rhône are sprinkled with British, Dutch and German names but this does not as yet seem to upset the Proven-

18

çals who are as welcoming to the twentieth-century invaders as the Ligurians were to the Phocaeans. At least, that is how we find them.

'My' Provence covers an area of approximately 8,500 square miles, which sounds huge. In fact it is 152km (95 miles) from Grignan, in the north, to the Mediterranean, and 144km (90 miles) from Nîmes across to the Bouches-du-Rhône/Var boundary. A contemporary prefect would find no difficulty in traversing the territory of two departments three or four times in a single day. If he did he would pass through a wondrous variety of country.

There are two high peaks, Mont Ventoux, in the north but visible from the sea, and Montagne Ste-Victoire, which stands guard over Aix. In the centre, running east-west, are the Luberon ranges facing, northwards, the Plateau de Vaucluse across the fertile valley of the Coulon (sometimes called the Calavon). To the west of Ventoux are the hills of the Dentelles de Montmirail with their savagely sharp peaks, matched south of Avignon by the Alpilles. Other, smaller mountains rise behind Marseille and from the left bank of the Rhône. The latter mighty river flows down the western part of 'my'region and has two outlets to the sea; the now tamed Durance joins it near Avignon. The waters of both have been manipulated to help irrigate the once stony and desolate Crau and other plains. Only the Camargue, much of it reclaimed marshland and salt-flats, is relentlessly close to sea level. The richly cultivated land varies between gentle undulation and steep foot-hills. Parts of northern Vaucluse give an impression of one vast vineyard. Elsewhere orchards and olive groves alternate with fields of cereals and vegetables. There is little woodland except on the mountainsides but many trees, planted as windshields or to provide shade. Typical of the region are tall thin cypresses, umbrella and other pines, almonds and the great planes which still line the roads so spectacularly though many are now diseased. In the *garrigue* country, close to Marseille, around Nîmes and also on the Vaucluse plateau, two short but sturdy species of oak proliferate among the lavender and herbs on the limestone heathland. There is not much pasture land, and the decline of sheep rearing has unfortunately increased the danger of fire because the animals are no longer there to nibble away the highly inflammable undergrowth.

Wild, haunting gorges are a reminder of primeval times when Tyrrhenia sank to become part of the Mediterranean and high folds formed above an emergent Rhône valley, long, long before the Ligurian chieftain affably awarded his daughter to a visiting Greek. They contrast with narrow lanes leading to remote abbeys. There are also nature reserves and forest walks on high ridges whilst almost anywhere you happen to be in Provence you will be close to a stupendous view. Nor will you ever be far from an

19

impressive Roman remain, several clutches of Romanesque churches, numerous châteaux bearing the scars of a tempestuous history, and culinary delights emanating from both land and sea.

Marseille and Avignon have already spread too much and most towns are following the national pattern of spilling into industrial and commercial complexes on their perimeters. Despite these monstrous growths of enormous cheap metal buildings painted in strident colours which deface the urban scene, there remain wide stretches of country dotted with small communities. A particular feature of Provence is the *villages perchés* (hill towns); another is the special light about which writers have often waxed lyrical and which some painters have at least partially succeeded in capturing on canvas.

Then there is the mistral, the fierce north wind which blasts down the Rhône valley, permanently bending trees, scattering garden furniture, tearing at shutters, sweeping away dust and leaves and, in some instances so it is related, bludgeoning individuals into black, murderous rages or insanity. That is the mistral (the word derives from the Provençal 'mistrau' meaning 'master') at its worst. There are times in the long hot summer when it is a relief to body and spirit. And it does not always blow. There are other winds of Provence; postcards are sold naming them, but the mistral is the one which is talked about, the one blamed for all excesses of temper both in man and nature.

I have recommended some hôtels and restaurants from personal experience but I do not attempt to compete with the indispensable Michelin Red Guide, or with its companion in green which is the most reliable I know for current opening times and admission prices to museums, public buildings and archaeological sites. During my bookselling years I sold thousands of Michelin guides, I wrote in praise of them in the trade press, I lectured about them enthusiastically to an audience seated on cane chairs in a library in Muswell Hill. I was that dedicated. Michelin's regularly updated guides should be part of your baggage; so should their 1/200 000 – 1cm:2km maps, especially now that they are indexed. (For this region use nos. 81, 83, 84.)

So this is a personal assessment of the region, probing into corners ignored by the standard guides and stirring up dust in areas cursorily brushed by them. Next-time-round itineraries are suggested but readers will adapt them to their requirements because that is part of the fun of travel. Four of the cities rate separate chapters; parking is easy in all of them except Marseille. For historical and personal reasons that's where I ought to start my journey – if you come by air to Marignane and hire a car, perhaps *you* will – but I will approach from the north, a latterday descendant of the Celts and Normans, come hither with peaceful intent.

20

1   A pocket of Vaucluse and some of the Drôme

Grignan : Valréas : Nyons : Vaison-la-Romaine

It is appropriate to begin with Grignan because that was next time round for us in 1989 when we drove south to buy a house. It had not lain in our path before because I favour routes approaching Provence through the Ardèche, and staying west of the Rhône until close to Vaucluse. But Grignan is legitimately named the northern gateway to the region and the view from the castle terrace makes a magnificent introduction. To reach it from the right bank of the Rhône you cross the river near Donzère and strike eastwards. All the set pieces are to be observed with the great plain of the Venaissin far ahead bordered by papal palaces. To the left are Mont Ventoux and the Dentelles de Montmirail, the latter from this angle looking more benign than from east or west. Nearer on the same side is the Lance Range with Mont Rachas its highest peak. In the foreground the belfry of Chamaret stands out clearly above copses and fields in which gleamingly smart villas are set. From the south-west terrace, below which are the tiled roofs of the village in various colours from grey to terracotta, the hills of the Rouvergue can be seen and, to the north, the Grignan woods and the heights of the Ardèche.

Grignan is also an appropriate starting point because it exemplifies the adjustable boundaries of Provence. The Adhémar family who built the château here in the mid-sixteenth century provided governors for the region. Grignan is no longer officially part of Provence but its Comte in the late seventeenth century was lieutenant-governor. He was also son-in-law to Madame de Sévigné who wrote many of her letters from his château or, when the detested mistral blew, from the nearby Grotte de Rochecourbière. The castle was so much altered in the Renaissance that its medieval origins were almost totally obscured. Later it decayed, to be restored just prior to World War One. It dominates the village to an even greater extent than do most châteaux, overlooking concentric terraces of narrow streets, some with the houses forming the uprights of frequent flying buttresses.

Madame de Sévigné paid several visits, adored the cuisine and spoke enthusiastically of doves, partridges and quails which were served to her. She died here of exhaustion after nursing her beloved daughter. She had

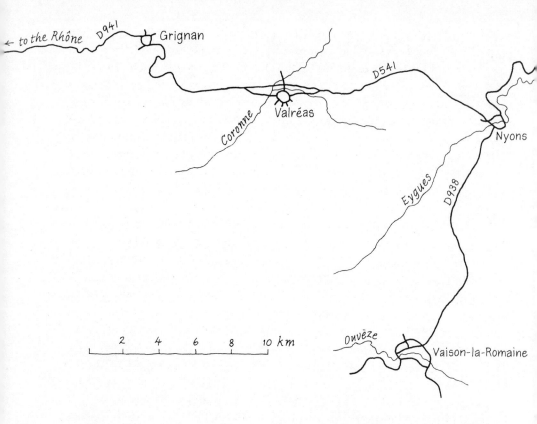

wished to avoid this particular fate because it was the local custom for a dead woman to be buried with her face exposed. Her body was to suffer further indignities when phrenologists vandalised her tomb in the eighteenth century and carried off a chip of her skull to Paris for examination. Her remains lie in the sixteenth-century church of St-Sauveur which was once connected to the castle.

The Comte de Grignan and his successors were recklessly improvident, making additions to the castle of costly architectural subtlety. The shape of many of the chambers defies geometrical definition. The first attempt of restoration in this century was by an American who also ran short of money, but after the first world war a Madame Fontaine completed the work as a labour of love.

The guided tour takes an hour, starting in a vaulted chamber a few steps up off the grand staircase. A table is laid with candelabra on a white cloth but that is the only adornment to distract you. I found the fifteen-minute introductory lecture in very rapid French unintelligible and, because there was nothing to look at, tedious. The visit came alive when we were released on to the staircase hung with paintings, one of them a portrait of the benefactress, Madame Fontaine. You are then shown bedrooms, ante-rooms and a King's Room with an enormous billiard table at the centre. Apparently, to French monarchs, billiards was a form of croquet adapted for playing at table level to obviate having to bend over the royal paunch. There is a draughty Bishop's Room with a small chapel conveniently beside it and a finely panelled music gallery which is used nowadays for live concerts. In another chamber is a Pleyel piano. Almost everywhere in Provence you will find evidence of music-making – from opera and Dixieland performed in the open air, to quartets and vocal ensembles in churches and theatres. At Grignan you can spend the intervals during recitals on the spacious terraces, perhaps admiring the roof where, instead of balustrades, there are *pots à feu,* carved to resemble vases holding flaming torches.

We stayed at the Hôtel Sévigné which Michelin rates as 'quite comfortable'. it doesn't have a restaurant but there is a garage. The patronne takes seriously the new regulations about hoteliers being required to speak some English and goes further by providing sharp-flavoured home-made marmalade at breakfast. She cannot tolerate the stuff herself, so she said, nor did it draw looks of envy from elderly, cloth-capped men who looked in for a pastis and a read of the morning paper. But I found it a welcome change from the sugary substance usually offered in tiny, plastic containers with the bleak so-called continental breakfast. Not far from the hôtel is the restaurant L'Eau à la-Bouche with a beamed dining-room and, when seasonal, open wood fire. Herbs and everlasting flowers hang from the ceiling, pictures of rabbits and cats decorate the walls. There is a handsome 'period' dresser. The food is excellent, but all comments on catering are subject to the warning that a change of management and/or chef may invalidate them.

Madame de Sévigné's grotto lies to the south of the town down a turning, marked No Entry Except for Residents, just off the road to Valréas (D941). In true French style you ignore this admonishment and take a bumpy ride for a kilometre until parking is indicated under trees beside a field of lavender and a new plantation of poplars. You then search for the grotto calling on such resources of wolf-cub initiative as may be latent in you. Reached up stone steps it lies under an overhang of rock. It is not one of the major sights of the region. Your reward comes on returning along the lane and seeing the château high, high above you. Now you will understand why Grignan has been called 'The Gateway to Provence'.

Grignan is in the Drôme which entirely surrounds a pocket of the Vaucluse. Valréas is the principal town, proudly proclaiming itself a papal enclave. Holy Father John XXII purchased it with the long-term intention of joining it to the Comtat, but in the following century Charles VII of France thought, not unreasonably, that such expansionist leanings should be curbed and forbade the sale of any more land to the Church. It did not, however, become a part of France until the rest of Vaucluse was surrendered by the Vatican after the Revolution. The ramparts of the town have gone, replaced by a broken circle of plane trees now lining the ring road. The basically Romanesque church, set at an angle to a scruffy square, is a riot of differing styles. The overall design is obscure but pleasing. It has, like many others in Provence, evolved with the centuries but whereas most show clear scars of battle, and some have made little attempt at recovery, Notre-Dame-de-Nazareth at Valréas seems to have enjoyed loving care at every stage of its metamorphoses, both inside and out. The decoration is sparse thus highlighting what is in fact a fairly simple carved south door. As if to compensate for a lack of architectural grandeur there is a massive organ at the west end of the nave in spirited Baroque, with three trumpeters rising from it. The octagonal bell-tower is veritable Romanesque. Close to it, standing alone, as is often the case in this area, is another. Note the beautiful tiling of the church roof; also the carvings, albeit badly eroded, on either side of the south door.

The free-standing bell-tower was built for the Cordeliers in 1459 and used as a barracks in the Revolution. It is now a theatre. There is another theatre, open air, in the Place de-l'Hôtel-de-Ville, and a third can be erected in a small courtyard which is also a through passage behind the town hall. (There are almost as many stages as there are concert platforms in Provence.) The wings of the Hôtel de Ville, which has a fine façade, now house municipal offices but the upper parts of the main building are used for exhibitions. Formerly, this was a residence of the Marquis de Simiane who married Madame de Sévigné's granddaughter.

Valréas is a busy commercial and light industrial town, also a market for the Coronne Valley which we leave as we take the hilly road back into the Drôme. It leads to Nyons, a centre of the olive oil industry and famous for its black olives in brine, an ingredient of *daube de Provence*, as the delectable local stew is called. Nyons is on the river Eygues at the point where it emerges from a gorge and enjoys a micro-climate excluding the mistral. (Did Madame de Sévigné know?) There are several mills close to the water and two large car parks. Some of the mills not only have sales rooms for products of the olive tree but also offer conducted tours. We visited one named Autrand where there is a video on which you may watch the various processes and perhaps understand them better than if you were shuffling along in a column. Almost next to the mill is a passage into the old town with its many narrow streets lined with tall buildings, several leading from the Place du Dr-Bourdongle which is arcaded against the sun.

The church is of minimal interest. Pass it to reach the Pont Roman which is neither Roman nor Romanesque but fifteenth century though it looks older. It has a single humped-back ('Devil's) arch of beautiful proportions,

Nyons: Tour Randonne

superbly spanning the Eygues and still used by motor traffic. Return to the church and take the steep Rue des Petits-Forts, a cobbled way rising to the Rue Cavalaire past houses which you may well feel pleased not to inhabit when you think of bringing home the shopping. (One resourceful resident has a pulley below the high wall of his home.) Halfway up, if you turn very sharply left and walk a few paces, you will suddenly see the Tour Randonne leaping at the sky. It is a tripartite skeletal stone steeple topped with a madonna, standing on a small chapel erected upon one of the old forts. The chapel was built as a sanctuary and opened in 1863 by the Curé of Nyons. The interior is tiny and occupied mostly by a gaudy altar set between two narrow staircases rising to a platform. The forecourt has a little shady garden. The cobbled way (don't miss the Passage du Ha! Ha!) is probably preferable to the more smoothly-surfaced but steeper path which runs roughly parallel. The latter is solely for the very sure-footed. It leads to an eerie covered passage, Rue des Grands-Forts, where many houses are built into both the rock and the remains of the Château féodal. A massive well-preserved tower lies at the end of it. Nyons is well worth a detour.

Cross the river and make your way to Vaison-la-Romaine – unless you feel an urge for further panoramic views from the Promenade des Anglais et de Vaulx, a narrow five-mile stretch of road to the north-west of the town. The journey to Vaison is through soothing olive groves and farms.

Vaison is different from other towns in Provence with extensive Roman remains. At Arles and Nîmes the medieval towns grew, literally, in and around the great amphitheatres. At Vaison the people of the Middle Ages built on a hill across the river Ouvèze, away from the Roman sites which are now surrounded by the modern town.

Vaison-la-Romaine is a marginal first-time-round date, and if a visit was made it was probably confined to the excavations. For next-time-rounders it is not only rewarding in itself but makes an ideal centre for touring the northern Vaucluse and the Dentelles de Montmirail.

Overlooking the principal Roman site is the Hôtel du Théâtre Ancien where we stayed in 1979. Min recognised the bar as that used as a setting in a BBC-TV French Course. This was confirmed by the patronne who was still outraged, years later, by the fact that, with characteristically auntyish discretion, the name of the town was changed to Montmirail. She brooded on the lost publicity but was pleased my wife had identified her establishment. Attached to it is a restaurant where we have eaten more recently. A friend wishing to lunch us well poked her nose into the dining-room and inhaled aromas coming from the kitchen. They were proclaimed 'authentic'. She was right.

When the Romans arrived 'Vaison' was occupied by a Celtic tribe,

26

Vaison-la-Romaine: Old Town

the Vocontii, who accepted them peacefully as conquerors. The settlement, then as now protected from the worst ravages of the mistral, soon became prosperous and fashionable, an important Roman outpost and a major city of the Provincia Narbonensis. Vasio, as it was known, flourished until the fall of the Empire when the Burgundians took it, followed by the Goths. Yet before the Romans departed it was already, in the fourth century, the seat of a bishopric.

In the twelfth century the Counts of Toulouse imposed their authority, erecting a castle which was rebuilt in the fifteenth, and the remains of which still dominate the upper town. The cathedral of Notre-Dame-de-

Nazareth, founded on the site of a Roman temple, was abandoned when life in the valley became unsafe. The populace looked to the protection of the lords in the castle and settled in terraces of houses around the hill, where another church was built and also a palace for the bishop. There is a clock-tower, too, of great elegance apart from its clumsy base.

This was Vaison for several centuries until it was again deemed safe to live beside the river. By the 1890s the upper town was all but aban-doned. The new cathedral which had acquired a Baroque frontage was closed and eventually deconsecrated. The houses fell into ruin. Notre-Dame-de-Nazareth was once more the centre of spiritual life. But, as happened elsewhere, the zest for rehabilitating decrepit structures and transforming them into ateliers for painters and potters manifested itself. In its wake came the restaurateurs and hoteliers so, today, the town on the hill lives again. The church is still in a poorly way although exhibitions are mounted there, and the castle is no more than a gaunt keep reached over slippery terrain. But the freshly cobbled streets have a central track of asphalt making for easy walking, small gardens are maintained beside some of the restored houses and the whole has an air of prosperity. From the castle there is a view of the newer new town and also of the Roman sites which, at this distance, look to be smaller than the car parks between them.

Notre-Dame-de-Nazareth apparently gets older the more the experts examine it. Apart from the use of Roman columns and foundations, which to medieval masons was obviously good stone husbandry, excavations in the 1950s brought other features to light. When the choir was lowered to its original level, foundations from the fifth and sixth centuries AD were discovered. The beautifully preserved apse, with an ancient altar in an arched nook over the bishop's throne, and various wall tombs, are quietly impress-ive. In the centre is a larger altar table behind which lies the sarcophagus of St. Quenin, a native of Vaison who became bishop from 556-575. On the north side is a cloister which is also a small museum. To enter you must leave the cathedral, walk past the east end and pay a few francs (unless you have an overall ticket which takes in the antiquities as well). The exhibits include a finely carved marble tomb. Some of the capitals of the actual cloister have been well-restored or, perhaps, newly imagined. Against the north wall of the nave of the cathedral can be seen a lengthy inscription not easily comprehensible. It seems to be an admonition to the monks to 'watch out'.

The exterior of Notre-Dame-de-Nazareth is equally appealing, another of those superbly simple Provençal churches which do not quite fit to a pattern. There are, as so often is the case, unexpected additions to the apse. The architects were never inhibited by following a style book, if one existed, so here we have a rather low, square tower joined to the end of a side aisle and a semi-circular kind of oubliette, with one tiny window, climbing part of the way up it. Another side of the tower meets the chancel from which a slightly lower apse protrudes, to be buttressed on either side of its windows. The roof is fun, heralding many to come in other towns we shall visit. In the lofty outer pediment of the nave there is an opening at door height leading to unguarded steps which have become a pigeon's cakewalk.

To the north of the cathedral, now surrounded by contemporary dwellings, is St. Quenin's chapel with a triangular apse. It is best viewed from the hilltop of the old city.

The Roman sites are named Puymin and La Villasse. Although the novelist Prosper Merimée, visiting the south on an official tour in the 1840s to report on ancient monuments, noted that excavation had begun, the serious work did not commence until 1907, and then on Puymin only. You will not, on your first visit, even now have seen all because the dig continues on both sites. Puymin is not only the larger but the more attractive, set as it is against a hillock covered in cypresses and other greenery. The foundations of the various houses are not satisfactorily labelled and puzzled visitors, guide book plans on their laps, may be seen sitting on walls attempting to make sense of what should be visual aids.

It becomes apparent, however, that those Roman citizens of Vasio, if they were wealthy, spread their property over considerable areas but were not bothered by having the rented houses of the proles close by. The House of the Messii, with extensive gardens, is separated from them only by Pompey's portico. The statue of Emperor Hadrian's wife Sabina, which once stood in it, is now next to one of himself, in the refreshingly uncluttered museum. The finest exhibits therein are two intact mosaic floors, one with a peacock in full plumage; the most haunting is a tragic mask from a tomb. There are heads and statues, and statues without heads, cases of gorgeous red pottery and all the usual artefacts lying behind glass. And on a wall close to the entrance is the informative map of Provincia Narbonensis in the year 118AD.

On an outside wall near the museum is a plaque to the Abbé Sautel under whose supervision the excavations of 1907 began.

Compared with that of Orange (see Chapter 3) the theatre has to be disappointing. The most interesting features of what is left of the stage are a gulley (*logement de rideau*) into which the curtain was lowered, and a rectangle (*fosses de scène*) where scenery was stored. The auditorium is, as at Orange, still used and the acoustics are perfect. In the hillside behind is a tunnel coming out above the nymphaeum from which spring water was piped to the Roman town. This was an entrance to the theatre – an eerie approach indeed – but is now closed to the public.

La Villasse is reached across the Place du-11-Novembre and can be viewed in its entirety before entering from a terrace at the side of the carpark. In it is a shopping street, hanging gardens, a covered canal and the very large residence and lands of the Patrician of the Silver Bust. Excavations to the west indicate that he had an equally prestigious neighbour in the Dolphin House.

Well away from both sites is an original Roman bridge with a simple arch over the Ouvèze. It is still in use for two-way vehicular traffic even though, in 1944, the retreating Germans attempted to dynamite it. The charge exploded but failed to harm the basic structure.

It also survived the catastrophic freak storm of September, 1992, when torrential rain burst the river banks sweeping away a camp site and part of a housing estate. The Pont Neuf, and other bridges down stream, built in modern times, were either destroyed or severely damaged.

2   Les Dentelles de Montmirail

Séguret : Gigondas : Vacqueyras : Notre-Dame d'Aubune :
Beaumes-de-Venise : Le Barroux : Suzette : Malaucène : Crestet

A minor turning to the left on the D977 out of Vaison leads into a rolling area of vines stretching south and east for mile after mile. The first stop is at Séguret, a town on the slopes of a hill beside another which was a Roman settlement where a huge statue of Jupiter was found. The remains of a castle are on the summit and there is a road leading to it but you will see equal and superior ruins of the same sort elsewhere. So concentrate on the village which, like the upper town at Vaison, is now mostly inhabited by artists and craftsmen. Séguret is especially known for its *santons*, the Provençal figurines often used for decorating crèches at Christmas time. (Some of these are elaborate and assembled with artistry; some are tawdry.)

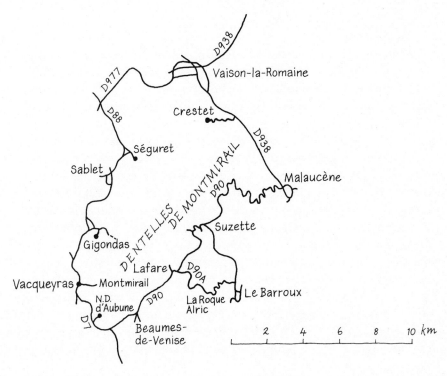

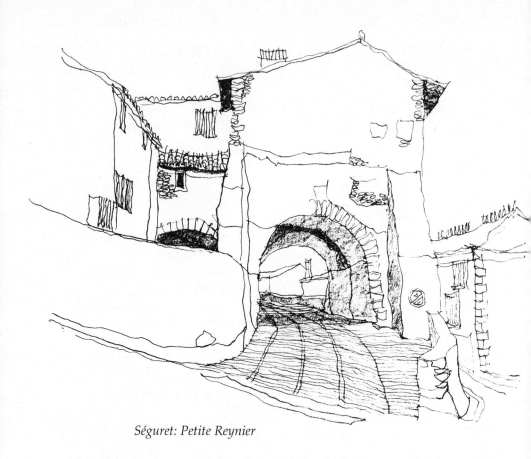

Séguret: Petite Reynier

They are on sale at several ateliers and we shall see more of them in shops and museums all over Provence. At others of the stone houses with thick walls you can buy the local wine which has its own *appellation contrôlée*. In October there is a wine festival after which, in the winter months, the town is almost deserted.

Leave the car in the ample parking area and enter through the twelfth-century gateway, the Petite Reynier. Ascend, at first gently, by a narrow roadway, past antique shops and the Fontaine des Mascarons. Séguret is, perhaps, a little self-consciously picturesque, but it has much to be proud of with its fifteenth-century courtyards and pretty vistas. High up is a simple church (St-Denis) with a vivid gilt altar and, close by, a very detailed *table d'orientation* which puts order into the beguiling views. During the season there are resident art courses and a theatre festival. Most of the permanent population live below the old village, close to the vineyards.

The next town, Sablet, is on a slight eminence with terraces of streets around a church typical of the region. It also sprawls into as much of the land as can be spared from the grape. On the way in and out as elsewhere on this heavenly plain, there are points of *dégustation* but the wine is not cheap, either bought at *caves* or in the shops. There are separate vintages but it all belongs, generically, to the Côtes du Rhône, and the production is enormous. For my palate most of it is overpriced compared with the house wines from Bordeaux available at many British wine importers.

Sablet can be admired well enough without stopping, so continue to Gigondas. Park in the small *place* and take a perambulation. In fact most of the village is between quarter and half way up the hill and there are hardly two houses on the same level in any one street. Its wine was known to Pliny the Younger. The village was for long under the rule of the House of Orange and has had a turbulent history. The castle ruins are being restored. The little church beneath them was sacked in the Wars of Religion by Protestants led by Baron des Adrets whose fiery faith caused much destruction in the Vaucluse. Above the firmly closed door there is a touching statuette of a crowned madonna. The Catholics now worship at a chapel, also savaged in

Gigondas

the conflict, on a hillside close by. The village is small and well cared for; the wine is considered, by modern Plinys, to be one of the best of the region. I find it both heavy and heady.

A road leads from Gigondas towards the Col du Cayron but peters out after a couple of kilometres. You can walk from here for hours up the Dentelles in the direction of Suzette where, if willing, your driver can be instructed to collect you later. Much later.

Then to Vacqueyras (another prestigious vintage) where the viniculturists advertise their product in tall, vulgar red letters on the tree-clad slopes above the village. The wine motif is pronounced in Vacqueyras but the son of one of their medieval village idiots is also celebrated. He was the troubadour Rambaud (1180-1207) whose statue is in the village square. There is also a florist's – Jardin de Troubadour – and a *cave* which offers Vin de Troubadour.

A side road leads to Montmirail where a spa was established in the nineteenth century. The water was bottled until 1919 and hôtels still exist. As with most places there are signs of old fortifications at Vacqueyras (also a Saracen cemetery) but you can afford to be blasé about them and proceed to Beaumes-de-Venise, after stopping to admire an exceptionally beautiful church standing sleekly against the mountainside. It is just off the D7. You can drive to it along a narrow track without passing places, but it is better to leave the car at a farmhouse, La Fontenouille, where you obtain the keys. There is no indication that this is the procedure; you just have to know. You then climb up through fields and someone's back garden to Notre-Dame-d'Aubune, a gem of Romanesque architecture which some date as early as the ninth century. The tower is Italianate and perfect, with four tall, slim openings on each side at two levels, the lower ones having support from columns with decorated capitals. The smaller key opens the iron gate to the roofed-over porch; the larger one, the heavy wooden door. Inside it is unexpectedly light and high. There are bold, crude paintings. The apse is probably at least one thousand years old; in the Wars of Religion it was used as stables.

Beside a house with blue shutters, joined to the chapel, is a board listing the activities of conservationists who care for the hillside and path up to the Devil's Rock on the Oppidum des Courens. On this plateau archae-ologists have made finds dating back to 1,000BC.

The town of Beaumes-de-Venise, famous for its sweet dessert wine made with the muscat grape, is only a kilometre away. It has a pretty name, and a prettier setting. The church, rebuilt after the ravages of the Revolution but not until 1849, is spruce and clean. Anne of Austria wor-shipped in its precursor and presented its clergy with church vestments because she thought so highly of the local wine. The relevance of the gift is obscure but no doubt the priests were grateful.

You are now at the southern tip of the Dentelles. Proceed northward to the hamlet of Lafare which does not warrant a stop. From here, climb through lush country, with pines and ferns abounding, to the spectacularly situated La Roque-Alric, a mere settlement but memorable for the fact that church and houses appear to spring from a huge slab of stone pointing arrestingly skywards. Certainly worth a short stop to click the shutters, then on, over the hill to a different view of the Dentelles and a winding road down through vineyards (no picnic spots) to Le Barroux, whose castle heaves into and out of sight with the twists of the thoroughfare. The picturesque little town is, for once, dominated not by a ruin but by a well-restored, privately owned château.

There is a very small car park on the north side of the village and a larger one on the south. I recommend the latter for the sake of a perambulation through the streets before climbing the rugged path to the castle.

La Roque-Alric

Turn left at a three-storied mansion which has a heavily eroded coat of arms above one door, then walk around the massive wall until you reach arrows pointing, one way to the château, and the other to the terrace. From there the panorama takes in Mont Ventoux looking lower than its neighbour Mont Serein, but that is an optical illusion; the Auzon basin with Carpentras and other towns easily identifiable; the Plateau de Vaucluse and the Dentelles. Below you are the pink-tiled roofs of the village and the Romanesque church with a feature reminiscent of the cathedral at Vaison. Steps on its roof emerge from inside the nave and lead, like a gulley, between two walls to the belfry.

The terrace is open all the year from 10.00 – 19.00, or dusk; the castle only during July and August.

The château, basically sixteenth-century, has survived appalling mishaps. The de Rovilhasc family who lived in it for hundreds of years still owned its ruins until 1929 when it was sold to one M. Vayson de Pradenne. He devoted the next ten years to restoring it, just in time for German soldiers to use it as a luxury billet in World War Two. In the confusion of retreat officers of the Wehrmacht abandoned bedding and other signs of their presence. Comrades of theirs who came after believed this to be evidence of a Resistance hideout, so they ordered those villagers who had not fled to assist in firing the building, which burned for ten days. Thus, the castle had to be restored for a second time in this century. The job was splendidly done but the interior, alas, is of no great interest. A visit was made worthwhile for me by the opportunity it afforded of overlooking a superb three-storied country house in very large grounds, with vines and cypresses on a slope – a quintessential Provençal setting. The property, the guide informed us, is owned by an Englishman. Some second home!

Just beyond Le Barroux – famed, incidentally, for its apricot fairs – on a minor road to Suzette, is Ste-Madeleine, a Benedictine monastery founded in 1970 and still under construction by the monks. I stress that the road is minor – almost a track – but it takes little traffic and descends to rich farming land before climbing to the wide-spread village. At first sight, on its cross-roads high up the hillside, Suzette appears to be no more than a few houses, a farm, and a chapel, so that it is surprising to find even a modest-sized *mairie*. But in the intensely cultivated surrounding land are many villas and farms. The road down to Malaucène winds through *garrigue,* fields and woodland. Where it emerges above the Groseau valley, at the Cirque de St-Amand, there are concrete picnic tables. It is a good place to eat and from which to savour another wide expanse of distant country, with fold after fold of mountains away to the north-east and Mont Ventoux opposite. On the hillside there are pines, holm oaks and deciduous trees; in the fields mauve mallow and scarlet poppies.

Malaucène is a small but lively town which is the starting point for the ascent of Ventoux either by car or on foot. In 1336 Petrarch, his brother, and two servants, made the climb and were back at Malaucène for bed but not until after nightfall. It was a clear day on which the poet claimed to have seen the Mediterranean from the summit. When a mistral is blowing you may enjoy a similar experience, but will you wish to drive up to that exposed position when the wind is at its mightiest? In any case, a trip over the Ventoux is almost certainly first-time-round so we will look at Malaucène.

There is a massive church built as a fortress by Pope Clement V. It has a long, bleak, south-facing wall, whose austerity is emphasised by six blind windows just below roof level. This effect is slightly mitigated by a similar number of openings below. The interior is simple and lofty but also lowering to the spirits. Towering above it is the hill with remains of a castle. Climb the hazardous path to the top where there is an abandoned stone altar and three wooden crosses bent by the wind. Here you can observe from whence you came over the Dentelles and look down on the little town which lies in a maze of narrow streets. Terraces of houses lurch and lean upon each other and there are gaps where they lean upon the air. Surviving gates from the original walls are to be seen, and beyond them a heavily tree-lined boulevard with cafés, restaurants and hôtels skirting half the town.

Crestet

On the road back to Vaison turn off on the left for Crestet which clings to the eastern side of the Dentelles. The bishops of Vaison who once owned the castle at Entrechaux across the valley also held one here, when it wasn't wrested from them by the ever-predatory Counts of Toulouse. Today it is in private hands and being restored. It dates from the twelfth century and stands at one end of a square above the church, which itself is squashed between terraces. The village is reached up a narrow road from which coaches are prohibited after a certain point. You can climb to the castle from a small parking lot by dodgy steps and footpaths, past pretty houses and gardens, some with little courtyards. There are no cafés, let alone hôtels; not even so much as a *boulangerie* unless one lurks down some alley which I failed to explore. There is a track road to Séguret but you are not advised to take it. Return instead by the way you came, to the Carpentras-Vaison road and enter the latter town over the Roman bridge.

Crestet gets only a paragraph here because I have nearly 150 places, large and small, to include, but one proud inhabitant has produced a survey covering in detail every facet of his *village perché*. It is handwritten, cyclostyled and pleasingly illustrated; a further volume is in preparation. Thus Crestet is being as lovingly documented as Avignon or Arles, and is setting a fine example for local historians elsewhere in the region.

3 Between the Rhône and the Dentelles

Rasteau : Camaret : Courthézon : Caderousse : Orange : Bollène : Barry : Sérignan : Ste-Cécile-les-Vignes

This second tour out of and back to Vaison takes in far more than you will be willing to endure on a single journey, unless you have been conditioned by rigorous package touring. Orange is almost certainly known to you but don't miss Sérignan or Barry.

Leave Vaison by D975 to reach Roaix most of which is on and around a hill on your right. Only stop if you wish to visit a former house of the Knights Hospitaller where there is a fountain whose façade includes a fragment of a marble altar decorated with illustrations of religious observances in the sixth century. Or if you have a taste for the macabre and gain admission to the church where, through a hole in a commemorative slab, it is possible to observe the thorax of a long dead man. That is, if you have a candle handy to lower through the hole to illuminate the chamber beneath. (I have not done this but have the information from M. Bailly – see Bibliography.)

You may prefer to luxuriate in the pastoral scene and contemplate the vines as you take the winding narrow road, which passes a small wine museum, to Rasteau. This larger village highlights its indebtedness to the grape by a sign close to the door of the church, noting that it was in the twelfth century that the first vines here yielded fruit to be trodden. Adjoining the church, to which the ascent is not as arduous as in some places, is a laboratory for analysis and labelling of the local vintage. The climb takes you through a typical clockhouse gateway, once part of the defences. In Roman times this was a residential district perhaps providing week-end homes for the patricians of Vaison. The village faces the Dentelles, commanding views of gently hilly countryside, wooded in those parts not taken over by the vine.

The road runs, almost straight, to Camaret-sur-Aigues where there is a medieval gateway now incorporated into a Baroque archway above which is a clock in a rounded pediment. This extravagant item of wrought-ironery is crowned with a ball and an emblem. Beyond the gate-way is a dull shopping street and a grim-walled eighteenth-century church which once housed the statue of a black virgin holding the infant Jesus. A bishop of

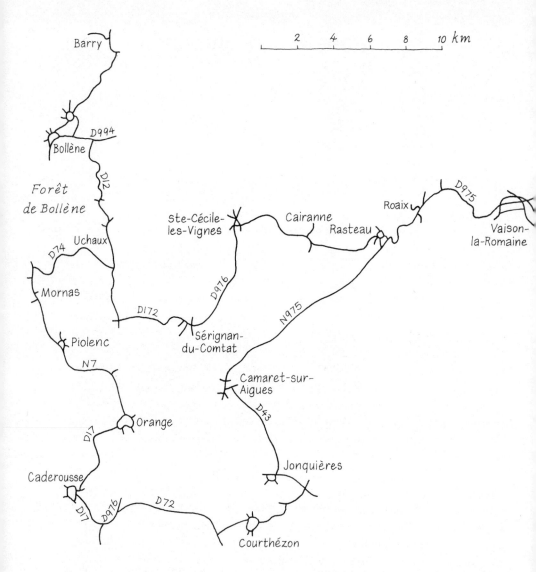

Orange declared this indecent and had it destroyed.

    Instead of proceeding directly to Orange take a roundabout route to Caderousse, the low-lying walled town at a point on the Rhône where Hannibal and his elephants may have crossed it. This takes in Jonquières and Courthézon, passing through characteristic Vaucluse countryside. On high ground, close to Jonquières, seventy Roman tombs were found; near Courthézon is the site of the first open-air village known in France, dating back to 3,000BC.

    Courthézon derives its prosperity from the Beaucastel vineyard which produces a highly-praised Châteauneuf-du-Pape. At the Porte-des-

Rasteau

Princes hôtel/restaurant I have enjoyed excellent lunches over many years both in the typically rather dingy dining-room and on its forecourt.

From Courthézon you pass over both the autoroute and the N7 before turning right on to the departmental road 976, which is the kind of minor route I adore, going beside farmyards and cottages, winding along past fields of abundance, to reach the turning for Caderousse on another stretch of *chaussée deformée* (D17).

The Hannibal connection is ignored by most guidebooks. *Provence Mystérieuse* mentions it but prefaces the descriptions by the ancient Greek historian Polybus with the words, 'At Caderousse *it is said*... Hannibal prepared and carried out his famous crossing'. It does claim, though , that in rocks beside the Rhône can still be seen the deep, square holes into which the anchoring posts of the elephants' rafts were driven. That is as may be. Certainly Hannibal crossed the Rhône somewhere.

Caderousse is about 6.5km south-west of Orange and has walls as protection against severe flooding. An inscription on the Hôtel de Ville notes that one inundation in 1856 reached to first-floor level. In early times the villagers protected themselves by building a dyke. Nowadays there are formidably high embankments, although since the hydro-electric installation further north the danger of flooding has become negligible. But tell that to the oldest inhabitants.

The church is the chief attraction, though you may only peer at the inside through glass doors unless there is a service. It is basically Romanesque with a simple frontage but develops Gothically at the side and rear, sending arches over an alley to adjoining houses which act partly as buttresses. It has an enormous bell which can deafen the neighbourhood.

The Resistance hero, Jean Moulin, lived here in hiding in 1942. A wall plaque on a house near the church notes that he was in radio contact with de Gaulle in London for six months.

Orange is certainly first-time-round on account of its Roman theatre, the best preserved in the world, and triumphal arch. The finest view of the former is from the Colline St-Eutrope. This hill was home to the first settlers, the Cavares tribesmen, and there was a castle from the first century BC until Louis XIV ordered its destruction. The remains at the north end are close to the platform where you can look down upon the great stage dominated by the figure of the Emperor Augustus. This statue was re-assembled from fragments.

The Romans built their town at the foot of St-Eutrope with the auditorium fitting neatly into the hillside. Beside it are continuing excavations which have so far revealed a gymnasium and at least two temples. The entrance ticket covers them as well as the museum opposite.

The seating capacity of the theatre was between nine and ten thousand. The stage is 61m wide and 9m deep and the back wall, named by Louis XIV 'the finest in my kingdom', is 36m high. It was once covered in marble. The building was vandalised over the centuries and used as a refuge in troubled times, which means for most of recorded history. Miraculously, it has been left relatively intact. In the nineteenth century the *félibres* were responsible for its restoration. Operas and choral works are performed here in the summer.

Opposite the theatre is a museum which owns a rare item in the surviving pieces of a Roman *cadastre* (land register) showing how the town was settled. This has enabled historians to deduce much about ancient Arausio. It needs explaining to those lacking specialist knowledge. There is also a small gallery displaying – surprisingly – many paintings by Sir Frank Brangwyn who is described as an 'English impressionist'. In fact he was a Welshman noted for his murals which adorn many public buildings on both sides of the Atlantic. The collection here, donated by Comte William Belleroche in 1939, celebrates his preoccupation with drawing the working man at work. One particularly memorable canvas is of a railway siding at night. The pictures deserve better care. They are dusty, badly hung and lack captions. (Min saw a French couple walking swiftly past them in bored, half-derisive incomprehension.) Worse neglect may be found at the cathedral of Notre-Dame which you may pass on your way to the triumphal arch. That is, if you even notice it. Crowded around with shops and houses, it has an actual garage in the apse. In contrast, the Hôtel de Ville nearby has been attractively redecorated. An extremely handsome three-storied mansion, four bays wide, with arches under the outer two and a pillared entrance between them, it is absolutely symmetrical with a dignified balcony and balustrade below the city arms. Surmounting it is a perfect example of a Provençal stone clock-tower and ironwork spire.

The pedestrianised shopping area of Orange is a pleasant haven away from the dreadful through road from which lorries are officially banned. (Not all drivers have read the instructions.) Take it to reach the triumphal arch which stands in a declivity with the traffic kept at bay by a large, round garden. So it is possible to stand and stare without feeling hemmed in. Here the N7 was once the Via Agrippa with Orange an important stage upon it. This splendid monument commemorates battles fought by the Second Legion and is decorated with sculptured scenes of fighting on land and sea. It is over two thousand years old; in the Middle Ages it became a castle but all traces of this misuse have been removed.

Orange has been not only Roman, Provençal and French but also Dutch, thanks to the fortunes of war and marriage. The House of Nassau (William the Silent amongst others) owned Orange from the mid-sixteenth century until 1713, although it was thrice confiscated during that period. It was another William, a descendant, who gained the throne of Britain after the Glorious Revolution of 1688, when James II was deposed.

When you have gazed your fill (and the arch is definitely worth re-visiting) take the N7, going north to Piolenc, the garlic capital of Provence, and Mornas which lies beneath a cliff face, a dramatic sight. Alas, the town has little else to offer although you may be lured to stop by signs proclaiming Village Historique. It is squeezed between the mainline Paris-Marseille railway and two major roads. Its Grand Rue is a near slum, with many of the buildings derelict or crumbling. In a truly civilised community alternative land would be found to re-house the population, leaving the rail and road administrators to squabble over the abandoned territory. The two old gateways could be incorporated into a new town as memorials. But such drastic rehabilitation would not affect the castle, which is high above the neglected old town centre. I must add that Mornassiens may feel differently about abandoning their town. In August 1990, their mayor was televised campaigning against the TGV extension through Provence and exuded much local pride.

Beyond the northern extent of unhappy Mornas turn right into the tranquillity of a wooded road through farmland leading to the many-faceted township of Uchaux, which consists of seven hamlets, each with its own name. One has a church whose beautiful frescoes were removed long ago, another has one which a local abbess converted into a sheepfold. Various lords, temporal and spiritual, owned parts of it in centuries past and took refuge here from plague and war. You would scarcely notice these Uchaux but for the *ralentisseurs* sensibly installed by the affluent landowners to deter speed. Go north on an undulating road through the Forest of Bollène where there is a shady picnic spot with tables, and a marked walk. You can also reach Bollène by N7 but my way is more agreeable.

If it did not back on to a great spur of rock, old Bollène would be swamped by the new town which sprawls out to meet the hydro-electric workings of the Donzère-Mondragon Canal. This has brought industrial expansion to the Rhône valley and beyond. The river remains navigable for tourism and commerce but has become one of the chief sources of pollution of the Mediterranean.

Old Bollène, on its hillside, an obvious homestead for ancient tribesmen, retains a spectacularly sited church which is best admired from without. It suffered grievously in the Wars of Religion when Baron des Adrets sacked it. Although rebuilt, the faithful Catholics became loath to make the steep ascent, so in the nineteenth century a new and architecturally inferior place of worship was provided for them. Old St-Martin's was then neglected apart from having its comely bell-tower refurbished. This stands today, overlooking a wooded garden, and set at an angle of about 45° to the body of the church, a feature to be noted at Ménerbes and elsewhere in the region. The church has a great, high nave with side chapels and two apses, one growing out of the other like a massive chunk of fungus. Inside, the building is in a serious state of decay. The whitewashed walls are flaking and there is no evidence that anyone cares. Services are held but twice a year; at other times the crumbling interior is adapted for art exhibitions. On the west side, across a roadway, is a newly created memorial garden and park in honour of de Gaulle.

The replacement church at the foot of the hill is ponderous, with a gloomy interior. If I were a believer I would wish to puff up the path to the still beautiful, though flawed, old St-Martin's.

Another enormity, in every sense, close to the nineteenth-century church is the blatantly Louvresque Hôtel de Ville, pompously dominating a small square. It has a badly scarred right wing which is now a cinema named Le Clap. (In fact the town hall is not that different from hundreds of others in France but seen so soon after the one at Orange it jarred on me.)

According to quite recently updated guide books, drawings by Chagall and Picasso are to be seen at the municipal museum on the Belvedère Pasteur, but they were stolen in the late 1980s. The museum, once a Romanesque chapel, is now closed. Louis Pasteur is commemorated in Bollène because it was whilst working here that he discovered the vaccine against swine fever.

On a hillside to the north of Bollène is Barry, an interesting relic of life during several centuries but now uninhabited. (Do not confuse it with another site above the village of St-Restitut.) Barry is signed at a most

Barry

complicated roundabout just outside the old town and reached by a rough mountain road which peters out under an overhang of red rock. You then clamber, at times steeply, to a twelfth-century ruined castle, way, way, above. The interest begins at once with the remains of houses built into the rock and a small chapel in front of them. Then, stretching up and round the hillside is a complex semi-troglodytic site dating back to the Celto-Ligurian tribes but, like the Village des Bories below Gordes (see Chapter 6), inhabited until comparatively recently. The dwellings are more sophisticated than at Gordes and, indeed, there are the shells of quite handsome houses, some standing free from the rock face which makes a natural fourth wall for others.

The views of the Rhône valley are stupendous. Looking down on the neat network of villas and roads directly beneath, and at the huge cooling towers of Tricastin and other paraphernalia of industry and technology, you may well wonder what more the Romans might have achieved had they harnessed electricity.

Return to Bollène and the road to Uchaux which is pretty enough to experience twice in one day. Note the new plantations of trees and the sleek villas with smart gardens all of which, along with Bollène and Barry, you will miss if you opt for reaching Sérignan direct from Orange.

Sérignan-du-Comtat is a 'must' because of L'Harmas Fabre, the house and garden of a great naturalist. It lies on the Orange road behind a high wall and closed gate. It looks forbidding but when you ring the bell you will be admitted most civilly. Up a short drive with plants and trees all lovingly labelled, is a rather shabby two-story house, on one wall of which a trumpet flower climbs luxuriantly to the eaves. From this angle the building, in an inverted L, faces an arbour with a lily pond on a mound.

Jean-Henri Casimir Fabre (1823-1915) was a polymath whose remarkable achievements should be more widely celebrated. He was not only a naturalist, but entomologist, mathematician, teacher, writer and much besides. He published 95 books, many of them translated into numerous languages. He completed at least 700 watercolours of mushrooms and other fungi. He wrote poems, composed music. He was a prodigious collector. On the first floor there are cases of neatly arranged shells, beetles, birds' eggs, fossils, marine animals, plus dozens of albums containing his extensive herbarium.

In the room below are displayed 262 of the watercolours, copies of most of the books in their various editions, letters from Charles Darwin and Mistral, and to his daughters and others; memorabilia of a visit to Russia in the 1880s; the menu of a dinner given in his honour (listing 15 courses); his coin collection (numismatics was a hobby, though it is a wonder he had time for it) and the medals he was awarded.

The garden beyond the arbour is a riot of flowers, trees, herbs and water plants. Fabre liked it to resemble a wilderness. This is still the intention but is achieved only at the cost of constant labour. Visitors may wander along its narrow paths and inhale the glorious aromas. In the house you are also left much to yourself. The custodian introduces each room briefly, then there is a generous length of time in which to study the exhibits whilst he dusts an object here and there or tidies some misplaced artefact.

Fabre was an astonishing man, born to peasant parents who, to escape penury, were constantly on the move. They became café owners in Rodez, Toulouse, Montpellier, Nîmes, Avignon, so that the boy's education was constantly interrupted. Despite this Jean-Henri won a scholarship and became a qualified teacher. He was employed at a school in Carpentras, where he married, started a family and embarked upon an intense course of

Sérignan: L'Harmas Fabre

higher education leading to appointments in Corsica and then Avignon. There he had a seeming setback to his career by falling foul of prudery. Citizens complained when he gave a lecture on the fertilisation of plants, and he was forced to resign. Whatever would have been his fate had he got to the birds and the bees? In fact, this incident made him. Having a family of eight to support, he began writing textbooks, gaining the economic freedom to do so by accepting a loan from John Stuart Mill (then resident in Avignon). He moved to Orange where his success soon allowed him to buy the house at Sérignan. Here, over the next thirty-five years, he acquired more wealth; more fame and even two more children, by his second wife. He died, aged 91, a year after Mistral.

L'Harmas is administered by the Musée National d'Histoire Naturelle, through its Entomological Laboratory, and was bought for the nation in 1922. It is truly representative of Provence in the infinite variety of its exhibits.

In the town itself are the remnants of a castle which once belonged to Diane de Poitiers, but most of it was destroyed by the Huguenots. Diane came here but once towards the end of her life. There is nothing else of note in this pleasant small town apart from a statue of Fabre. This is near a café where you may take a break and read more about him in a handout provided by L'Harmas.

Sérignan suffered from the overflow of the skirmishes at Ste-Cécile-les-Vignes which until the 1920s was plain Ste-Cécile. It has a religious past of particular ferocity but is now, as the name implies, a wine town. A church was dedicated to Ste-Cécile in the late twelfth century and belonged to the Knights Hospitaller who, in 1317, handed over their domains to the Avignon pope. In the Wars of Religion the town changed hands several times. At one period there was a garrison of 600 Italian soldiers. The 'original' church, rebuilt twice, is a charmingly diminutive edifice framed by a nineteenth-century stone gateway. There is a public garden, with children's playground, in what was a cemetery. The official contemporary church is a boring item of the 1850s. Of the town walls all that remains is a stone clock-tower above a gate, but spread about the centre may be found many old doorways and pediments.

The road to Cairanne is dotted rather ridiculously with single cypresses placed at intervals of about twelve feet. They provide neither shade nor protection from the wind. The vines of Ste-Cécile have rose bushes planted at the ends of rows to give early warning of mildew formation.

Old Cairanne stands on a knobby hill just sufficiently spacious to support the dull ruins of a castle, two places of worship, and a few streets of houses most of which show signs of considerable antiquity, though that may be a hangover from earlier in this century when much of France looked deliberately neglected in order to fool the taxman. One chapel, Notre-Dame-des-Excès, was restored in 1979 by a special team of cavalry of the Foreign Legion which is an odd instance of diversification. It is a dumpy, rectangular building bearing a plaque to one 'Frédéric Alary, Vigneron, Historien, 1900-1987'. His name appears again beside vineyards down on the plain.

Take the road back to Vaison, past Rasteau and Roaix, and bend your thoughts to what the chef at the Hôtel du Théâtre Ancien is preparing.

Vaison-la-Romaine

D938

Mont Serein

Col des Tempêtes

Malaucène

D974

Groseau

Le Chalet-Reynard

MONT VENTOUX

Belvedere
le-Paty

Bedoin

D974

D14

Sault

Mormoiron

Villes-
sur-Auzon

Monieux

D943

Gorges de la Nesque

D942

D150

Malemort

Blauvac

D5

Méthamis

Javon

Venasque

D4

Col de Murs

D177

PLATEAU DE VAUCLUSE

D24

Murs

St-Saturnin-
lès-Apt

Sénanque

2   4   6   8   10 km

4   Mont Ventoux and the Plateau

Groseau : Mormoiron : Venasque : Col de Murs : Sénanque :
Gorges de la Nesque : Sault : St-Saturnin d'Apt

Almost wherever you go in western Provence there is the presence of Mont Ventoux which is a sentinel over the region and, on the whole,
a benign influence. The summit is 1,909 metres above sea level and at any
time of the year it appears to be snow-capped. But it is only so in deep mid-
winter, and then not always: the impression comes from the limestone. It
rises to a massive cone and commands incomparable views. Nowadays the
natural beauty of the peak is marred by huge items of technology that spoil
the experience of being at the appropriately named Col des Tempêtes far
more emphatically than does the small souvenir shop which at least serves
as a shelter from the wind. There is also a small church-cum-chapel which
has been rebuilt many times since a hermitage was first established in the
fifteenth century.

Many visitors, before going up and over, opt for the picnic spot
and camping site at the foot of the mountain at Groseau, where the river of
that name first emerges in a spring of clear water. The Romans built an
aqueduct to carry it to Vaison but nothing remains of it, or of the pagan
temple which was nearby. The latter, however, may well be hidden by the
ancient chapel of Notre-Dame-du-Groseau which belongs to an abbey dating
from the seventh century. The doorway incorporates a stone from Celto-
Greek times, whilst inside is a fourteenth-century fresco commissioned by
Pope Clement V who had a residence here. But the door is locked and there
is nothing to indicate even what the building is, let alone where the key to it
may be found. The chapel stands, beautifully preserved, in a field a few yards
from the road.

The mountain path, the Grande Randonnée, starts at Groseau.
Petrarch's description of his expedition is thought to be the first extant record
of a climb, and helped to gain Ventoux the magical qualities which appealed
so to the *félibres*. The first road to the summit was from Bédoin. Then, in 1933,
the way from Malaucène was laid so that nowadays a round trip is possible,
although between mid-November and mid-April the section from Mont
Serein to le Chalet-Reynard, a ski resort, is closed. As next-time-rounders

will know even in high summer the trip provides a very sudden change of temperature within a few miles. Never go without an anorak or jersey however stupefyingly hot it may be on the plain.

A monument was erected recently to commemorate the English cyclist Tommy Simpson, who had a fatal heart attack during the 1967 Tour de France.

Fabre of Sérignan wrote in detail of Mont Ventoux and its plants, contrasting the flora of the far north, to be found on its upper levels, with the purely Mediterranean trees at its base.

As you descend, the arid limestone soon gives way to a thickly treelined road with plenty of stopping places. At le Chalet-Reynard continue to Bédoin where we are back into wine country. The little town is a resort and noted for the seventeenth-century altar-piece by Pierre Mignard in its Jesuit church. You can also reach Bédoin from just beyond Malaucène on a poorly maintained but attractive wiggly road. At Le Belvedère Paty it overlooks quarrying sites in rich red and yellow ochres, and beyond them the small hill town of Crillon-le-Brave. The road later passes by the eleventh-century Chapelle-de-la-Madeleine which, a notice states, is private property.

Just off the road south from Bédoin is Mormoiron where there is little to see apart from a couple of mid-sixteenth-century houses beside and opposite the *mairie*. It has a wide main street with hôtels and gift shops and also what claims to be an Alimentation Générale. The prospect of experiencing that celestial aroma associated with old-fashioned grocer's shops led me into it but there was only the faintest whiff of the smells of yesteryear. Deep freezing and hygienic storage have put paid to them. A sign to a Musée led me to an ancient church which seemed partly inhabited and constructed over a public tunnel with paving steps. That was worth the detour but I didn't discover the museum. (Close to Mormoiron is a newly-constructed artificial lake wherein you may bathe, unsupervised.)

Head for Malemort where inevitably there is a Romanesque church and neolithic site. You can't stop for them all but if you do, note the seven-headed fountain by the imposing gateway which is all that remains of the wall. The church is in a poor way but has a certain hangdog nobility.

On to Venasque, high on a spur of rock above the valley of the Nesque. Before you make the ascent there is a religious community to be visited by the river. It is private, but you may go into the Baroque chapel to see a rarity from an earlier sanctuary. This is the tomb of Bishop Boethius who died in 604AD and whose remains lie in a fine Merovingian sarcophagus with motifs of rosettes and wheels. This chapel is Notre-Dame-de-Vie. Up a lane beside it is an interestingly shaped modern church built in local stone. It is roughly polygonal and has narrow, gullied slices of roof reminiscent of the hats traditionally worn in *The Barber of Seville.*

Venasque, which comes high on my next-time-round scale, gave its name to the Comtat Venaissin at a time when bishops moved there for safety from Carpentras, thus effectively making it the capital of the territory for varying periods between the sixth and tenth centuries. One prelate was St. Siffrein, a former monk, who built the cathedral, the only remains of which are now incorporated into the baptistery. He also gave his name to the cathedral at Carpentras, and is buried here in the fine church which defies the usual lunchtime curfew by staying open all day. The piped music includes an unaccompanied singer rendering what sounds like a prim version of a cheerful cabaret song. A crucifixion of the Avignon school is much admired; it is late fifteenth-century.

Opinions differ about the origin of the baptistery which adjoins the church. There may have been a pagan temple dedicated to Venus on the site and the first Christian building was either a baptistery or a funerary

Venasque: The Baptistery

chapel. It has four apses partly supported by Roman columns and at the crossing, an octagonal sunken font. The interior has for me a slightly eerie stillness, a sense of time momentarily stopping, despite a recorded commentary with a backing of sacred lala-ing. This is for the natives. Foreign visitors are handed notes in their own language. In a corner niche is a statue of Bishop Siffrein looking superior and holding a horse's bit in both hands. It is, we are told, made of one of the nails of the holy cross and explains his equestrian prowess. It came from Constantinople around 1205AD; 'the fact that he was able to use it testifies to an extending of divine privilege.'

The village, a visual delight at almost every point, rises gently from a dip outside the church to a ruined castle, through narrow streets and a modest central *place* with a small fountain. Since World War Two it has put on a cheerful and self-respecting face probably indicative of a prevalence of *résidences secondaires*. This trait, to be observed elsewhere, is said to have detracted from the quality of community life; it might be equally fair to say that it has brightened it. Venasque already attracts visitors. On a lane leading to the castle is the Hôtel des Remparts which has a dining terrace facing tree-clad hills. Posters of old films decorate the walls of the bar. The welcome is cordial.

The Plateau de Vaucluse is nothing of the sort, especially at its western end. It is mountainous with gorges, to one of which we are bound next via the Col de Murs (627m). This is a lonely road with a rapid descent at first, on little more than a track from Venasque, after that through a winding, low ravine into the forest where, for many kilometres, only a single dwelling is to be seen. Then it climbs to a view of farmland before coming down through meadows and orchards on what, at last, suggests a plateau. The first settlement is Murs, a village grouped about a privately-owned château which, with turrets, towers and mullioned windows, looks in splendid condition. At the ungated entrance heraldic beasts stand on low pillars. In caves around Murs the Vaudois from the Luberon sought refuge from persecution. But, so Jean-Paul Clébert relates in his *Provence Mystérieuse*, their Catholic pursuers killed them in their hideouts by asphyxiation.

Now go by even more minor roads to Sénanque, crossing the river Sénancole twice. This cuts the gorge in which the abbey lies in its serene simplicity, at the end of a vast field of lavender, almost straddling the valley from west to east. It is built of limestone, whose greyness seems in summer to absorb colour from the lavender. It is beautifully proportioned and not quite symmetrical. There is nothing superfluous nor decorative; neither is it austere. It is about as perfect a building as you will find in the whole region.

The abbey was founded in 1148, fifty years after the Cistercian order came into being, and thirty-six after it accepted the strict discipline of

Sénanque Abbey: The Cloister

St.Bernard of Clairvaux. It was built by a dozen monks from Mazan in the Vivarais. They copied the design of the one they knew, a prototype for well over three hundred other abbeys whose whereabouts are shown in a display in the chamber beyond the ticket booth. Despite the asceticism advocated by St.Bernard, including the renunciation of all wordly goods, the order amassed huge wealth and became decadent. At Sénanque there was a revival of original aims and ideals at the beginning of the sixteenth century, after the Vaudois heretics had murdered the brothers and inflicted damage on the buildings. It was rebuilt, survived the Revolution, when it passed into private hands, and then again came under ecclesiastical ownership. There followed a further spell as a monastery until anti-clerical laws forbade its continuation.

From 1926-68 the monks were back again before leasing it for twenty years to a secular organisation who made it a Centre for Sahara Studies whilst also attracting visitors. Their success was such that the lease was not renewed and the Cistercian Order took over what appears a thriving business. There are coaches in the car park at all seasons and the shop is well stocked. On the floor above it is an exhibition about St.Bernard and the Order.

So Sénanque is once again a functioning Cistercian monastery with a few monks who observe divine service seven times a day. They work on the land where they are assisted by lay brothers, and use the original refectory, now restored. This is not open to the public. But they no longer sleep in the abbey, which visitors enter by the former dormitory. This great rectangular chamber has steps leading down into the church at one end and wider ones, in the centre of the floor, take you to the beautiful cloister. The monks' cells were flimsy partitions behind which they slept on straw mattresses. On the walls now are visual aids to an understanding of the entire building with illustrations of the processes of construction. Also displayed are models of the implements and tools used. There are guided tours but they are rendered superfluous, in my view, by the excellent signboarding and the simple, informative brochure, available free in several languages.

The church has been restored to the condition it was believed to have been in when first completed. There are no paintings, sculpture or stained glass. Nor is there a public entrance because this was (and is) a private place of worship. (The monks also have a chapel, not open to visitors.) A door from the church leads to the cloister, off which lies the chapter hall and monks' hall, the latter the only chamber that had heating because there the inmates copied manuscripts.

A path at the side of the abbey enables visitors to view the lovely complex from the rear. It is a tranquil place to take a walk before returning to the dustbowl of a car park. (Perhaps some of the profits from the shop could go towards a better surface?)

I think, despite the coaches which will soon necessitate widening the road from Gordes, you will find Sénanque a highlight.

Return to Venasque up the west side of the valley ignoring all signs to Murs and its Col, taking instead another secluded road through a different gorge. Then, but surely after a night's rest, go back to Malemort where there is a choice of routes to the Gorges de la Nesque. One way goes around a massive quarry, seemingly encompassing an entire hill, to the tiny ancient village of Blauvac; the other by way of Methamis, situated on a hill on the lower slopes of the northern side of the Plateau, amongst vines and farmland. South of it can be seen sections of the great dry-stone wall built in 1720 in a desperate but ineffectual attempt to protect the Comtat from plague.

A ruined castle still has high stone windows and much wall and there is a well cared for church with a three-part bell-tower. Two wings appear to be inhabited; between them is the entrance, up a grand double staircase suggestive more of a noble homestead. The hillside has pleasant houses and gardens but rather too many barking dogs, some of them unleashed.

Whichever route you choose, when you reach D942 turn right for Villes-sur-Auzon where, again, you have a choice of ways to Sault. The 'touristique' one through the Gorges is the more southerly. There is nothing to detain you in Villes.

The Nesque has cut deep into the Plateau of Vaucluse for almost twenty miles from close by Villes to Monieux. The road runs high above it and there is scarcely any sign of habitation – just a farmhouse and a gîte near the start. It is all but entirely wooded with coniferous and deciduous trees, some newly planted in official forestry rows. It is hunting country, without cultivated land apart from the plantations. There are plenty of stopping places from which to admire this savage natural phenomenon, a heady experience for some of us. The most celebrated view is from a platform, with panel quoting from Mistral's *Calendau*, beneath the Rocher du Cire which rises 872 metres above sea level. I find it a relief to be out of this oppressive terrain and on to the gentle Plateau d'Albion, where there are farms and camping sites overlooked by the imperiously placed Sault and facing the shady village of Monieux. Here there is a very small circular chapel now in the centre of a car park, and on the hillside above the ruins of, not a castle for once, but a medieval watch-tower.

Sault has a reputation for its lavender mills – and its sausages. The importance of the latter is certainly reflected in the *boucherie* housed in the very frontage of the church of St-Sauveur. I am sure this leaves ample room in the church for the faithful even if some of them have to crowd into the reconstructed *borie* next to the altar. The little town features several low round towers (once part of the castle) adorning the ends of buildings. There are two or more hôtels. Beyond one of them, behind a rampart, is a park with seats, and views over fields and wooded foothills, then more rugged heights and *garrigue* up to Mont Ventoux.

The museum at Sault, featuring ancient remains, is open only on some afternoons of high summer. Leave it by D943 again through hunting territory and more woodland, where there were Resistance battles in 1944. Further on is the château of Javon standing alone in the countryside. Built in the sixteenth century and restored in this, it is now privately owned. There is a mostly untamed garden with stone gateways adorned by stylish female heads, and a wall low enough to see over and enjoy the lily pond. Javon has four round towers and an air of impenetrability.

The road goes into another gorge, much less impressive than the

Nesque, but I prefer it. You can see ahead across the Coulon valley to the Petit Luberon. There is nothing to invite claustrophobia. It gives way to more *garrigue* and as soon as you see pink-tiled roofs you know you are approaching something urban. It is St-Saturnin-lès-Apt which sprawls against a spur of plateau where there are extensive remains of an eleventh-century castle. This may be visited but the way up from the Place de-l'Eglise is very rough indeed, without barriers or railings. A number of doorways and arches with ribbed stonework are extant; there is a well-preserved chapel, with bell-tower and cemetery. Beyond the lower west wall a dam has been made; from the other side you look down upon the church and town, far below.

St-Saturnin-lès-Apt does not seem a prosperous town. Many houses are decaying, others are closed in winter, there are some fine, or once fine, doorways. Much rehabilitation is needed to make it attractive but the church, with its classical portico, at least is well cared for. So is the adjacent Maison Commune which has a curious decoration of cherubs above the entrance. In a square lower down the hill is a modern sandstone sculpture of a man kneeling to play *boules*. He is A Joseph Talon, a father, so the inscription declares, 'of trufficulture.'

St-Saturnin, in its lovely situation, could become worthy of its past. The Celts were here, the Saracens have left their mark, remains of mammals which pre-dated the elephant have been unearthed, so has an Iron Age tomb. Perhaps the local bard, whose Maison de la Poésie behind the church has window displays of his verses, should be invited to sing its praises in municipal literature.

On down the hill into the valley, and to Apt. The approach is marred by garishly coloured factories and hypermarkets constructed in metal. There is a local ruling which prevents owners from painting houses on new estates in colours unsuited to the environment. You may not, for example, use bright yellow, vivid blue or scarlet. Why cannot the same restriction be applied to the stridently hued hives of commerce which are making the outskirts of most towns hideous?

5   Apt and environs

Rustrel Colorado : St-Christol : Simiane-la-Rotonde : Caseneuve :
Fort de Buoux : Sivergues : Mourre Nègre : Saignon : Petit Luberon :
Vidauque

Apt is not the most interesting of Vaucluse towns but is a convenient centre. Its strategic position in the Coulon valley, at a crossroads between the Plateau and the Luberon, accounts for its glorious past – tribal capital in Celto-Ligurian times, Roman colony built at the order of Julius Caesar and named Apta Julia, place of pilgrimage in the seventeenth century when it was still a bishopric. Today nothing remains from ancient times apart from a few artefacts in the archaeological museum and the lower crypt of the Church of Ste-Anne. From the car park at the eastern end enter by the Porte de Saignon, which has a bell-tower and a stone crest and is all that is left of the walls, apart from the Tour Hôpital. They stood, often restored, for nine hundred years and the medieval street pattern they enclosed remains, including the Rue des-Anciennes-Prisons where a corner of tiny cells, one above the other, can be seen. A superior tower to the Hôpital awaits you indicating the presence of the church, a former cathedral, which you might miss if you are window shopping. It spans the road above a section of Romanesque brickwork beside the almost inconspicuous secondary entrance into the gloomy, much altered church. The interior, which has plain vaulting, is spoilt by dull, dark paintings surrounded by dirty gilt trimmings. A side chapel with a dome was added in 1660 and contains relics which attracted Anne of Austria, mother of Louis XIV, here. It is not recorded that she went overboard about the local wine as she did at Beaumes-de-Venise, but her visit is commemorated in the Baroque tympanum. She is not to be confused with the saintly Anne after whom the church is named and whose shroud is in the chapel sacristy. One legend has it that Charlemagne, no less, brought it from the East. Other treasures are enamels from Limoges and an Arab standard appropriated by a crusader.

For me, the chief interest in the church lies in the two crypts below the main altar. The first is Romanesque and perfectly maintained with a neat serving table and sarcophagi in a small ambulatory. Below it, reached by symmetrical narrow stone staircases, is an older one, with a block bearing carved lettering from early Christian times. This may well have been the site of the Roman basilica.

The archaeological museum, behind a dismal frontage along the road from the imposing Bibliothèque Nationale, is underprivileged. Some of what should be there has been removed to Avignon, Paris and the United States, with copies, in a few instances, left to indicate what has gone. Yet it has been permitted to retain items found at St-Saturnin and elsewhere. Rows of Gallo-Roman oil lamps – votive offerings – are neatly displayed; so are two heaped fragments of them. There are tombs with ancient skeletal remains, pieces of Roman paving, a lot of heavy china, a room of ex-votos, another of pharmaceutical jars and many hunks of masonry. Don't feel guilty at giving the museum a miss.

The Bishop's Palace is now the Hôtel de Ville, standing graciously in the Place Gabriel-Peri, with two delightful fountains. Facing the bottom of the square is a bookshop with so much stock that little space is left for customers, though it is said to be a centre of cultural life, as is the Café Grégoire in the Place de-la-Bouquerie. On Saturdays there is a market which draws huge crowds, especially for its candied fruits and truffles.

From Apt one looks up, not down, which makes for variety in this land of panoramic views. To the east is Saignon, jutting out of the mountain on a crag of rock. Just across the Coulon is a small peak, its woodside covered with villas and apartment blocks. To the southwest is the Avénue des Bories, rising steeply to the Grand Luberon and leading to Fort de Buoux; an adjacent road, lined with vineyards producing some of the best wine of the region, goes to Bonnieux.

Two excursions from Apt involve lengthy walks. For the first take the road to Rustrel (D22) along the valley of the Doua. Before it reaches that small town there is a crossroads with a minor turning leading to one car park for the walk along the 'Provençal Colorado'. Further on the D22 there is another; at Gignac, a few miles on, a third. The 'Colorado' is an ochre cliff where there are quarries similar to those at the more famous Roussillon (see

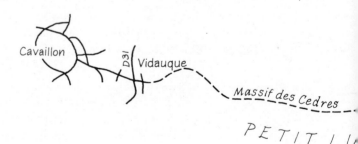

Chapter 6). The signs to it are not clear except to advise that this is all private property, so stick to the footpaths, if and when you can find them. If you start at Gignac, a hamlet where tradition is so strongly upheld that the few streets are labelled only in Provençal, descend to the valley down a steep meadow, after which the walk is often arduous and sometimes vertiginous.

On rejoining your car drive up to Rustrel, a village at the foot of

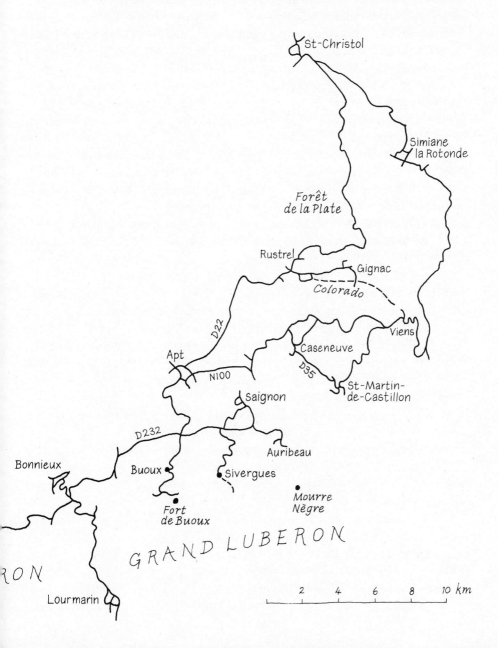

the Forêt de la Plate which spreads over the eastern end of the Vaucluse Plateau. Rustrel has a seventeenth-century château, now the *mairie,* with four towers coloured by the local ochre. Joined to it is a handsome dwelling painted in green.

For six kilometres above Rustrel the road climbs through dense, uninhabited woodland to emerge on the Plateau d'Albion where a farmhouse may be discerned and an isolated auberge. Surrounding them are great fields of lavender. Some kilometres on, comes St-Christol. The peace of the Plateau has been disturbed by the installation in the 1960s of a rocket missile base whose administrative blocks scarcely enhance the landscape. However, it has brought work and new housing to the outskirts of a village which is still what one would expect of an old settlement – it has a breathtakingly lovely church – except that it is now partly spruce. In it is a restaurant that is a hunter's delight; on the menu, one day in January, were venison, wild boar stew and partridge.

Drive back a short distance for the turning to Simiane-la-Rotonde lying beyond the borders of Vaucluse, in the department of Alpes-de-Haute-Provence, but too good to miss, a jewel of a little town overlooking a fertile plain and facing the Montagne de Lure, beyond which the Alps go on and on and on. The approach is through woods and olive groves until you arrive abruptly in front of the impressive Rotunda (probably 13C) whose purpose is much discussed by experts. Some insist it was a keep; others, a chapel, mausoleum, state apartment of the Simiane family's castle or, more prosaically, a storage chamber for weapons. The walls are of rough brick with a staircase built into them, apart from a central tower of much later date which protrudes like a submarine's conning tower. The dome just below it is irregularly vaulted with four long, stepped light-shafts, reminiscent of the openings in a classical tomb. On a mezzanine floor concerts are given and exhibitions mounted. Opening hours are severely restricted even during the high summer.

The town lies below the Rotunda. Halfway down the hillside is a small car park from which you can walk to the church. This has a wide frontage and a wooden door carved with chalices, mitres and incense shakers. There is a typical Romanesque apse and buttressed nave. Walk around the entire building and go down through an archway to the frontage again, before taking well signed paths to the Clocher St-Jean (1585); the Place du-Four (with a very fundamental baking oven in one corner); the old covered market with tall openings through which to admire the plain; a little chapel with a no-nonsense, simple carved door below a rough stone pediment; and an elderly tower block of apartments, the Maison Eyroux de Pontèves (designated 'early 11-16th centuries'). The paving is better underfoot than in most villages. The hill is steep enough to allow the housing to be terraced with a minimum of masking. There is a bar, a bistro, a shop or two. It feels lived in.

Return towards Apt via Viens, a rather sad hill village with ancient ramparts and an air of mourning; St-Martin-de-Castillon, which looks romantic viewed from down in the Coulon valley but is largely drab and

Simiane-la-Rotonde

dark; and Caseneuve, where it is worthwhile stopping. Here is a magnificent castle (owned privately) of tenth-century origin, presenting a massive front to the world, towering over the village and countryside. What is left of the keep is over 20m high and the well is 35m deep. According to Bailly, the latter was bored by hand out of the rock. There are three towers, two round, one square. The gleaming appearance of the whole will offend those who object to restoration but I think a marvellous job has been done. It was completed by two men of Caseneuve, name of Ripert. They deserve, if such exists, the Order of Viollet-le-Duc. Facing the village is a triumphal arch standing alone in a field; it belonged to a nearby chapel said to be the largest in Provence.

A narrow, winding, extremely minor road leads back to the N100.

There are three recommended walks within a short drive from Apt. For the first take the Avénue des Bories to Buoux. The road comes to the Plateau de Claparèdes between Saignon and Bonnieux, where there are lavender fields, farms growing cereals, oaks, mostly of the smaller varieties, and occasional small dry-stone walled structures, often conical, known as *bories*. (For more about them, see the next chapter.) Descend to the small settlement of Buoux which consists mainly of holiday homes for the Marseillais but also has a restaurant about which Peter Mayle writes as though thrown into a gastronomic trance. Do not be lured for the moment but drive along the bottom of a steep gorge beside the river Aigue Brun, noting intrepid climbers ascending the vertical rockface, to the turning for Fort de Buoux. There is a rough-and-ready car park on a clearing under the trees and from there you walk a short kilometre, at one point beneath a vast overhang of cliff, up to the ruined fortress with its views over mountain, plain and valley. The Ligurians were here, so were the Romans, so was a medieval castle until the destructive Louis XIV came along. In earlier times it was of strategic importance because it commanded the pass over the Luberon.

The lone house on the hillside where you pay for admission has in its small garden a red plastic swing hanging from the branch of a tree. This has made as vivid an impression upon me as the great gorge overlooked by the fort, the magnificent rock face with strata of varying colours and the panorama from the keep. Is that because it struck a note of comforting domesticity in an awesomely rugged setting?

When I made my way up the jagged path to the lower end of the fortifications I supposed I felt something of the sense of security experienced by early settlers. Then I noticed a defensive trench facing away from me so, presumably, there was danger of attack from the other side of the hill, too. Between this first fort and the higher battlements and donjon lay the medieval village. Partly hidden in the undergrowth is the shell of a thirteenth-century church with a discernible apse, and some bricked-up pointed windows half sunk into the ground. There are several caves which sheltered farm animals, a series of silos cut down into the rock and many cisterns, although no evidence of water. There has been just sufficient restoration of castle and ramparts to give a strong impression of the past but the whole has a compelling beauty of ruins which have been left to time and the weather. Vegetation has been allowed to intrude on to the ancient masonry except where rough paths have been trodden. There is just enough signposting.

Fort de Buoux does not draw crowds and you may find yourself almost alone there. The descent from the postern of the castle is perilous and if there is but little of the mountain goat in your movements, descend by the same path you climbed up. It is possible to walk on from here to the summit of the Grand Luberon but for the present I suggest returning down under the huge overhang of rock (note the pitons) and up the valley, beloved of mountaineers in training, to take the Saignon direction. When Sivergues is signed, approach this enchanting little place via a wiggly road, winding round a gorge. At the entrance to the hamlet there is a car park with tables, also a notice stating that the road ends here. A few houses are visible beyond a tiny chapel where I once heard a musician playing the harmonium for his own delight. Its sound followed me as I explored the only street, with stone paving laid in patterned strips. It leads past a gîte to a path which is the start of the ascent to the summit. This will take a good hour but if that is not sufficient you can walk for at least as long again on the track to the Mourre Nègre (1,125m above sea level) where a television mast of great complexity slightly spoils the grandeur.

The Luberon is a limestone ridge running from near Cavaillon to overlook Manosque about fifty kilometres to the east. Here it extends in fragments to the Durance. It is divided by the Lourmarin Gap, that part to the west being known as the Petit, that to the east, as the Grand Luberon. The whole area, plus much of the Coulon valley and also the Plateau, is designated the Parc Natural Régional du Luberon. It was formed with the intention of protecting both people and wild life. In the mountains here men have sought refuge since the Iron Age, some dwelling from that time until the eighteenth century in *bories*.

You can also ascend the ridge from Auribeau, another diminutive community at a lower level than Sivergues, a few miles to the east. Here you park at the end of a track, where a gate should be closed against vehicles. It is usually left open with the inevitable result that some motorists make a nuisance of themselves on the long, winding narrow approach to the top. Not far from Auribeau, on a densely wooded hillock, are ruins of a church or château all but hidden amongst the foliage. It is an exhilarating walk because at every turn on the way you see either a new angle or a familiar view or a fresh one entirely, and it is fun to pick out, on the hills to the north, places already visited – Viens, Caseneuve, St-Martin, St-Saturnin and the road above Rustrel.

When you have descended to either Sivergues or Auribeau, drive to one of the most astonishingly sited of all *villages perchés*, Saignon. It is said that from the edge of the spur you can see Avignon on a clear day but you cannot reach this point because it is private property, and also perilous. You are permitted only as far as the former church which, with the abbey it served, is now residential or used as offices. Views there are, nonetheless, and why not turn some ruins to practical use? You can walk amongst the conversions and at least climb the steps of what was the charming little Benedictine church of St-Eusèbe. The abbey was founded a thousand or so years ago but the monks had gone long before it was confiscated at the Revolution. On a lower perch, the other side of the town, is the parish church with a fine carved doorway and, within, two richly red marble pillars on either side of the altar. It is the usual hotchpotch of Romanesque, Gothic and Baroque, with an interestingly shaped rear of Provençal-pragmatic. The north side, above a steep cliff, is well buttressed and restoration of other parts is in hand. Between it and the abbey remains, in the dip wherein much of the town lies, is a bell-tower which belongs to neither. There is a pretty square and a number of narrow winding streets, one of them leading past the Ancienne Auberge de Rocher, to an occupied gloomy remnant of château. The *centre ville* has a delightful fountain, a potter's atelier, a large covered communal washplace, cafés and a hôtel. It should be an agreeable place to spend the night.

From Saignon to Cavaillon (where the next chapter begins) is a short journey mostly along the Coulon valley but if one of your party is willing to meet you below the western edge of the mountain you can walk along the Route de Petit Luberon for part or all of its length, (27 km). Return by D232 and stay on it until it meets the road from Bonnieux to Lourmarin. A partly tarmacked track opposite is open to traffic as far as the Massif des Cèdres. On your way you will pass a tall, seemingly medieval Italianate tower. In fact it was not erected until the 1880s when an eccentric sculptor, Philippe Audibert, built it so that the Mediterranean could be seen from his property. It is 30 metres high, has one hundred steps to a viewing terrace but is not open to the public. There are other buildings just off the road, a gîte, a pizzeria, but that is all and at the end there are no cafés or restaurants, only signs begging you to be tidy because the municipal dustcart does not come this far. In spring and early summer especially the roadside resembles a vast, closely planted rockery of herbs and flowers in abundance.

Once amongst the cedars, which came from the Atlas mountains of Morocco, you must abandon your car. The walk is often enclosed in woodland so you are unaware that you are at an altitude of 700 metres above sea level but later, on the way west, it gives way to scrubby terrain. The distance from the cedar forest to the hamlet of Vidauque is 15km and crosses the path from the Gorges de Regalon to Oppède (see Chapter 10). At the Tête des Buisses, by a radar station, the road is again in use but mostly only in an easterly direction. Go down the steep hill to Vidauque with the Alpilles and Cavaillon as part of the panorama. At the bottom is the restaurant Les Quatre Saisons where they grill corn on the cob and serve it with butter and lemon sauce as a starter. Or you may prefer the *feuilletté de saumon* – the pastry melts on the tongue. You can follow with the traditional *daube* or perhaps a white fish in a brown sauce, and finish with *fromage blanc* in its *coulis de framboise*. And all accompanied by the excellent organically grown wines of La Canorgue from a château close to Bonnieux. More to the point, after such a trek, Les Quatre Saisons has a swimming pool which can be used for the price of a drink.

Vidauque lies off the D31 between Robion and Cheval Blanc. If your car and driver refuse to budge out of Cavaillon a taxi fare will not ruin you; the walk to that sprawling town is not recommended.

6   Hill towns above the Coulon

Cavaillon : Robion : Oppède : Ménerbes : Lacoste : Bonnieux :
Roussillon : Goult : St-Pantaléon : Gordes

The Coulon is a tributary of the Durance into which, when in business, it flows close to Cavaillon, so it is fitting to start from that town to tour this clutch of *villages perchés*. Another reason is that Cavaillon has its own small hill town on Mont Caveau, a select suburb with prosperous villas, a pizzeria, terrifying wolfhounds but, more importantly, the twelfth-century chapel and hermitage, St-Jacques, which sits on the very edge of the cliff. From the mighty rock, which faces the end of the Luberon range, you are pointed in the direction of many of the towns on the itinerary. Up here there were tribal settlements but the Romans built their town on the plain. Virtually nothing of it remains. Only two arches, one of them, finely decorated, may have been part of a gateway elsewhere. They were re-erected late in the nineteenth century in the Place François-Tourel from which there are wearying steps up to Mont Caveau.

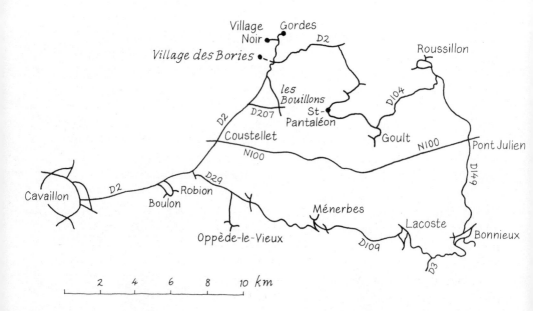

Cavaillon is said to be the wealthiest town *per capita* in all France which is something you might not guess from driving into it past streets of poky houses and dreary blocks of flats. Perhaps the inhabitants like to keep a low profile. One of them provides a touch of unconscious humour with a motor accessories establishment named GAY PNEUS.

The demoted cathedral of Notre-Dame-et-St-Véran has a typical octagonal Provençal tower, and beside it a complementary belfry, but its best feature is a small cloister with a garden. The paving around it is uneven and exudes the same air of neglect as the stonework of the entire building, some of which is in a parlous condition. If this were Britain there would be a hoarding at the entrance pleading for hundreds of thousands of pounds for essential repairs. On the south wall, in good shape, is a sundial worked into the stone, surmounted by a senior looking angel. The interior is dingy but worth inspecting for the four hundred years old carved pulpit and choir stalls.

There is a synagogue and Musée Judéo-Comtadin, also an archaeological museum. They can be visited on one ticket. The museum has coins, pottery, prehistoric stones, a human skeleton with embryo and, because the former chapel in which it is housed was once attached to a hospital, rooms with medical items. The synagogue and Jewish museum are in a street which has recently been re-paved with small oval stones in various colours. The former is reached up an outside staircase on to a balcony with three high arched windows. The pretty interior, in silver and turquoise, has a wrought iron gallery. It is no longer used for worship so the tabernacle will be opened in your presence. During the Occupation its treasures were removed and hidden in a cellar. The 'synagogue' then became a tea-room with an orchestra behind the railings enclosing the tabernacle. The transformation fooled the Germans. A most charming building, it dates from 1772/4 and is still used for weddings. Beneath it, entered from under an archway, is the museum in which may be seen the oven where unleavened bread was baked, a six-teenth-century Old Testament printed in Paris, and objects from an earlier synagogue on the same site.

The religious buildings do not reflect the alleged wealth of the town; many of the shops do. Some of these are in a pleasantly pedestrianised area. Cavaillon is famous for its melons and it is worth noting that market day is Monday when, unusually for France, the centre is bustling and alive.

On leaving, once you have reached the ring road, encompassing not only the town but also Mont Caveau, take the D2 for Apt. After a few kilometres you will come to Robion, situated on and around a modest-sized perch, standing slightly away from the sheer cliffs of the Petit Luberon, against which there is an open-air theatre. The caves above were inhabited long, long ago. Sections of ramparts remain, merging with buildings of many periods. A clock-tower-cum-belfry, formerly part of the Chapel of the White

Penitents, is now the high end wall of a house. Old defences have become garden boundaries. The church, of Romanesque simplicity, has suffered the usual modifications and alterations of time and was burned by the terrible Baron des Adrets. Robion is a place for a gentle stroll, to admire the prettiness and to note the plaques erected in 1989 to commemorate its most eminent citizens of two hundred years before. Near the theatre is a path up the mountain. Above the church an ill-kept road leads to Boulon, a hamlet where rivers rise, their sources concealed, as at Fontaine-de-Vaucluse, within the mystery of the mountain. Boulon today has one or two ruined buildings, a concrete stage marked Private Property standing in a large paddock, and the shell of a very old Renault. There are many picnic tables in a placid setting.

Stop at Robion if you can, though there are more remarkable places to come.

The inhabitants of the tortuously-sited Oppède-le-Vieux agreed, understandably, to be officially re-housed on the plain nearby between 1907-1911. Hence the growth of Oppède-les-Poulivets. In World War Two, however, the abandoned settlement, lying beneath the ruins of the castle built around the end of the twelfth century by the Counts of Toulouse, became a place of refuge for artists hounded by the Germans and the Vichy government. It has since become fashionable to restore old houses on the hillside and many now display signs of affluence.

Enter under the archway of the old *mairie* which has wooden beams, supports a bell-tower and has apartments, one boasting a smart door with a heavy brass knocker. Turn right, starting your ascent of – at its best – steep, roughly cobbled terrain and then uneven slippery track. Mostly it is the latter, so if you are at all unsure of foot, turn back at once. This is a not much inhabited part of the old town and if you climb it alone you may well be lulled into a sense of wondering unreality. You pass dishevelled houses and gaping ruins, overgrown with weeds, and you may come upon a licensed car parked in what the owner thinks of as a lay-by. How it got there or will be removed is a mystery. Shortly, on the right, is a flight of thirty steps, some broken, leading to the church and château. These were laid by a Christian writer of stories for missionaries who wished to divert tourists from a right of way passing his house. Above them are many, many more, some in perilous condition. You will find yourself brushing past foliage up unlikely narrow openings and hoping you are taking the correct route. You are, and you soon come into a clearing beside the church, a stolid edifice of twelfth-century origin. The key can be had from the *mairie* but a custodian may be showing customers around already, allowing you to slip in unofficially. There are orderly pews, a furnished altar with paintings above and behind it, side chapels, one dated 1691, and hymn books piled ready for use. It is not in the best of nick but the roof and buttresses look sound. From a balcony behind the apse there are fine vistas. Look up at the ruined château and you will see a window with stone framework almost intact. There could be someone watching. In the background is the thickly tree-clad mountainside. The going is heavy, nature mingling inextricably with broken masonry.

The Counts of Toulouse and Provence supported the Albigensian heresy and, when it was suppressed, forfeited the castle to the Pope. The Vatican, in due course, awarded it to one Jean de Meynier who became the first baron of Oppède and celebrated his authority by massacring the Vaudois Protestants here and elsewhere in the Luberon, as a curtain-raiser to the Wars of Religion.

On the descent from the château, pass the church again before taking another path towards a semi-derelict chapel standing, locked, beneath umbrella pines, like a stage backcloth. Or, I should say, like yet another stage backcloth because Oppède is essentially theatrical. Below lie houses in various stages of resuscitation. One, with its shutters and roof intact, looks inhabited, but is it? It has outhouses and a cellar, wonky walls and rough brickwork. Is someone inside at work on a Gothic novel? Higher up the hill is a handsome Renaissance mansion with a small corner turret, crenellations and a large decorated doorway. On the roadway taking you back to the car park are several well-kept houses, one with a shady, Spanish-style courtyard, studded oak doors and an ironwork balcony on stone supports. Another, perhaps an atelier, has a small neat garden, with lawn, rose bushes and a swing. Oppède is, at every turn, surprising.

There is a choice of two minor roads through vineyards and farmland to Ménerbes, which is built on a hill, roughly oval in shape. The privately owned citadel dominates the centre of one part of it, with the other main buildings strung out along the crest above steep, narrow alleys of shops and houses, all of which should deter drivers, and some of them do.

Ménerbes passed through the familiar ownership of the Counts of Provence and Toulouse, who acquired it from the Comte de Forcalquier and passed it on to the Avignon popes. None of these owners fortified it and the castle was not built until the 1580s after the town had been besieged during the Wars of Religion. The Huguenots held out for five years.

The castle was bought, in 1962, by the art historian John Rewald who restored it but visitors are not admitted. The best view is from a path on the south side of the town or from below on the plain. The front gate, unimposing behind a well-watered small lawn and fir trees, is at the end of a path along the centre of the hill. This is as close as you can get.

On the way to the church is the official town centre with the Hôtel de Ville in pleasing stone but having unfortunate double-fronted glass doors.

Close by is an archway beneath a clock-tower leading to the ramparts. Between the *centre ville* and the church stands one particularly handsome house with a turret, and a garden planted with welcoming cypresses that rise almost to the roof. (In Provence *two* cypresses are a symbol of hospitality; if both flourish, your virtue in this respect is evident to all but if only one does well your generosity of spirit has fallen short.)

The church, usually locked, has a squat bell-tower at an angle of 45° to the nave, a feature noted elsewhere in the region. Several of the windows have been bricked up, the forecourt is dusty and it stands, on weekdays at least, forlorn. Next to it, equally neglected after vandalism in the 'eighties, is the cemetery. Here the sense of desolation is heightened and the tombstones, standing above graves so untended that their outlines have vanished, resemble menhirs. Walk through them to the far wall to look down upon Le Castellet, a fifteenth-century small castle, now owned by the widow of painter Nicolas de Stael. It doesn't look grand enough to warrant the fortified walls surrounding it, but once it was part of the town's defences. It is also associated with a Danish count who fled his country after being involved in an attempt to kill his queen's lover. To the left are trim vineyards, a large farm complex, then, on the slopes above, woodland dotted with villas. Further south the mountain rises above a quarry which from this distance suggests a display of abstract sculpture. To the right is the gleamingly prosperous valley stretching away to the Plateau across more vineyards, orchards, woods, and some scrubland with habitations, large and small.

Another aspect may be appreciated from the car park below the restaurant Clementine where benches face a smaller hump of hill forming a backdrop to a scene of cultivated land with farm buildings and houses. If it were a painting you would commend the artist for his perfect composition but it is thus for practical or legal, not aesthetic, reasons. A *mas*, shabby, apparently neglected, has a complexity of outbuildings clinging to the once handsome farmhouse. Only from the height of the car park can its diversity be perceived. Others are more spruce, with clipped hedges and cypresses, a smart new wing here, a modern barn there, both in their soft Provençal hues, blending with older parts. This is a favoured land. Linger to stand and stare awhile.

Behind the car park is a street which leads to a track round the south-east side of the hill, then returns to meet another steep road with houses facing the Luberon. This makes a pleasant forty minutes' walk, mostly beside fields or prosperous villas set in spacious, abundant gardens. Away towards Bonnieux is the farmhouse converted by Peter Mayle, author of the hugely successful *A Year in Provence*.

Descend from Ménerbes and take the D109 to Lacoste, a town which owes its present prosperity at least partly to the notoriety of the

Lacoste: Bell-tower

Marquis de Sade but some also to the presence in it of a school associated with the Cleveland Institute of Art. It is here that Michael Jacobs, who has written an excellent guide to a larger Provence than mine, taught, and it is common to hear American accents resounding against the stones. The de Sade family comes into Lacoste's history only in the early eighteenth century. Before that the castle was variously owned during four centuries. There were ramparts as early as 1038 which, in time, made the town eminently defendable during the Wars of Religion when it was a Protestant stronghold. The besieged surrendered after being offered safe custody. They were then murdered and raped.

The Marquis de Sade converted the château into a manageable house of forty-two rooms and a private theatre. It was all but destroyed during the Revolution when the most famous member of the family was absent, and is being very slowly restored by one André Bouer. It can be reached the easy way, by a track road leading to a small plateau from which there is a bridge across the dried-out moat, but ascent from the town is to be preferred. Park by the post office and climb, first to the Portail de la Garde which leads to an evenly cobbled street. At the old *boulangerie,* now a residence, bear right and then, at the clock-tower, perform a U-turn, pass beneath an arch and prepare for a haul up stony, uneven ground that becomes increasingly wooded as you approach the castle. On the north wall is an unguarded, wide stone staircase with a locked door at the top. There is evidence of new stone blocks but vastly more is to be done before it becomes habitable again. Not far from the rear entrance is a disused quarry overlooked by a tall *borie*-style building. In its grounds, so far as they can be defined, are a few strange sculptures by Malachier, a miller who lived here about a century ago.

Return to the town by the tortuous path and enjoy its buildings. The main street winds and undulates from a trim, square *mairie,* through the Place de l'Ancien Temple (no remains visible), past Les Studios de Justine, a hôtel and the Café de Sade, back to the car park. Outside the café, an arbour has been created at a dip in the street; beneath it are served good, simple, cheap meals. It is all intensely picturesque and atmospheric. The church, with its typical early seventeenth-century belfry, is not remarkable but is an essential item in the townscape. Unlike Oppède, Lacoste has been continuously inhabited since early times. It faces Bonnieux across one valley, and Goult across another. We once overlooked the former, seated at a rusty, sloping table on a terrace with a gradient of about 1:5. There three of us were served with vast omelettes, each sufficient for a family, and mountains of *frites,* as we drank in both the fabulous view and litres of white wine.

Bonnieux stands at one approach to the Lourmarin Gap and is dominated by a partly Romanesque church which offers one of the most relentless of all climbs in these hill towns, although it can also be reached by road. From the winding, drab main street, go under an arch with directions to the *Mairie, l'Eglise* etc, and after a steep, straight, slippery cobbled path you turn right to face eighty steps leading to the church whose door is almost certain to be locked. It attracts few, if any, worshippers because the faithful use a much larger but by no means more beautiful edifice near the foot of the hill. This also tends to be locked. It has recommended fifteenth-century paintings. The custodian's door, at 17 Rue Voltaire, was so heavily shuttered that I didn't dare disturb him.

Down one of the many flights of steps joining the various terraces is a fine house, crowded into a corner, with a small, stone lion guarding its doorway. On the wall is a coat of arms bearing a motto; Hauteur N'Est Souch. I am unable to explain its meaning.

A singular feature of Bonnieux is its Musée de la Boulangerie. The exhibits are housed on four floors of an ex-bakery and you are encouraged to begin at the top although the great ovens, of course, are in the basement. Every aspect of baking is touched upon, from engravings of Christ performing the miracle of the loaves and fishes, down to an advertisement for Fernandel's film, *Le Boulanger de Valorgue*. Other posters proclaim conditions of sale at various dates. Bread plays a particularly vital rôle in the daily life of France so it is not surprising to note all the literature it has produced. It may be freely consulted, with tables and chairs provided, but the non-professional visitor will probably be content to read pages from some of the ledgers, and to study a few invoices. One *facture* dated 22 Nov 1929 bills 10 Farine Supérieure, each weighing 1,000 poids, and costing 218 old francs. (An explanation of the weight of a poid would be helpful and also a note of the comparative value today.)

On the ground floor are spotlessly clean rooms, with white marble tiles, displaying costumes, furniture, rock specimens and artefacts having no obvious connection with *baguetterie*. I prefer the gloomy cellar where there are blackened ovens and curiously shaped vessels used daily in performance of a ritual dear to every French person's heart – and stomach.

A minor road to the N100 leads from Bonnieux, past the Château la Canorgue, where I occasionally drop in to buy a case of the excellent *vin biologique*, to the Pont Julien. This perfectly preserved Roman bridge, still in use (though not for lorries) has three arches over the river Coulon. The middle one is higher than the others and there are additional openings for taking the water when the river was in flood. Turn into a track at one end, park the car and gaze at its simple beauty and the ingenuity of its design. It is a small masterpiece, a gem surviving from the ancient world.

The places mentioned so far in this chapter were probably not seen on a first visit. Roussillon, to which we are coming through fertile farming land, a few small woods and hills in bright hues, may well have been.

The most colourful of the hill towns, by nature of its ochre cliffs, the dozen or more shades of which are present in the buildings, Roussillon is also in my estimation the most beautiful. There is near perfection in the grouping of its church and houses on the eminence dominating the gorge where the sand is mined. At the start of a path by a large car park there is a splendid new sun-dial, and notices explaining the colour formation of the rock. They relate how the industry, started in 1780, declined in the 1930s but

Roussillon

was revived after World War Two. Diagrams show how the ochre, discovered by Jean-Etienne Astier, is worked. It is non-toxic and used to colour linoleum, wall paper, cigarette papers and other materials. By a decree of the municipality samples of rock and sand may not be removed. The path is mostly unfenced and slippery. Discourage children from playing in the sand, which stains clothes, but take the walk, even though some of it is vertiginous, because of the aesthetically satisfying experience of beholding this weird landscape, partly natural, partly man-made. If you complete it you will come to the quarries where open-cast drilling takes place. There are more ochre cliffs on the other side of town above the Aiguilles du Val des Fées (the Fairy's Valley).

Roussillon has not had a particularly dramatic history by local standards. There are a few remains of a château and the church goes back to 1048, although some of it fell down the hill when an adjoining building was blown away in a gale in 1858. At the top of the town is a pottery and gallery, just beneath a spectacular viewing point. The church lies below it and the bell-tower lower still. The latter has an archway which frames the incomparable countryside. There are several restaurants. We once enjoyed Sunday lunch at a kind of pub where real life hunters sat at a long table with their families. There was no menu. Large, succulent cutlets were served with *pommes frites* and mixed salad. The bar was crowded with locals gossiping over their pastis and beer. It was out of season and we were treated as though we belonged.

One of the most interesting items of Provençal literature. *Village in the Vaucluse,* is by an American professor, Laurence Wylie, who lived in Roussillon with his family for a year in the early 1950s. The way of life it describes has altered markedly since it was first published but the village looks substantially the same as it was then and, although the book is now a period piece, the contemporary reader will learn much from it which is relevant. One revealing fact relates to the days of retribution following the Liberation. The mayor was ordered to arrest a number of citizens for collaboration with the enemy. He tore up the instructions. The Roussillonnais were not to be allowed to settle old scores or perpetuate feuds on a wave of fervent nationalism. They were one village; they were rebuilding their lives.

Roussillon has another claim to fame because of Samuel Beckett who, as an Irish citizen, was not interned but spent part of the war here lying low. The boredom of village life led him to a nervous breakdown, and memory of it can be found in dialogue in his most famous play, *Waiting for Godot*. But he also helped in the Resistance.

The departmental road 104 leads to Goult which is usually ignored by the guide books. It is a gentler experience than the other hill towns. The streets are tarmacked and none of them is especially steep. There are few ruins and most of the buildings are well maintained. The original settlement was remote from the entrance to the present town where church and *mairie* stand. The church is simple Romanesque. There we have enjoyed many chamber concerts under the auspices of the Friends of Music of the Luberon.

The château is built on the rock and extends above the road to join a wing, with a turret at one end, and a well-groomed courtyard beside it. It is privately owned. Higher up the hill, reached by a drawbridge, are some remains of another castle. A road beside the first leads to a panorama via well cared for gardens open to the public, many old dry-stone walled houses, a few arches and a segment of ancient rampart. The large viewing area could be mistaken for someone's back yard but you are not trespassing. It is a tranquil spot.

A rough cattle track beside a sailless windmill beyond the walls leads to terraces first cultivated some 1,500 years ago when the Romans had departed. They were worked until soon after World War Two. Then the dry-stone walling deteriorated and the olive trees were petrified in the great frost of 1956. In 1988 a seven-year project of restoration and conservation was energetically undertaken by an association (with a long, easily forgettable name) backed by funds from the EC, national and regional government and local councils. The work achieved is a triumph for those dedicated citizens who have contributed to it. There is a small herbarium at the start of a well-signed itinerary, much of which is over rough paths and up and down rudimentary steps. At frequent intervals are notice boards drawing attention to what is, or was, grown here and to the finer points of dry-stone walling. You are shown where beehives were attached to the walls; you are taken to a cistern hewn out of the rock centuries ago to store precious water. The remarkable resilience of the olive is illustrated countless times. The trees were frozen to extinction yet the roots stayed alive and put out shoots which, now bearing fruit, surround the stump of the original. An attempt, so far unsuccessful, is being made to reintroduce the almond. You will come across *borie*-style houses partly used for the protection of toiling workers retreating out of the sun but also as leisure shelters. As you make your way gingerly about the terraces you will certainly appreciate the harsh conditions endured by those who lived off the produce grown on them. At the end of the trail is a massive chunk of rock bearing a metal cross and the brief message MISSION 1935 GOULT. Presumably it commemorates a latterday evangelistic endeavour rather than the arrival of Christianity in these parts.

Goult lies immediately above the hamlet of Lumières, where there is a pilgrimage church of Notre-Dame with a large collection of ex votos. Motorists who pass by on the busy N100 are mostly unaware of the next-time-round treat on the terraces above them.

On your return to the car park in the centre of Goult note a veteran Bureau de Poste, now disused, with stone benches outside. It also deserves restoration.

You may have time to deviate from the road to Gordes to a curiosity which is not a hill town though it is on a slope. The church at St-Pantaléon, almost lost in the rich countryside, is twelfth-century or possibly earlier. It stands by a road junction at the top of a hamlet which is about to become village-sized by the provision of new housing estates. It is minuscule, with room for only three rows of short pews facing the altar. At its rear, apparently part of the rock, is a necropolis in which are said to be the tiny tombs of stillborn babies. The legend is that the little corpses miracu-lously came to life for sufficient time to receive baptism before burial. (So why didn't a merciful god breathe more air into their lungs and allow them at least a childhood?) Another explanation of the tiny tombs (60-70cm long) is that when space ran out in the 'normal' cemetery, remains buried there were cast higgledy-piggledy into the graves hollowed out of the rock. The key to the church can be obtained from the auberge down the hill. The villagers are proud of the church's survival. In 1907 some insensitive person tried to purchase it for conversion into a barn. There was an outcry and today there exists an association committed to its maintenance. The modest charge for membership should be increased to cover the cost of a few large dusters. It is a charming building, but also sad because of those diminutive tombs.

On to Gordes, the most spectacularly sited of all the hill towns and, like Roussillon, it may have been 'done' first time round. It lies on a spur of the Plateau de Vaucluse and can be seen from miles around until it is momentarily lost in the final ascent. Then, suddenly, as the road curves, it is there again in close-up, an unforgettable sight. A few spaces are provided so that those in cars can stop a while to fix the scene in their minds and take photos. You'll see small terraces with cypresses and bushes, tiny lawns, many supportive man-made walls and chunks of natural rock on which some of it openly lies. Amongst the orderly hôtels and villas are some ruined houses, all in pink stone; at the top is the plainly buttressed church and the great château. It is another utterly unplanned yet harmonious composition.

The car park lies a half-kilometre on and is heralded by a double hexagon of blue cubes alerting you to the fact that you are about to enter the village of Vasarely. He is a painter who had a severe attack of the abstracts in the second half of his life. This made his fortune and gave rise to the Vasarely Foundation at Aix. More importantly for Gordes, which was partly destroyed from reprisals when a German soldier was killed, the painter helped to rebuild the Renaissance castle, some part of which still showed eleventh-century origins. The price the town has to pay for this is a permanent exhibition, on four floors, of Vasarely canvases, tapestries and constructions. In the basement, confusingly reached *up* steps from the main *place* but *down* others through the Hôtel de Ville, is the Musée Didactique, where entry is free because this is a saleroom for the master's works. On the three floors above, in the high-ceilinged chambers with beamed roofing, are more and more of Vasarely's designs, which may be of surpassing interest to textile manufacturers but, in this setting, are dull, monotonous and incompatible. Then on the first floor the admission price becomes acceptable because, at the end of the vast chamber, is a carved chimney-piece covering almost the entire wall. It has pediments, niches without figures, a frieze, cornice and medallions. It is rich in its whole and in its detail.

On the next floor, in both rooms, Vasarely is at his most yawn-worthy but above comes some reward although not until the far room is reached. There, facing the doorway, is a delightful painting of tigers (1939), and around it portraits and other canvases reveal a master's touch. There is also a self-portrait with the head surrounded in glowing light.

Other painters associated with Gordes were André Lhôte, who made the village an artistic centre in 1939, and Marc Chagall who lived there after World War Two.

From without it is difficult to ascertain the precise shape of the massive church because it is embedded closely with other buildings. If you enter be sure to wear dark glasses. Apart from the ceiling at its highest point, where it is dirty white, it is garishly decorated throughout, crammed with gaudy altars, bad paintings and inferior statuary. Retreat at once into the extremely hazardous streets and alleys (*calades*). Turn right to slither down to the Théâtre des Terrasses, stopping to cling to a wall, as you take in the stunning views over patchwork-quilted countryside. Return to the *centre ville* by another set of steps arranged in the local style, with cobbled ways on either side of ramps, and the whole bordered by shallow runnels to take away occasional rain. As you look again at the château note the fairylights on the topmost wall, a ludicrously kitsch addition.

The enlarged town plan in the car park indicates both the Village des Bories (here spelt Lories) and a Village Noir. The former is a must, the latter is difficult to establish as fact although it also appears on IGN Map 67. It is not signposted but I spent an enjoyable hour in boisterous weather striding along lanes of dry-stone walling looking for it. I encountered no one but a free-range dog who, mercifully, considered himself more wary of me than he supposed I was of him. I came to a field at what I reckoned was the position of the map reference. There were ruined hovels but no evidence that they had been burned. Returning a few months later, I found them not only inhabited by touring cyclists, but fitted with bunks and lockable wooden doors.

The actual Village des Bories nearby is reached through scrubland down a narrow track off the D2, although that also we found difficult to locate at a first attempt. However, it is there, so persevere along a thoroughfare on which it is a relief not to meet oncoming traffic, cross a little bridge and park before walking up a short path to the site. It is open all day, all the year round.

Although prehistoric in appearance, the *bories* here are only three to four hundred years old. They are dry-stone huts with pointed roofs, and can be found at various places in France, as well as in other European countries and on other continents. The examples below Gordes are unique in Provence for comprising an entire settlement. On the approach road you will see isolated *bories*, but it is not until you have climbed the uneven terrain bordered by umbrella pines, holm oaks and olives, that you come upon the several groups of buildings, surrounding a central baking house, which have been painstakingly restored over the last twenty years. There are five clusters each with a different arrangement of dwelling, barn, pigsty, goat or sheep pen and storage space. Some have mezzanine areas which were bedrooms, two have places where silkworms were bred, one boasts an actual two-story house, the upper part reached by unrailed rough steps. This is now a museum recording the progress of restoration and displaying photographs of similar dwellings elsewhere. You have to bend almost double to enter some of the buildings, several of which have glassed-off sections in which are shown various artefacts relevant to the life and work of the settlers. Occupations were not only farming the surrounding land, tending the olives, vines, almond and mulberry trees, but also making agricultural implements and shoes. The site is lonely. The buildings owe much to folk history but were

Gordes: Village des Bories

81

constructed between 1600-1800, remaining inhabited until the last century. They could have been refuges in troubled times or the peasants who lived in them may have felt themselves a part of Gordes because there is no trace of a church, a burial ground or a formal meeting place.

On a day when there is a light breeze to mitigate the fierce sun it is a placid place to be. Shadows cast on the beautifully simple stone walling acquire an almost mystic quality enhanced by the presence of an almond tree petrified in the course of an unusually harsh winter.

Silence prevails.

Following this experience you will probably drive past the turning to Les Bouillons where, in a farmhouse and on its grounds, are two museums. They are of contrasting nature, one being devoted to the history and development of stained glass, the other to olive oil. You do not have to visit both in order to see one of them but the admittance fee covers the two.

You go first to the farmhouse which is an old mill set at an attractive angle to the road and surrounded by trees. Most of the ground floor is a celebration of the olive – its hardware, its software, its anointed place in religion. The Route of the Caesars, declares a poster, is the Route of the Olive. The prize exhibit is a tree trunk almost ten metres long which supplied the pressure to the grindstone extracting the oil.

The stained glass museum is in a super-shed with a drunken floor following the contours of a rocky slope. The permanent exhibition traces the use of glass in early Egypt and Mesopotamia to the revival of the craft of staining it in post-Second-World-War Europe. There are reproductions of the windows at Chartres cathedral and elsewhere which enable those who are not technically minded to enjoy the museum visually without comprehending some of the processes demonstrated.

By now the road back to Cavaillon may well call. Once in that town again, visit the café-restaurant Fin-de-Siècle, in the Place du Clos. Thirty-three steps lead to the elegant first-floor dining-room which seems to be under separate ownership from the ground-floor café where, at lunch time, they serve a delicious, copious, and inexpensive *plat du jour* (steaks, cutlets, chicken casseroles, with *frites* and salad). The café is wide and high (hence those 33 steps) with a bar like a battlement and marble-topped tables, some in low-sided alcoves. There are extravagant chandeliers and huge wall mirrors which reflect the ceiling and cornices, and also the fine double doorway to an inner saloon. On its ornate pediment a wicked-looking cherub brandishes a loving cup in one hand and a bunch of grapes in the other. Beside the door are delicately painted panels in the style of Redouté, one of which has unfortunately been partly removed to allow for a service door into the kitchen. Then there are the enjoyably atrocious late-eighteenth-century pastoral paintings. One shows a lover serenading a lady who seems to have become detached from her legs. In another the beau is concentrating on the minutiae of his belle's high mop of hair whilst an improbable sheep looks on. I call it 'Nit-Picking'.

It is not difficult to imagine Manet's barmaid from the Folies Bergères behind the counter, but what would she make of the modern nut-dispenser? You are more likely to be served by a pleasant young man in jeans.

7   The Sorgue and Auzon Basins

L'Isle-sur-la-Sorgue : Le Thor : Aubignan : Caromb :
Mazan : Carpentras : Pernes-les-Fontaines : Le Beaucet :
Saumane-de-Vaucluse : Fontaine-de-Vaucluse

The Sorgue is a short river which begins mysteriously, ends ignominiously and thrusts about extravagantly in between. Whether its source is deep inside the Plateau de Vaucluse, or further away in another mountain, has not been ascertained. When in full spate it gushes from a cave at Fontaine-de-Vaucluse and very soon splits into five strands at L'Isle-sur-la-Sorgue. These receive other waters as they flow, mostly in a north-westerly direction. One joins the Ouvèze at Bédarrides, another makes a brief appearance at Avignon before diving underground into the Rhône. The river is at its best at the town which was once an island in its midst.

From having lived in it, I know L'Isle better than other towns in the region. On the morning bread-and-newspaper run I exchange greetings with upwards of a dozen residents. The kids on our *lôtissement* meticulously ring the bell to request permission to retrieve their footballs; when we are absent they climb the fence. We have been accepted on the estate. Neighbours invite us for drinks, forward our mail when we are in England; we have even played *pétanque* together. So I am biased in L'Isle's favour; I have also proved its convenience as a centre, which is why I recommend its Hôtel des Nevons (no restaurant but it has both garage and car park) and the Café-restaurant Bellevue. At the latter, opposite a confluence of Sorgues, you can eat simply, cheaply and well, but avoid the house wine. In summer there is a charcoal grill, with its chimney lost in the branches of a plane tree. Waitresses jaywalk between restaurant and riparian terrace. Ducks and occasional kayaks float by, boys dive into the river from a road bridge over which, on Saturdays, wedding motorcades make their raucous way, all horns blaring.

Inevitably, L'Isle has been dubbed 'the Venice of the Comtat' but the comparison is superficial. Pope-Hennessy wrote that its ten banks give it 'a false, fresh air of Holland'. I don't think that is an accurate description either. It is a town which happens to lie beside water. Its first inhabitants were probably fishermen. It once had walls above its natural moats. They protected it from Baron des Adrets during the Wars of Religion although that rampageous warrior was further deterred by a scorched earth policy

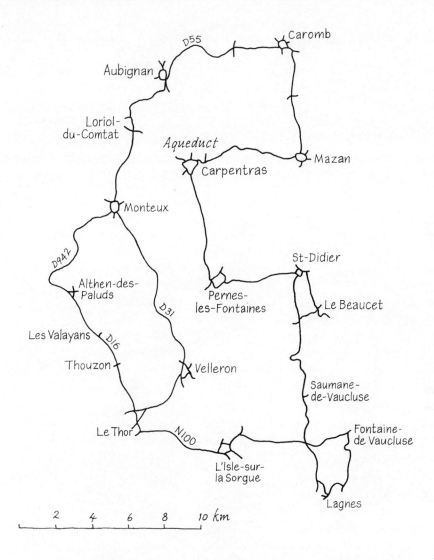

which destroyed monasteries and mills and also flooded the surrounding countryside. During the Terror it was besieged and, later, the walls were demolished; in World War Two the railway was seriously damaged by allied bombing. (L'Isle, incidentally, is the railhead for the more famous Fontaine-de-Vaucluse.)

Architecturally, the town is noted for its Baroque church, its eighteenth-century hospital and the Hôtel de Campredon. Baroque churches are rare in these parts. This one was built on to an existing Gothic edifice, incorporating its fifteenth-century bell-tower, in 1647. The interior is magnificently beautiful or excessively garish, according to your taste. The predominant colour is gold, overlaid with cobweb; above the west door are

85

cherubs on glittering clouds. The walls and columns are busy with saints and angels.

The stone gateway to the Hôtel-Dieu frames a pleasing two-story building with a chapel, an old pharmacy and a fine staircase. The Hôtel de Campredon, also eighteenth-century, has a handsome frontage and a pretty courtyard, softly gravelled, with niches where statues once stood. Its three levels are used for art exhibitions. There are also, between two strands of the Sorgue the pretty Caisse d'Epargne, Italianate, and late nineteenth-century; the earlier palace of the Dukes of Palermo, now devoted to antiques, and a

L'Isle-sur-la-Sorgue: Caisse d'Epargne

dull Cardinal's Tower, another of the town's many art galleries.

To understand how accurately the town is named you must wander about it. The alleys and courtyards leading off the main streets wind and bend, breaking into occasional squares, some of which have been strikingly transformed, their restored apartments now coloured in bold yellow, red or orange ochre. In places there are still stretches of ancient walls which probably were always out of line. A few overlook narrow inlets, unnamed tributaries of the Sorgue. The medieval street plan has been maintained but much of what was frankly squalid to behold only a few years ago has been cheerfully modernised without any hint of tarting-up. And why not? These are homes or offices for the citizens of a prosperous, busy town in the late twentieth century. As you stroll about you will see a number of the great iron waterwheels which still revolve. They are a reminder that L'Isle, long before the industrial revolution, was a town where silk, oil, corn, paper and dyes were processed.

Today the prosperity of the town comes increasingly from its importance as a centre for antiques and junk; and where the one category ends and the other begins is a grey area. More and more properties are being converted from filling stations and shops into showrooms for *antiquités* and *brocante*. Throughout the year the permanent sites are joined on Sundays by stalls set up on the Avénue des Quatre Otages; at Easter and for a long weekend in August the fair goes on for five days, spilling over into the park and elsewhere, sharing pavement space with illegally parked cars. On the day before it officially begins massive quantities of bric-à-brac and larger items of furniture (like a church pew or a row of ex-cinema seats) are de-livered ready for display to the invading hordes who descend upon L'Isle in search of bargains and rarities. Certainly there are treasures to be found but much of what I have examined seems to me either grossly over-priced – e.g., a battered cricket bat at £50 – or ready for the tip. Or both. I have seldom seen transactions being concluded, yet the stall keepers sit contentedly, usually in the sun, sipping champagne at noon, gossiping to each other, then, in the evening, driving off in their BMW's and Volvos. So it must be worth their while.

On Sunday mornings the ordinary produce and clothing market merges with the *brocante* fair, spreading through the streets, squares, and quays, and cluttering the entrance to the church, a regular exhibition of the innate wastefulness of the system. Large quantities of what is unpacked before breakfast is carted away at lunchtime. Many stalls offer identical goods; some, I suspect, don't sell anything. Yet there is an ambience of good humour to which the street musicians contribute, especially Philippe, the baritone with the musical pram and a repertoire of pre-rock *chansons*. At the Café de France, opposite the church, you can withdraw from the seething crowds to have a coffee. On Wednesday evenings this is a rendezvous for live jazz. A few doors along is a double-fronted draper's shop which has resolutely declined to move with the times. Its stock of traditional Provençal materials is stored in or on the original Belle Epoque shop fittings. Not only are credit cards unacceptable, but a notice on the counter states that payment may not be made by cheque in any circumstances, and la patronne still quotes prices in old francs.

The poet René Char was born at L'Isle-sur-la-Sorgue and lived here for most of his life, dying in 1988. He is remembered for his brave rôle in

Le Thor

the Resistance, as well as for his books. As is customary in France many other citizens are commemorated in the street names of this especially appealing place.

L'Isle, regrettably, is expanding apace, with new commercial developments lining the road to Le Thor, a town noted variously for its daily grape market (August-October), its colleges of music and its church. Attached to one musical academy is the Plein Air Théâtre de Jean Moulin, one of many memorials to the Resistance leader. It also has an interior auditorium seating several hundred. We were once present as two of fourteen people attending a piano recital. It has been remarked that there is an over-provision of musical entertainment hereabouts.

A pleasing feature of Le Thor is the clock-tower entrance to the main street. Rightly, it has not been widened to allow two vehicles to pass through it at the same time, even though it is only a replica of the original. Beyond it is the bulky Romanesque church with a beautifully proportioned short spire upon double octagonal lanterns. Albert Camus likened it to a bull: his description is quoted in the lobby beyond the intricately carved doorway with decorated capitals. The road curves round it to a hump-backed medieval bridge over the Sorgue which itself winds about the church precincts. Outside the *mairie,* on the N100, are crumbling statues of Molière and Corneille, duplicates of the ones at the theatre at Avignon.

On the D16 from Le Thor, past the Departmental School of Music, is the much advertised hamlet of Thouzon, with its cave discovered in 1902 when mines were being worked in the hillside. The entrance is from a meadow by a café where the walls are adorned with posters of many other caves. The stalactites within the Grotte de Thouzon are highly admired; the guided tour takes half-an-hour. Before taking it you can picnic on stone seats and tables in the meadow. On the hill-top are the ruins of a Benedictine monastery. The approach is from a lane close by. It is a rough climb up the scrubby hill to what is left of a chapel, part of a single tower, a well mostly filled with rubble and a few walls of patterned brickwork. The twelfth-century monastery was in use until the 1640s.

On through Les Valayans, Althen-des-Paluds and Monteux, perhaps not stopping at any of them. Or you can reach the last-named direct from Le Thor by heading north through orchards, vineyards, fields with high protective rows of cypresses and sheaths of rushes, past Velleron which lends its name to one strand of the Sorgue and passes, in this low-lying neigh-bourhood, as a hill town. Velleron is also known for its weekly agricultural market held austerely on an asphalt enclosure without shade. Monteux rates a note in the history books, not for its dull square tower and extant gate-ways, but for a colourful twelfth-century legend concerning a simple farming boy named Gens who could cause water to pour from rocks, and had such a winning way with wild beasts that when a wolf killed one of his oxen he tethered the creature to his plough and set it to work. Because the Montiliens, then unaware of his amazing gifts, thought him stupid and harried him, Gens became a hermit near Le Beaucet, some twenty kilometres away, and was subsequently canonised. It is to the hermitage there that a pilgrimage is still made on a week-end in mid-May. On the day before the anniversary of the saint's death the young men of Monteux remove his statue from their church and run with it to Le Beaucet. There follows a night of feasting and vigil. The next day they run back with the statue to Monteux. Probably a day to avoid trying to drive through the town because the French have a way of closing streets, and even entire towns, for celebrations of this nature. And quite right too.

Having passed the wittily named Café du TGV, close to the level crossing over a little-used branch line, leave Monteux by a minor, pretty road, almost entirely rural, to the village of Loriol-du-Comtat. It has a little church on a hillock, with two bell-towers, but doesn't warrant a stop. Proceed to Aubignan which, if you have the time and need to buy a picnic, does. It has lost its ramparts but retained two gateways, one of them incorporating a covered meeting or wash place below a clock-tower. There are narrow streets and *impasses* to be inspected on the way to the Place du-Château-du-Pazzis. There were seigneurs d'Aubignan in the fifteenth century but their château has gone, so has the first church of 1095, although an ancient back wall remains as part of the rebuilding of 1732. Next to it is a chapel now used as a theatre.

After Aubignan cross grape-laden countryside to the attractive hill town of Caromb whose vineyards are irrigated by a reservoir, the Etang du Paty, formed in the eighteenth century by a complex of walls and locks. The simple, podgy church of flaking sandstone encloses a highly decorated interior. It lies below the fragmentary remains of the château which was mostly destroyed in the Wars of Religion. Gates of the old walled town remain, and there are eerie, narrow streets, off which run courts and alleys. The Hôtel de Ville, sixteenth-century, has a familiar iron belfry and overlooks an equally typical fountain. The local white wine has a distinctive flavour and can be obtained from a *cave* on the Carpentras road where, attached to it, is a small museum. You cannot go far in Provence without coming upon a museum.

Take minor roads to Mazan on a lower hill dominated by a fine church whose octagonal bell-tower is surmounted by a spire. This has a spacious interior round which runs a wide ambulatory decorated with sculpted reliefs of the Crucifixion. To one side of the church across a small *place* is a deconsecrated chapel with a perilous outside staircase rising to a small belfry. It houses a museum open, under voluntary supervision, on afternoons in high summer. The exhibits are mostly rural – agricultural implements, peasant costumes, stuffed birds, and so forth. The most interesting item can be peered at through the gates if the museum is closed. It is a *four banal*, a fourteenth-century communal oven of formidable size.

Ancient Mazan is perpetuated on the walls of the cemetery, on another hill facing the town. These are lined with sarcophagi of Gallo-Roman origin. The chapel of the graveyard, Notre-Dame-de-Pareloup, is eleventh- or twelfth-century, and was restored in 1456. Little, obviously, has been done to maintain it since. It takes its name from a tradition that it was built to ward off marauding wolves. Partly submerged, which may be due to subsidence, it is overhung by pine trees and is more pleasant to behold than the lovingly tended, opulent tombs nearby.

All this time we have been making a ring around Carpentras, for long the capital of the Comtat, and the largest place by far on this itinerary. It has an aqueduct which goes one better than the Pont du Gard in successfully negotiating a bend. It also has a famous library and the second oldest synagogue in Europe.

Over the centuries Carpentras has proved impregnable although it lies not much higher than L'Isle-sur-la-Sorgue and at only half the altitude of Vaison-la-Romaine.

The Ligurians were here, one of their tribes making it their capital long before the Romans colonised it about 45BC. Prior to that it came under the jurisdiction of the governor of Gaul. The Roman presence is now marked only by the much diminished remains of a triumphal arch tucked away in a corner between the cathedral and the law courts. This is worth noting for its relief figures of prisoners but, during the season, difficult to locate because then the square beside it has a stage and seating for open air performances of music and opera. Carpentras, like many Provençal towns, has an annual festival. It is also famed for its confectionery, the *berlingots*, in mint, caramel, aniseed and other flavours.

There were two layers of ramparts (one is now part of a new one-way system) which successfully defied Baron des Adrets when Carpentras, as capital of the Comtat, was a Catholic stronghold. Nor did the revolutionaries, marching two centuries later, conquer it easily. Avignon had turned on the Pope but Carpentras remained loyal. A fortuitous storm dispersed the attackers but time was not on the defendants' side and the following year the city became part of France. Not only that. It lost status when Avignon was named capital of the Vaucluse.

From Mazan you approach Carpentras on the plain which became a fertile garden in the nineteenth century, following the river Auzon for some of the way. Just before arriving, deviate to the Mont Ventoux road to admire the fine eighteenth-century aqueduct which is 631.50 metres long and rises to 23 metres at its highest point. During the plagues of 1720-22 a *mur de la peste* was built around the entire environs of the city to ward off the epidemic, stretching over the Plateau and beyond to Monieux and villages on the southern side. (See Chapter 4 under Méthamis.)

Where the road from Mazan approaches central Carpentras is the rectangular market place (Allées des Platanes). Except on Fridays it provides ample parking. Close to the north end is Les Marchés de Provence, a super greengrocers' with produce proudly and lovingly displayed. The old town is to the west. Enter it from the little garden beside the Office de Tourisme (town plan available) on the Avénue Jean-Jaurès. A passage leads between a music college and recently rehabilitated apartment blocks. On some of the latter can be seen traces of the original stonework. La Charité is more, in fact, than a college of music. Built in 1669 to cater for the poor and needy, it is now a centre for all the arts. The festival is administered from here. There is a theatre, an exhibition hall and, surprisingly, a large aquarium.

Ahead, on the corner of Rue St-Jean, is the neat Chapel of the White Penitents, with a decorated pediment, eye window and single bell-tower. It is now used as a conference centre. Continue past it to the Place Charretier where, tucked into a corner, is the Synagogue. It dates from the fifteenth century but was largely rebuilt in the eighteenth, then restored in 1954. A gallery, lit from within and without, runs all round the interior. A rich red cloth covers the tabernacle. There is a very small chair of Elias. The short tour does not include a visit to the *piscina* or to the oven for baking unleavened bread but the guide has a fund of interesting stories. He will tell you that during the Black Death, when persecution started because the Jews were accused of poisoning the water, the Pope stopped it by pointing out that they too drank from the wells. But, adds the guide, the official pronouncement cost the Jews a large sum. He tells also of 1942 when the Germans marched into Unoccupied France. The city librarian, a Christian, removed all the treasures from the Synagogue in a wheelbarrow and hid them until the Liberation.

More splendidly sited in the square is the Hôtel de Ville which you can literally pass through to reach the colonnaded Rue des Halles. Off one side is a street lined with exclusive looking shops and an arcade at third-story level. Go on to the Rue de l'Evêché which slopes gently down to the Porte d'Orange, almost the only relic of the walls, dating from 1360. This leads on to the Boulevard du Nord where you get the best impression of the height of the town and of its impregnability. From here, either follow the wide (but busy) main road into the Place Gambetta or make your way, with the help of the town map, through narrow, terraced streets where you will form a good idea of how the Carpentrassiens have lived for centuries. Emerge at the Porte de Monteux on to the Boulevard Albin-Durand where, opposite a Baroque bank (Caisse d'Epargne) is one of the city's proudest possessions – the library of Bishop d'Inguimbert, a local boy who, when made bishop in 1735, brought home with him from Italy the collection of books and manuscripts he had amassed there. Ten years later his ever-growing library was opened to the public; when he died in 1757 it comprised 230,000 items of which some 5,000 were in manuscript. Nearly half of these are very early works and about 200 rate as incunabula (printed before 1500). There are also books of hours, drawings and prints, a later bequest.

In the same building, Allemand House, across a rather gloomy courtyard with statuary, is a dingy museum displaying keys, daggers, *santons*, caps and other objects, many in shabby old glass cases. The ground floor collection is said to be representative of life in the Comtat. Upstairs, there are dozens of mediocre paintings, a few items of furniture and a collection of statuettes which may be Roman but the labelling is sketchy. The ticket is supposed also to effect admission to the archaeological museum down the road in the former Chapel of the Grey Penitents but that is sometimes closed.

At the top of the Boulevard Albin-Durand is the Place Aristide-Briand flanked by the imposing Hôtel-Dieu with dashing *pots-à-feu* adorning the roof. It too was founded by Bishop d'Inguimbert and is still in use but you don't have to be visiting the sick to inspect the old pharmacy and wall paintings. There is a fine central double staircase, with iron balustrades, and three simple stained glass windows at the first landing.

Cross to the municipal theatre (period public loos at one end), a forbidding building because all the windows have been bricked over. Next to it is the Musée du Vin with a sumptuous wooden door. You are now back in pedestrianised Carpentras at the Rue de-la-République, leading to the Place Général-de-Gaulle and the cathedral. First, deviate briefly into the Rue du-Collège where the great bulk of the early seventeenth-century chapel glowers over the narrow street. On one side of it is a cloister, on the other a small public garden where someone has erected a lump of stone of indefinable shape. It may be a student jape.

The cathedral, built 1404-1509 after an earlier one had collapsed, is fifth-rate. The Gothic south doorway, through which Jewish converts entered to take baptism, is its highlight but the west front is a mess. The tower is pathetically skimpy, the interior dark and dull, though not badly proportioned. The church is attached to the massive Palais de Justice, formerly the Bishop's residence erected in the 1640s. Both overlook a more or less oblong *place* which has new fountains with double-headed ogres spewing out water. Not a pleasant addition to the many older fountains dotted about the town. Turn right to see the cathedral from the north, its best aspect. Beside it is the

Roman arch already mentioned. Then return to La Charité via the Rue de-la-Sous-Préfecture, noting the ancient doorway at No.40.

Carpentras is still a medieval city in its layout but bustles with contemporary activity. Although it has no single feature so arresting that a visit becomes imperative, it is an historical palimpsest of great interest, supporting the proud claim that it remains Capital of the Comtat Venaissin despite being departmentally ruled from Avignon since 1791.

Return towards L'Isle-sur-la-Sorgue via Pernes-les-Fontaines where, on an approach road, lies a fifteenth-century *croix couverte* charmingly

Pernes: Fontaine du Cormoran

set in a public garden. One guide book states that this accurately named town has 36 fountains, another 33. I haven't counted but if you like a walk to have a purpose, a perambulation through the narrow, hilly streets, ticking them off, gives an innocent objective to a stroll. The first you will see is in the Place du Cormoran close to the well-preserved Porte Notre-Dame near which you will have parked. The church Notre-Dame-de-Nazareth is, curiously, outside the walls and always has been. It merges with what appears to be the presbytery and is usually closed. The apse is eleventh-century and part of a rich architectural jumble which is not well maintained. The walls of the town were first built in the fourteenth century; the Porte Notre-Dame is reached over a bridge embracing a small chapel. There is also a viewing platform over the river Nesque, one bank of which is lined with willows. (Willows in the Vaucluse have a glorious translucence at all seasons; when the leaves have fallen the fronds have a bright green or sometimes vivid orange glow.)

Pernes' greatest glory departed long ago. From 968 to 1320AD it was the capital of the Comtat. A plaque unveiled in 1968, in the courtyard of the Hôtel de Ville, records that one thousand years earlier, following the death of the little-remembered King Boson II of Provence, the town entered an era of prosperity lasting until Carpentras succeeded it as capital. Today its main industry is concerned with the preservation of soft fruits grown locally. Adjoining the town hall is a theatre with a covered stage but open auditorium. The most prominent building is the Tour de l'Horloge, topping what was the keep of the castle. Far below is the Tour Ferrande, once part of a palace belonging to the Knights Hospitaller. In it are late thirteenth-century frescoes which can be seen, during the season, on a guided tour. Note, near the entrance, the multi-, sometimes comically-headed Fontaine de Gigot. Also note, near the cormorants' fountain, on a wall of the covered market, a list of statutory weights and measures showing what were once the going rates in Pernes. Before 1840 when the metric system became law different areas had their own standards, which was confusing and could lead to skulduggery.

Much of the town wall is well cared for, as are the three gateways. Some older buildings need face-lifts but, for the most part, the town is not neglected and the new does not conflict with the old. The public garden near the Tour Ferrande has a lovely arbour with stone tables and chairs and, in the spring, magnificent irises, purple, blue and white. Pernes should not be missed.

East of Pernes is the charming little spa of St-Didier which has more sleeping policemen (*ralentisseurs*) per square metre than anywhere else in this part of the Vaucluse. You are thus forced to drive slowly as you approach it, probably along a fine avenue of plane trees leading to the ancient town behind an arched gateway and bell-tower. Within the walls are well-preserved streets of terraced houses lying between the church and the château. The latter was enlarged and restored many times from the fifteenth century onwards until, in the nineteenth, it became the headquarters of the spa. It now caters for sufferers from nervous diseases and digestive ailments. The property is private but can be admired from the courtyard. The three-storied L-shaped building is just small enough – at least from this viewpoint – to create an atmosphere of domesticity combined with gracious living.

Outside the town on the road to Venasque is an impressive edifice which has been a monastery, a glass works, and a school. It began more modestly as a church, Notre-Dame-de-Ste-Garde, in 1666. After the vicissitudes of three centuries it changed hands yet again in the 1980s to be restored by the Institut Notre-Dame-de-Vie-à-Venasque. It is huge, rather forbidding and anonymous. It could be a barracks or a hospital; no sign reveals its present status. However, our road from St-Didier takes us in a different direction, through farming territory for 5km to a small *village perché*, Le Beaucet, which clings to an outcrop of rock belonging to the Plateau. The remains of the castle are still impressive with a clearly discernible chunk of keep, and they have been softened by the umbrella pines which shade them. Most of it was destroyed by fire after being struck by lightning in the 1780s; it would probably have been savaged in the Revolution anyway. Below it, houses nestle into or under the crag of rock. The ascent from the car park is hard going up steep cobbles but there is another entrance from the rear of the village through a gateway by the *mairie*. This leads past an auberge to a small church which stands almost as high as the castle. In the car park is a statue to

Le Beaucet

96

Gens, the saint especially revered in Monteux. Drive a few more kilometres into the hills, leave your vehicle in a field, then walk to the hermitage where the saint's statue is carried in homage every May.

From Le Beaucet is yet another minor road leading to Saumane-de-Vaucluse. This is a most attractive route through *garrigue* country to a hill village on a narrow promontory detached from the Plateau. It clusters traditionally around the high walls of a château and has an air of quiet prosperity suggestive of dormitory status. There is a small Romanesque church at one end of the spur. High above, at the other, is the castle once in the possession of the de Sade family. An uncle of the notorious Marquis lived here, a learned, loose-living cleric who neglected his Benedictine monastery. It has latterly been restored by the patrimony department of the Conseil Général for the Vaucluse and is currently leased as a training and research centre to a tenant whose name is undisclosed. It faces a public right of way up the hillside and also a path alongside it which was until recently a nature trail. Growing there were seventy-two species of plants and trees all labelled in Latin, French and Provençal. It was a delightful place to be on a hot summer's afternoon, wandering in the shade, perhaps lingering beside *Quercus Pubescens Willdonow* to learn its French name, *Chêne pubescent*, and its Provençal, *Roure o Blacas*, which I could have been fooled into believing was Irish. One description read like a declension:

Asparagus Autifolius
Asperge Sauvage
Aspargo Faro.

It did not look at all edible but a friend assures me it is a great delicacy. My wife recommended the trail as a living reference work for many of the plants and trees mentioned in the Marcel Pagnol autobiographies but, to our regret, the notices have been removed, those species which remain are not identified and the path is blocked by fallen trees, some of them burnt. No one at the château or the tourist office knew the name of the society which had sponsored the trail, or if there was any intention of reinstating it here or elsewhere. At the château they were sincerely regretful. At the *syndicat d'initiative* they were neither helpful nor interested. A fine advertisement for PR.

Descend from Saumane, where the road has been cut through the rock, to Fontaine-de-Vaucluse but do not turn left when it is signed. Go instead to the village of Lagnes, picturesquely situated on a hillside at the top of which you do turn left, to join another road to your destination. This is by far the most dramatic of the three ways into the famous little town which is the one place on this itinerary you are certain to have visited on your first trip to this part of Provence. It is a prime tourist attraction but should not be dismissed for that reason, and it is well worth a return visit.

Fontaine, at the foot of the western end of the Plateau, has long been famous for the mysterious cave where the Sorgue first appears, and for its associations with Petrarch and Laura. It is safe to assume that the hundreds of visitors it attracts every day in summer – plus the dozens in winter – come to climb the rocky path to the 'source' of the river rather than to pay homage to the poet. This path is lined with souvenir shops which even forty years ago sent sensitive souls such as the late James Pope-Hennessy into a quivering rage, but I find them less offensive than the large derelict mill by the bridge, which is an eyesore visible from most of the restaurants. Also, by no means, all of the goods on display rate as junk and in the new underground complex there are shops selling useful and often beautiful handcrafted articles of quality. In the mill, which is part of it, hand-made paper is still produced and you can watch the processes.

It is supposed that, at the end of the path where the river emerges from the mountain there was once a high cavern which the action of the water over the centuries caused to collapse. The great stones on the bed of the Sorgue were probably once its roof. When in full spate the river rushes over these but in the dry season it makes its way beneath and surfaces a few yards further on. In 1950 Jacques-Yves Cousteau and a companion dived to seek the source and were nearly overcome when, having gone down sixty metres, they could still not touch the bottom. There have been many attempts since to plumb the depths. Workers at Renault built, in their spare time, an unmanned machine with cameras, computers and other technology but, unluckily, a cable snapped as it was being raised, and all the information sank. It has never been recovered. A four-language aural aid should be available beside the 'source' but this can be difficult to hear if many people are around, so to learn what is known about the caves beneath the Plateau a visit to the Museum of Speleology may be preferred. This celebrates the explorer Norbert Casteret's lifetime's work underground.

The most recent museum, opened in 1990, is not specifically related to Fontaine-de-Vaucluse. Its subjects are the Occupation and the Resistance, and its lower floor is a grim reminder of daily life under the Germans in France as a whole. There are reconstructions of shops showing signs, NO BREAD, NO EGGS etc, and of a stall with newspapers of the 1940s. There are notices of emergency regulations and examples of ersatz goods, some illustrating native resourcefulness in dealing with acute shortages. On the first floor a fifteen-minute film of the progress of World War Two is shown, relating it to the work of the Resistance. The exploits of Jean Moulin, René Char and other leaders are further recorded in exhibition rooms.

Beside the path to the great wall of mountain are plaques to Petrarch and Laura. It is unlikely that she came here but he did, as a friend of Philippe de Cabassole, who became Bishop of Cavaillon, and who stayed a while in the castle whose ruins overlook the village. Petrarch was a scholar priest (1304-74) who divided his life between Italy and the Comtat Venaissin. The house in which he supposedly lived at Fontaine-de-Vaucluse is now a museum, as you would expect. It is reached through an opening in the rock, just beyond the bridge, and is bordered by an attractive garden and the river. There is a clear view of the castle on its craggy peak at the top of so high and treacherous a path that it makes your heart ache for those who were made to build it. The upper floor of the museum is devoted to Petrarch and his Laura (who bore her husband, Hugh de Sade, eleven children, then died of plague, aged 34) and celebrates, if that is the appropriate word, a relationship which to most of us would be highly unsatisfactory. He is depicted wearing cloth-cap style headgear which also covers his neck, presumably a religious vestment. Not exactly dishy but did Laura ever see it? A plaque reminds us that the learned and maybe saintly priest was responsible for a classical revival and for popularising the sonnet. Good for him.

The church of St-Véran (who slaughtered a vile beast in the fountain) is ancient and simple and would have been familiar to Petrarch because part of it at least is twelfth-century. Antique columns are encased in the interior at the crossing; the vaulting is both oven-shaped and rounded. On the exterior of the nave the architrave has carved figures. It makes a perfect setting for the chamber music concerts given here late on summer evenings.

The L'Isle road forms a loop round the centre of the village returning, past the junction with the road from Lagnes, to the N100. Both parts pass under the aqueduct carrying the Canal de Carpentras. There are spacious car parks on the approaches to Fontaine – one of them is by a riverside meadow, ideal for picnics.

It is only eight kilometres back to L'Isle and a meal at one of the restaurants facing Le Partage des Eaux where the Sorgue divides to flow around the town it has encircled for centuries.

8   Avignon

Montfavet : Châteauneuf-de-Gadagne : Villeneuve-lès-Avignon

Where the ditch defensive to Avignon's walls once ran is now a ring road. Around the ramparts there is free parking although electronic signs woo motorists to garages above Les Halles and beneath the Palace of the Popes. From the latter you emerge into the heart of the city like a warrior from the Trojan horse. I prefer to find a space near the Daladier bridge and enter by a narrow opening, on foot, at La Poterne de l'Oratoire. It may feel like coming through the tradesmen's entrance but it gets you quickly to the Place de l'Horloge.

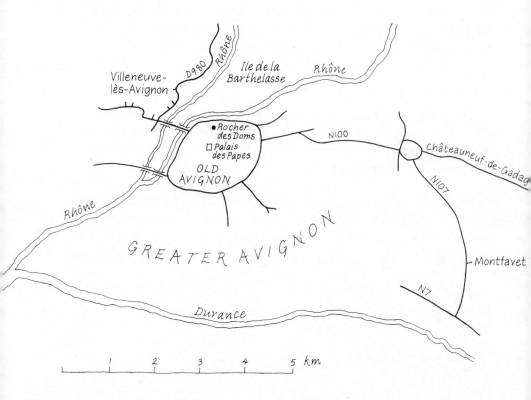

Avignon: Place de l'Horloge

That is where Avignon really starts, any time round. It did for us in 1962 when, though a mistral blew, we dined alfresco. I paid the bill with a bank note featuring Henri of Navarre. *'Voilà!'* cried the waitress, *'Un roi protestant!'* So much for papal influence. The Place de l'Horloge has an air of bonhomie but, nowadays, it is wiser to restrict your visit to a drink, although it has one restaurant of repute. Some of the buskers are a pain, others are sheer delight, such as the Dixieland group which played on the morning of the 1989 *quatorze juillet*. The leader, a stout young man wrapped into a euphonium, danced as he played, from irrepressible joie de vivre. We, who applauded, were the least revolutionary of mobs.

There is a two-tiered carousel of the Belle Epoque outside the nineteenth-century theatre which is immaculately maintained, its entrance guarded by the seated stone figures of Molière and Corneille. Next to it is the town hall, not quite pompous, with, high above it at an angle, the clock-tower, begun in the fourteenth century, raised higher in the fifteenth and offering visual accompaniment to the striking of the hours. The Roman forum was here but no trace remains. Avignon was less important than Arles and Nîmes, yet it ranked amongst the twenty cities of the Narbonensis, as listed by the emperor Agustus. The Romans fortified it. A tiny part of their wall is to be found in the churchyard of St-Agricol and close by, in the posh Balance district, is a vestige of an arcade.

Avignon has always had strategic importance because of the Rocher des Doms, inhabited by tribesmen long before the Greeks landed at Marseille; and from its position close to the confluence of the Rhône and the Durance. The courses of both rivers have been altered by man and nature over the centuries, and the ingenious hydro-electric schemes, plus efficient locks and dykes, now prevent the floods which recurred regularly until the 1950s.

If you are a newcomer you will go straight from the Place de l'Horloge to the centre of papal Avignon in the next *place*. If not, you have a wide choice of museums, churches, Renaissance mansions, shops and galleries. Nothing is far away because old Avignon, within the walls partly restored by Viollet-le-Duc in the nineteenth century, is a manageable size. There are no uniform times or days of opening. A start may be made by strolling down the wide Rue de la République, lined with smart shops, hotels and banks, to the Tourist Office where it is possible to visit all the major sights vicariously on video.

There are three outstanding churches, one of which, close to the Place de l'Horloge, is seemingly named after a Roman emperor, thus suggesting an early convert, but St.Agricol was mythical. It is possible to walk around it except for a section on the Rue St-Agricol where shops have been squeezed to its side. Steps up to its west door ought to be imposing but are not because too much hems them in; the door at the top is a beauty. From there a modern catwalk leads past the churchyard beside the impressively high nave. A notice claims seventh-century origins but most of it dates from the fourteenth when the popes were here. If it stood uncluttered in the space its height demands – which it never did in crowded, medieval Avignon – would it be improved? I wonder. It belongs so very much to its surroundings.

St-Pierre, behind the east side of the Place de l'Horloge, is taller and even more boxed-in than St-Agricol. Narrow alleys follow its great mass into a small, tree-packed square in one direction, and into the Rue Corderie in the other. Its west doors have superbly carved wooden panels featuring young angels, apparently in pain, an older one in smiting mood, heraldic beasts and caryatids with twisted legs. It echoes the papal palace in its complexity and is probably best appreciated from the roofs of nearby buildings; much craning of the neck is required to take in its variety. Its bell-tower has a spire decorated with crockets, such as are found adorning many local churches. At first sight they resemble gargoyles placed closely together but they are non-functional.

St-Didier has room to breathe and can be viewed satisfactorily from the *place* named after it. It is strikingly simple and handsome, then runs riot into a belfry so arranged that the three apertures for bells on each side are hung like traditional pawnbroker's signs. The south door has a fine, carved madonna and child above the lintel. St-Didier was built at the same time as St-Pierre (c.1360) and is the largest of Avignon's churches. The inside is as plain as the exterior with a large, wide, single nave. In one chapel facing the entrance are frescoes (school of Simone Martini, early 14C), discovered in 1953. Almost opposite, in another, is a highly esteemed altar-piece by François Laurana (c.1430-1502); its carving, for me, has an element of the crudeness of Spitting Image. The best of the stained glass depicts the story of the building of the Pont St-Bénézet which began when a shepherd boy had a vision. He started work in 1177, single-handed, but his efforts drew the help of others. Even so, the work took eleven years, and what remains of its successor can still, of course, be seen.

A feature of ecclesiastical life in old Avignon, as elsewhere, were the chapels belonging to various penitent brotherhoods. These came dressed in shades of grey, red, purple and blue, as well as black and white. The Greys have an oddly shaped chapel off the Rue des Teinturiers. Above it rises the crumbling tower of the chapel of the Cordeliers. The doorway features two monks in hoods with eye slits, reminiscent of the Ku Klux Klan, and leads to entrance lobbies like those of a low church hall. The interior is more colourful with a Peruvian gold glory. The Whites have a Gothic chapel near Les Halles and the Blacks are to be found beneath the Rocher des Doms beside a hospital. Their chapel also has a glory, but outside. It features busy cherubs and the head of John the Baptist on a dish. Opposite is the Rue de la Forêt, which is unexpected. Where was the wood, and when?

There is also the Chapelle Ste-Claire, mostly ruined, where Petrarch first saw Laura of Noves in 1327. A plaque quotes the poet Ronsard as authority. The refectory is now the Théâtre des Halles.

Of the other churches, St-Symphorien, on the Place des Carmes, has a pleasing cloister and crocketted spires. In its precincts is a colourful playground for children who go barefoot in it, unaware that in the fourteenth-century monastery to which the cloister was attached, the Carmelite monks, also unshod, trod the same ground. Facing the *place* is the strangest of the towers of Avignon: the remains of the Augustinian convent which lurches over the Rue de la Carreterie. It is now a working belfry with a modern clock-face. Not far away in the Place St-Jean-le-Vieux is another lone tower which belonged to the Knights of St.John of Jerusalem. Its base is currently used as a radio cab office.

Beside the Tourist Office lies all that is extant of a cloister once part of the convent of St-Martial. The church of that name has suffered conversion from a Benedictine monastery to a reformed protestant church. It overlooks gardens with attractive statuary and many benches.

The massive church whose high, gaunt side we passed before crossing the Rue Vernet, en route for the Place de l'Horloge, is the Chapelle de l'Oratoire, ponderously Baroque in its lower parts, happily neo-Romanesque aloft. Finally – on my list, that is – comes the little two-level chapel on the Pont St-Bénézet which acquired an upper part when the bridge was rebuilt in the thirteenth century and raised higher above the river. Not high enough, however, because most of it was swept away in the seventeenth.

I should also mention the synagogue, near Place St-Pierre, which is still used. It is an anonymous looking building, a heavy, windowless rectangle with a round Martello-style tower surmounting it.

The museums of Avignon are not in the top class although the Calvet may be by 1993. When the French reorganise their collections they do so with superthoroughness and close them for years. When I last visited the Calvet, in 1982, I admired paintings by Bosch the Elder, Vlaminck and Chassériau. I noted some early Dufys and Utrillos in dire need of cleaning and came away with an overall impression of rooms full of dark brown canvases. Phaidon records works by Canaletto, David, Géricault, Delacroix, Corot and Manet as well as 'fine collections of ironware....Greek antiquities' and 'prehistoric finds'. Michael Jacobs refers to paintings by Soutine and dotes on the atmosphere which he hopes wont be destroyed by restoration. I liked, as he did, the eighteenth-century mansion with a courtyard where peacocks roamed. Throughout 1989-92 I was unable to gain admission; once when I peered through the gates the scene was like the morning after the Blitz.

Calvet was a son of Avignon who became a distinguished medical academic. His bequest formed the basis of the collection.

Next door is the Musée Requien with natural history exhibits accommodated behind a shabby doorway and hall. There is no charge for admission which is reasonable for this limited display of leaves, plants, ferns, stuffed beasts, ammonites and fossils. The geological section has good photographs of the rocks of the region.

The third limb of the Calvet, the Musée Lapidaire, is housed in a deconsecrated Baroque church in the Rue de la République. It contains altars, friezes, tombs, Roman mosaics, heads, chimney-pieces, bronze pots and two cases of classical glass. There are Egyptian and Greek rooms and exhibits from all periods of Provençal history. Many of them are maddeningly labelled with the curatorial notices placed so close to the floor that they are difficult to read, if you need glasses, without lying flat. My favourite exhibit is a Renaissance chimney-piece from an Avignon house. The sculptor was hugely inventive and fanciful. Two caryatids whose heads 'did grow beneath their shoulders' support the entire thing. Ladies with curiously droll expressions adorn it. There are mythical beasts and birds one of which appears to be dancing with a lord. Elsewhere in the museum is the hideous Celtic monster, found at Noves, with its large paws crushing two human heads, and an inexplicable spare arm (its own or a human limb?) apparently supporting its villainous mouth and jaw.

The third museum in the Rue Vernet region (Vernet was an eighteenth-century marine and landscape painter) is in the Rue Victor-Hugo. Louis Vouland was a collector who left his treasures to the city in 1973. They are housed on two floors of a sombre mansion tastefully laid out with faience, furniture, silver, paintings and orientalia. Except for the Sèvres and Vincennes the china is too chunky for my taste but the decorations are pretty. There is an elaborate box designed to hold all that is necessary for brewing and drinking tea in the open air for one person only (!) but best of all is a group of utterly exquisite far-eastern ivories of two ladies and an old man. In the same case are smaller figures of Japanese workmen and, on a mantle nearby, a very tall woman, with a pagoda growing up to her waist, is holding a grizzled, elderly baby.

Another museum, like the Vouland free, is open even less frequently. This is the Théodore Aubanel which belongs to the family that has been printing and publishing in Avignon since 1744. Théodore himself, the poet, was a founder of the *Félibrige*. There is a guided tour (except on Saturdays and throughout August) when you may be conducted round by the present Madame Aubanel. The publishing offices are next door and the printing works along a nearby alley. The Aubanel family lives in an apartment above the museum. The three rooms for visitors have original presses, manuscripts of Théodore's poems, photographs of the entire dynasty, copies of all the books they have published and various memor-abilia; also a painting of a nude by Théophile Gautier. The Aubanel is reached, up a cobbled cul-de-sac, from the Place St-Pierre, and provides an example of a nineteenth-century enterprise still very much in business.

Finally, in my selection, comes the best of the museums open at the time of writing – the Petit Palais, housing what remains of a nineteenth-century collection of Italian Renaissance paintings, the works of the Avignon School which flourished at the time the popes were here, and much else. Not only does it occupy a beautiful building, formerly the Archbishop's Palace, with a charmingly intricate interior layout, but the paintings are excellently and sparingly displayed. There is no sense of overcrowding, each canvas is allowed to breathe and one *salle* leads into another up or down wide, winding stone steps, through unexpected doorways and formal staircases. From many of the rooms there are stunning views across the Rhône to Villeneuve-lès-

Avignon and far beyond. The ruins of the pontiffs' summer palace at Châteauneuf-du-Pape are visible – clearly so when a mistral is blowing. Having said which, it is a pity to record that, although the presentation cannot be faulted, many of the pictures suffer from the bane of their time, the virgin and child syndrome. How bored the artists became with that subject is evident by some of the results, yet the greatest used it to display their genius. Here, undoubtedly, the finest is a Botticelli, with a beautiful, thoughtful, unusually very young Mary looking down upon a chubby child who has, perhaps, a somewhat precocious worldly alertness about him. And the painter has gone as far as he dared in understating the haloes.

The Christ child was less fortunate in a charming manger scene by Bartolo de Fredi where the halo has become an apparently uncomfortable pillow. But what a lot is going on in the painting and how joyful the animals are! There are also many crucifixions and some narrative panels depicting scenes from the lives of saints. Carpaccio, a contemporary of Botticelli, boldly distances himself from a religious theme with a view of town, castle and hills seen through a rocky opening. In the foreground, almost an afterthought, is a bench of clerics. The Avignon School, also fifteenth-century, was more conventional. There is a portrait of Ste.Cathérine of Siena with what appears to be a red pepper in her left hand but it may be a bleeding heart. The same lady (I think) also appears holding a Bible and a sword. A linked painting of St.Michel shows him killing a devil by treading in its open mouth. Then there is Nicolas Dipre's *Jacob's Ladder* which rises a mere thirty steps to a low cloud. I think, no doubt perversely, that I prefer Enguerrand Quarton's *Virgin and Child*, plus saints: a bold, stylised composition.

By the entrance is a vast chamber in which the School of Avignon is again represented by a fourteenth-century fresco from a house at Sorgues. More importantly, there are carvings rescued from churches and abbeys, carefully displayed so that the features of angels and kings, once on high, can be enjoyed at eye level.

It is difficult to get lost for long in Avignon. Wherever you go you are certain to be confronted, sooner or later, by a rampart or a gateway which will enable you to reorientate. Also, maps in glass cases are part of the street furniture. So it is a joy to roam around the city at leisure, especially between midday and two o'clock when most people are enjoying *le déjeuner* – although the number of shops selling convenience foods is an indication of the prevalence of bad foreign habits. During those hours you can follow the twisting patterns of the medieval ways and chance upon one delight after another – noble, five-storied semi-palaces blocking the sunlight as much as in Florence, carved doorways, decorated stone frontages, inner courtyards, fountains, small gardens, contemporary trompe-l'oeil murals and even the

106

river Sorgue making a mysterious reappearance beside the Rue des Teinturiers, the quiet backwater where, in addition to the Grey Penitents' chapel, are antique shops and restaurants. (A *teinturier* is a dyer.)

To make a systematic study of the many fine mansions of Avignon you would need to consult one of the erudite volumes to be found in Roumanille's bookshop in the Rue Agricol. Joseph Roumanille was a *félibre*. He, Mistral, Aubanel and other associates held meetings in what is now the back room of the shop specialising in the literature of Provence. The stock is new, second hand and antiquarian with a few titles in English. The nearest to it of the mansions is the Palais du Roure from where Mistral published his magazine *L'Aioli*. The Roure was built in 1469 by Florentine merchants from whom the Marquis Folco Baroncelli-Javon was descended. When he joined the *Félibrige* he renounced his possessions to become a *gardian* in the Camargue, where we shall encounter him again, dispossessed perhaps but by no means undone. After his departure, and Mistral's, the Palais hit hard times from which it was rescued in 1918 by Jeanne de Flandreysy-Espéran-dieu, a collector who was married to a historian. She formed a *salon* for artists and intellectuals and there is now a museum of the treasures acquired by herself and her husband. An art college operates in the Palais, exhibitions are mounted and in a courtyard, which may be inspected, recitals are given. Go through the formidable archway and look up at the Renaissance windows and the lamp brackets hung irregularly on the high walls.

Other houses worth noting are one in the Rue Ste-Cathérine with a smaller courtyard than that of the Roure but boasting an attractive plant-covered well; a palace built by good King René in the street named after him; a grandiloquent stone-faced mansion at 5, Rue Galante and two former mansions of the nobility, facing each other across the Rue Viala. They are the headquarters of the Conseil Général and the Préfecture. On an even larger scale are the Ceccano, now a public library, close to St-Didier and, in a quite different genre on the Rue des Lices, a stone tenement block built in the sixteenth century to house the poor and the old but now part of l'Ecole des Beaux-Arts.

In addition to churches and elegant mansions, the city has a proliferation of theatres none of which, with the exception of the one on the Place de l'Horloge, and La Comédie (now only a façade on the Place Crillon) looks much like a conventional playhouse, although the Theatre of the Big Bang is, or was, in a 'thirties-style cinema. The existence of all these reflects the annual festival in July when the city seethes with activity, and hundreds of thousands of handbills are wished upon tourists and residents. The festival is administered from the Maison Jean Vilar, another seventeenth-century house at the end of a passage across the *place* from the town hall.

Your walk should include some of the roads immediately behind the walls. This will give you a sense of the security which inhabitants must have experienced in violent times. Much is in need of repair but the state of unrestoration of some sections will give solace to opponents of Viollet-le-Duc. Try, also, to approach the Palais des Papes from the rear. It is like an early skyscraper, belittling the cathedral beside it. There is a narrow alley with a sharp bend (watch out for traffic) to take you through the rock forming the foundations of the vast building, and into the square which is almost certain to be thronged with tourists, some of whom will be attending to the antics of jugglers and clowns or listening to itinerant musicians. Even if you have been here before you can bear to gaze again upon the unique surroundings, and perhaps remind yourself of how the popes came to Avignon. Or perhaps not – it is a complicated story.

In the early fourteenth century Rome had became a hot seat for the popes who were in dispute with the Emperor. Clement V, a Frenchman, having taken refuge in Bordeaux, came to Avignon en route for a conference and decided to remain, moving into a monastery in 1309. His successors, one of whom was the local bishop, enlarged the episcopal palace but that would not do for those who came later. By mid-century not one, but two, enormous fortresses were erected and Avignon had been purchased from Queen Jeanne of Naples, who was also Countess of Provence.

The fourteenth century was undoubtedly Avignon's finest hour despite the Black Death, in which thousands perished. For a brief period it became the centre of the western world. In the wake of the Pope came cardinals, priests and hangers-on. Trade boomed (so did crime), a university was founded, the arts flourished, Petrarch inveighed against conditions in the city but also wrote his sonnets to Laura, and the walls were rebuilt. The papacy returned to Rome before the end of the century but leaving a dissident faction of holy fathers until 1411. So, for a while, the Christian world had two popes.

In the sixteenth century Avignon was threatened again. François I occupied it in 1536 but withdrew when plague returned. It was not a battleground during the Wars of Religion, thanks to its formidable defences, but in the mid-seventeenth-century Louis XIV claimed it, only to return it to the popes twenty-five years later. They continued as owners until the Revolution, in whose aftermath it finally became part of France.

The exterior of the palace as seen from the *place* is an architectural feast, a devious building erected for devious purposes. No two sections of it are alike. It is a riot of invention and compromise, of windows, balconies, turrets, doorways, arches, crenellations, each representing some special need of the moment, or a papal vanity, the detail even more stimulating than Gilbert Scott's St-Pancras, because the patterns are less disciplined.

An explanatory pamphlet is available in several languages and there are many wall signs in English which language the French are now taking seriously, thus knocking a lot of the fun out of impromptu translation. So a guide is not essential but if you engage one they will certainly lack the colour of the old crone who conducted Charles Dickens in 1840, showing him the chambers where the Inquisition performed its tortures and the pit into which priests were thrown at the Revolution.

The second of the Avignon popes (John XXII) took up residence in the Bishop's palace in 1316. He enlarged it to suit his needs. His successor (Benedict XII) pulled it down to replace it with what is known as the Old Palace. Clement VI who came next added the New Palace and what we see today is based upon their work, plus much restoration. It is a massive building with vast halls, a dining-room the size of a small estate, a chapel as big as a parish church and, the most intriguing architectural feature, a monumental chimney in the upper kitchen, reaching high into the sky. In the courtyard performances are given against the marvellously rich wall of the new palace which has Gothic windows set irregularly about it. In various chapels are frescoes by Matteo Giovanetti, some of them sadly faint with time, and the papal bed-chamber has pleasing pastel shaded tempera designs on the walls. The adjoining room, the papal study, has frescoes with a hunting motif. This maze of an edifice cramps the style of Notre-Dame-des-Doms lying on a higher mound of rock to the north. Rated as a cathedral, it has a smaller nave than at St-Didier and has suffered heavily from restoration during eight hundred years. The altar and simple but ingeniously contrived octagonal Romanesque dome were unaffected by seventeenth-century improvements, but the imposing bell-tower has been added to – most unfortunately – by an enormous Mary plonked upon it in the nineteenth century. The side chapels are garish but have good monuments; the narrow gallery around the nave is subdued and unpainted. The west door is very fine but partly hidden by a large crucifixion on the embankment supporting the front of the church.

At the river end of the Place du Palais is a formidable building which became the cardinal's, and later the archbishop's, residence soon after the popes installed themselves across the way. It later served in defence of the city but was subsequently downgraded after the Revolution to become stables, whilst the palace itself was a barracks. It returned briefly to ecclesiastical use in the nineteenth century until church and state split. Then it became a technical school. It is now, as already recorded, a fine museum of paintings and sculpture, known as the Petit Palais.

Opposite the papal château is the Hôtel des Monnaies, formerly the mint, now a school of music. Exuberant cornucopias are carved on the walls.

Finally comes the ascent of the Rocher des Doms by foot, or on the little train, past well-tended flower beds and a notice stating that Avignon is twinned with Colchester, England's earliest recorded town. On the spacious hill-top there are no signs of an early settlement and there is little to look at apart from the views but they are sensational. There is a snack bar, a lily pond, seats in the sun, seats in the wind, seats in the shade, and a grotto. There is also grass but you must not lie on it. In the recent past Avignon was a hippy centre, a period in the late 'seventies and early 'eighties which its citizens recall with distaste. So although you may consider yourself kempt enough and cleanly dressed, remember that, in the eyes of an attendant on the Rocher, any sleeping form is a hippy.

There are a few items of statuary including Jean Althen (1703-74), Armenian-born agronomist who introduced *garance* (madder) to the region, a dye made from herbaceous climbing plants, and gave his name to the village of Althen-des-Paluds; also a naked lady, unnamed, in what can only be called a state of ecstasy.

Althen, on whose back is a memorial to the one-and-a-half million Armenians who died from Turkish genocide in 1915, looks towards the viewing platform below which is the Pont St-Bénézet, now little more than a jetty protruding into the river. Once it boasted twenty-two arches spanning two stretches of the Rhône, and the Ile Piot too, on its way to Villeneuve-lès-Avignon.

The Rocher des Doms is one place to relax (but decorously); another tranquil spot – permanently so for John Stuart Mill and his Harriet – is the cemetery of St-Véran, just beyond the ring road. It is so extensive that wide access avenues have been built to the hundreds of tombs, some monumental, some economy-sized. There are few, if any, new plots but there is room still in the family vaults. It is better to have this peaceful and not too sombre haven close to the centre of Avignon than yet another business park or shopping complex. The entrance to the cemetery is on the Avenue Stuart Mill, where he is named 'Philosophe, Economiste, Homme Politique Anglais, 1806-73.' In how many English towns are streets called affectionately after foreigners?

When the Mills first came to Avignon they stayed at the Hôtel de l'Europe, in the Place Crillon. Formerly a private mansion in the sixteenth century, it became, and remains, the city's best-known hôtel. Dickens, the Brownings, Henry James, George Eliot and Lewes, were amongst those who stayed there. After Harriet died, Mill remained for fiteen years fully en rapport with the people and with Provence.

Close to the Hôtel is a shop called London Bridge specialising in English goods of quality. The shops of Avignon are as varied and as pleasant as you would expect of a famous city, also as expensive. South-east of the Place de l'Horloge many are in a pedestrianised area which is respected by some of the traffic most of the time. Close by are Les Halles, the covered market. Covered, that is to say, by a monstrous concrete car park nearly as high as the Pope's Palace. On entering the large rectangular market floor it seems at first too clinically clean with its bright modern fitments, but then the close proximity of all that excellent produce with all those eager, knowledgeable purchasers makes the ambience a very agreeable one indeed.

Avignon-without-the-Walls, but with an unrivalled range of hypermarkets, is to be avoided. So unless you are furnishing a house there will be no need for you to unravel the mystery of how to reach Auchan, the superstore on its northern borders where every item costs a fraction of what it does elsewhere, and where you can have a meal called Flunch at a cafeteria. Nor should you need to visit the offices of the Sécurité Sociale lying close to the *périphérique* to reclaim medical expenses or, much worse, to make your way to an industrial estate on the south-western side where the Automobile-Club Vauclusien hides from its members. But you will need to pass through some of Greater Avignon to see certain places which, by a thin margin, are still not a part of the whole.

East of the Rhône the first stop could be at Montfavet where there is a well-preserved church of distinction. It has a placid bulk, flying buttresses, an octagonal belfry and spire, and a south doorway with suppliant figures above the lintel. The stone is much eroded, the faces severely pock-marked, but they are eloquent just the same. The church is closed except for services so you may have to take on trust the altar-pieces and vaulted nave. But you can see, at the west end, part of a surviving monastery with no-nonsense, squat, square towers which were once fortified. Below them, on the other side, mostly in the shade, is now the Boulodrome Municipal.

Slowly you leave Montfavet – the frequent *ralentisseurs* insist – heading for Châteauneuf-de-Gadagne, one of the lower hill towns overlooking the Sorgue-Ouvèze basin. It is not a 'must' but has its rewards and the Plateau de Campbeau above it is a perfect picnic site with a view of the ruined monastery at Thouzon (see Chapter 7). The Rue de l'Eglise, descending steeply into the village brings more visual pleasure, ending at a thirteenth-century gateway to the Grande Rue which, to be fair, is grander than some I have encountered. In it is the house where *félibre* Anfos Tavan was born. At one end of the *place* below the *mairie* is a bust of him on a fountain. Another citizen, named 'notre bienfaiteur', Alcantara Goujon, is also commemorated in this main square. He has an elaborate mausoleum on the Plateau, near the lane which leads to the Château de Fontsegugne a rendezvous of the *félibres.*

Another outing from Avignon, strongly recommended, is to Villeneuve on the right bank of the Rhône. You reach it over the Pont Daladier which, in 1959, replaced an earlier suspension bridge. (Daladier was prime minister of France in 1939-40 and represented the Vaucluse for thirty years in all.) It spans both branches of the Rhône and also the Ile Piot now joined to the Ile de Barthelasse. Barthelasse, once also divided by another strand of the Rhône, is now one island, a quiet, green enclave, mostly farming land, and safe from flooding although some parts of it are below the level of the river.

Villeneuve-lès-Avignon is a place in its own right, a 'new town' founded in the thirteenth century to rival the old when French territory faced that of the Holy Roman Empire across the river. Despite this endemic hostility, the king of France made no objection to cardinals building themselves mansions here when space was at a premium in Avignon. Philippe-le-Bel's splendid defensive tower dates from just before this time. There are 176 steps to the viewing platform but before deciding to climb them wait until you have been to Fort St-André where you can see the same panorama with rather less effort. And that visit should wait until you have been to the new municipal museum. Chief amongst the exhibits are the fourteenth-century ivory of madonna and child which is exquisite, a small work of perfection, and the Coronation of the Virgin, by the Avignon painter Quarton. The ivory is displayed on the ground floor (where you may wish you had ignored

Villeneuve-lès-Avignon: Fort St-André Gardens

another double-sided statuette with two imbecilic heads of the Christ child); the painting has a large room to itself on the first. It was painted on wood for the monks of the nearby Charterhouse and is an intriguing composition using striking colours, especially in the reds of the angels' cloaks. When the sun shines into the room, the gold patches below the Virgin glow excitingly. Choruses of worshippers, nuns and cherubs are grouped at each side and, below them, are pictures of Rome and Jerusalem, beneath which are the devils and the damned in hell. It has absolute conviction. Lucky museum to have room to show such a masterpiece unaccompanied. There are, though, more paintings elsewhere – a Visitation by Philippe de Champagne, for instance – and also a collection of early Bibles.

Villeneuve has other attractions – the Charterhouse and the Fort. You reach the former by the gateway off the Rue de la République. A Carthusian was elected pope but felt too humble to accept high office. That should have made if difficult for any other nominee, but Innocent VI consented to be put forward at the same time as donating his wealth and land to building a Charterhouse at Villeneuve. It is huge, with a church, three cloisters, numerous cells, service buildings and guest apartments.

The most attractive cloister is called the Graveyard and surrounds a green meadow; another, St-John, has a large octagonal fountain at its centre. In the chapel there are well-preserved frescoes. Several cells, surprisingly lacking in austerity, may be visited. One has a ground floor with living-workroom opening on to a small patio and garden, and an upper story with bedroom, study and balcony. Quite a bijou billet.

The entrance from the town, up a mulberry alley with a pharmacy bordering it, crosses a covered way into a reception area where tickets are sold. Leave by another courtyard where there is a persimmon tree (bright orange fruit in autumn), then turn a corner to reach the church. It has a whole side missing so that you may look into it as at an architect's model. The brick is unadorned and beautifully weathered throughout the entire complex. Much of the building has survived the turmoil of the centuries and it is now used, in high summer, as a cultural centre. It is possible to enter from the rear, where there is a car park, and begin with the bakery and St-John cloister before paying your admittance money.

From the Charterhouse car park you can walk up to Fort St-André which is entered between two massive medieval towers on a great eminence. This dominates the town whilst complementing the higher Rocher des Doms across the river. From it you can gaze upon Avignon and the mountain ranges of the Vaucluse and Bouches-du-Rhône. And there are but 85 steps to the tower top compared with 176 at Philippe-le-Bel's. Halfway up pause to observe the lofty chambers once used as prison cells. Within the walls of St-André are also the Tour des Masques, a chapel, a ruined abbey, the remains of a village, terraces, olive groves and a modern private house. An extensive, formal Italian garden has statuary – one dreaming lady drapes herself against a mound of rock, others beam from behind shrubs. There is a pergola, probably once belonging to a cloister, vast vaulting beneath which you can walk to another part of the estate, cypress avenues and dormitories of sarcophagi. (There were burials here from the seventh to the eighteenth century.) High above the lovely ruin of the cemetery is a small chapel. This is an exchanted place.

From the wide terrace look again, before you leave, at the incomparable view of Avignon.

9   South of the Grand Luberon

Lourmarin : Vaugines : Cucuron : Ansouis : Tour d'Aigues :
Grambois : Peyrolles-en-Provence : Silvacane : Cadenet

It might be appropriate to take in this itinerary, if you are staying in Apt, by using the Lourmarin gap between the two parts of the Luberon. Equally it is within easy reach of both Cavaillon and L'Isle-sur-la-Sorgue. I have placed it here because, although the places visited are nearly all in the Vaucluse, they are geographically closer to the Bouches-du-Rhône than the

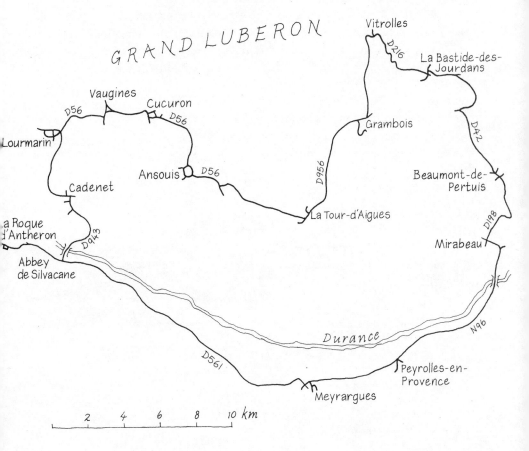

subjects of the previous three chapters, and most of the remainder of the book is set in that department.

Lourmarin has several hôtels and even more restaurants, some of gastronomic status, so that makes a good base. A pleasant winding road signs a Michelin 'red rocking chair' hôtel, symbolising tranquillity, but I suspect there is little in the way of riotous assembly in Lourmarin proper to spoil your sleep. It is a pretty town with its basically fourteenth-century château standing aloof from it, across a meadow and on an incline. In its present state, the castle is mostly restored Renaissance but encompasses an old watch-tower with a sentry walk from an earlier fortified building. It has a monumental staircase (91 steps) and high beamed rooms with enormous chimney-pieces, one featuring creatures with taloned feet. Having survived the Revolution, and a plan to turn it into a hospital, it was taken in hand in the 1920s by Robert Laurent-Vibert, an art patron. It is now a cultural centre administered by the University of Aix. On our visit there was a guided tour led by a gentleman using a microphone with faulty amplification. I turned him off by gazing out of the huge, handsome windows at olive groves and peaceful countryside, or by examining one painting whilst he discoursed about another. I was able to thus capture something of the thrill which those who attend courses in this admirably restored castle must experience.

Albert Camus had a second home in Lourmarin and is buried in the cemetery of the fifteenth-century church. The writer died in a car accident, as did M. Laurent-Vibert. The church (beautiful font) stands in a maze of tiny streets and was firmly locked when a long distance cyclist, who had got there before us, tried to gain admission. He had ridden over from the Dordogne and was not surprised, philosophically proclaiming it quite usual

Lourmarin: Château

because Christianity was on the way out. An Islamic takeover was to be expected because nowadays only the Muslims believed in God. He informed us of all this cheerfully and went off in search of refreshment.

Five kilometres distant is Vaugines, beside the river Laval which rises in the mountain above. A particularly picturesque village, it is in two parts. The older climbs the usual foothill with vestiges of castle and bell-tower, easy to lose in the confusion of terracing. The streets have names such as Rue de la Fausse Monnaie, which runs from top to bottom, sometimes beneath arches, and has an ancient gateway at its foot; the Aire des Deux 'Negro', the Rue des Amazones, and the Rue des Coquillages. On the Rue des Amazones is a very striking house (early Renaissance?) with a prosperous rusticated doorway and above it a twice (deliberately) broken pediment. The *mairie*, in the Place des Fontaines, is properly four-square but has the Epicerie du Luberon occupying most of one side at ground-floor level. Opposite are smart public loos. Ascending by the Rue Vieille, and then the Rue des Coquillages, you seem to be clambering about in private backyards, but this is not so. When you reach bare rock, go a little higher to a shady dell with a hedge of cypresses on the north side and evidence of terracing underfoot. A metal table and six rusting chairs seem to have been abandoned beneath the trees and it could be that this was (even, is) someone's garden. It is an idyllic spot from which to gaze upon the mountainside.

The other part of Vaugines takes off from one side of the Place des Fontaines to follow a low rise of the hillside. It consists of a single street with a shallow gulley for carrying rain water. For most of its length – about half-a-kilometre – it has buildings on both sides, and a very assorted collection they are, ranging from demure double-fronted villas and pretty balconied houses, to farm outbuildings, stores, apartments and a public wash place dated 1922. There are a few gardens and it is all backed above by pine trees. On the other side of town, across a field from the road, is the thirteenth-century church with an apse two centuries older, a charming building in a perfect setting. I didn't disturb its peace.

Cucuron, another 5km on, announces itself impressively with a keep. The road winds around it to the town which still has ramparts plus a gate or two. On a lower hill is a ruined tower partly obscured by umbrella pines. The keep – not a ruin – has a locked door and glazed windows and seems in a healthy state. Down wide steps from it, attractively built over the paved way, is the house of Queen Jeanne, she who was married to King René. Nearby is the clock-tower – sixteenth-century – which has, instead of the usual wrought iron framework to house the bell, an elaborate stone belfry with four decorated feet. It faces the Rue de l'Eglise and the fine doorway and patterned tympanum of Notre-Dame-de-Beaulieu. The interior of this church, part Romanesque, part Gothic, has been heavily baroqued with much coloured marble, but there is a good wooden *pietà*. Close to it is the Musée Marc Deydier mainly devoted to farming implements and small lapidary objects. A droll wooden horse, with a skeletal but unanatomical body, stands in the centre of one room attached to a wagon. On the stairs are life-size figures in folk costumes. Some rooms display works by Deydier, a local photographer. Admission free.

The chief joy of Cucuron is the Place de l'Etang. Here is a great rectangular pool, with fish, surrounded by plane trees nearly thirty metres high. On one side of it are the Bar, Café, Restaurant and Hôtel de l'Etang, where the food is good and the accommodation adequate. But beware, if you go out of season, to provide yourselves with a home entertainment kit, including corkscrew, for the bedroom. We contrived to make our meal last until 9.30. Then, when we announced we were going for a stroll, it was made clear that Madame would be locking up in ten minures. Another thing. She didn't accept credit cards.

Cucuron nestles under the Grand Luberon almost directly below the Mourre Nègre. It struck me, in early February, as having a particularly mild climate. Marooned in our room, we didn't use the heating or shut the window.

Ansouis which comes next ought really to be the climax of this delightful route because it is the best thing on it. Not only is the castle intact, it is also inhabited *and*, such is the claim, has been in the same family – the de Sabran – for more than 800 years. It is open at all seasons and the guide may be an old retainer, a member of the family or even Milady herself. You enter up a ramp, through a stone gateway. On the return this passes part of the garden, where there is topiary work, to reach a spacious courtyard with a line of chestnut trees and another of classical urns. They face the grand early seventeenth-century frontage of the château which has six bays at first- and second-floor levels, and numerous doorways reflecting in their decoration the detail of the stonework. The principal entrance is heavily porticoed and adorned with coach-style lamp holders of engaging elegance. The masonry is a lovely yellow. On an adjacent wall sits an amiable stone lion. A passage near the top of the second ramp leads through shrubs to a small turret at a corner of the wall, overlooking a formal Italian garden with box hedges. On the north and west sides the grounds are richly covered in foliage sweeping down to the boundary walls. (Note, at various points, how the construction has its foundations on a fault in the rock.)

The guided tour takes about forty minutes, starting in a lobby at the head of a Henri IV stairway. It is actually an armoury and not exactly homely. Firearms, swords and other villainous looking weapons are displayed but domesticity on the grand scale soon follows, with enormous and mostly hideous lumps of furniture occupying the high, wide chambers that are also adorned with tapestries. If you are fortunate you may be conducted by the guide Min and I encountered at an off-peak time when we were the only visitors. When he noticed us wincing at some of the items he relaxed and joined in our irreverence, though with dignity and always remembering to impart information, never failing to answer a question with a wealth of facts. He also reacted to our enthusiasm for the spacious kitchen, with over 100 copper pans and wall cupboards for every conceivable culinary need, as well as a cabinet of *santons*. It was good to learn that the family cook (on a large modern range) and eat there. The dining-room is for formal occasions.

The de Sabrans number among their medieval ancestors the hallowed couple, Elzéar and Delphine, who endured an unconsummated marriage and led saintly, celibate lives, despite which the line continued.

Ansouis: Château frontage

Portraits of the revered pair are hung in an austere room beside other works of art.

You may not care for all the furnishings but you are likely to warm to the house simply because it has been lived in for so long. The most striking part of the visit is to the oldest region, down grim stone corridors to the prison, with a solitary small door high in a wall. Nearby is a well from which in times past members of the ruling family had to make a quick getaway down passages leading many miles into the surrounding country. You are told that they employed wooden wedges to insert in the wall as they climbed down, removing them as they descended to prevent being followed. You are not told what happened when they reached water, which comes naturally to wells, or how they coped if the entrances to the passages were beneath it. Was there a hint of *Lettice and Lovage* in this anecdote?

There is a chapel, once a guardroom, and in it a glittering gold altar about which we had a good snort. At this sanctuary you are close to the Henri IV stairway from the entrance hall. Back down it, in the small lobby, we were shown a repellent stone model of a fountain. That clinched matters. I tipped the guide extravagantly.

Next to the castle is the parish church, once the court of justice. The walls of the nave are painted with innocent floral designs but the altar resembles an elaborate cocktail cabinet. The small hill town jostling around these two edifices is the usual charming hotchpotch of buildings leaning heavily together for support. Note the *mairie* down a passage just inside the ancient gateway, and the bell-tower.

Ansouis' other, lesser, feature is a Musée Extraordinaire, the creation of a deep sea diver, G Mazoyer, who lives in a house beside it. M. Mazoyer has convinced himself that he is also a painter and sculptor worthy of exhibition. His garden is set about with representations of ancient fishes and other creatures that roamed underwater in the Luberon area about ten million years ago. Inside there are rooms displaying items the diver recovered from the Mediterranean, the Indian Ocean, and other seas. They range from exquisitely simple shells to vicious subterranean beasts which can sever a limb with a snap of their bivalves. There is also a Blue Grotto in excruciating taste. On the first floor M. Mazoyer's paintings are on show. He may conduct you round himself; he is charming and informative, and his museum is certainly Out-of-the-Ordinary.

South-east from Ansouis is Pertuis, the largest town hereabouts, from which a main road leads to La Tour d'Aigues. Pertuis has nothing outstanding, only a run-of-the-mill Gothic church and castle ruins. There are better ones at La Tour d'Aigues which you can reach by a cross-country route. The layout of this small town is different from most others. The castle is not on a hill but stands beside a valley where flows the Lèze, and the streets are roughly on the same level with, if anything, the church standing slightly higher.

The Château is a vivid ruin with a giant gateway across a bridge, one façade of the original Renaissance palace with gaping windows to the left, a refurbished wing with coloured glass in its casements to the right. Centrally, behind the entrance, is an entirely rebuilt keep. Then there is all the ironmongery of the permanent scaffolding for seating at concerts, which adds to the impression of a film set. You almost expect to see a camera tracking along the dried-up moat. The architect was an Italian, Ercole Nigra,

La Tour d'Aigues: Detail of ruined Château

and the castle was the most famous in the district, encompassing a park and gardens the size of a village. In 1780 most of it accidentally burned down but chambers housing an extensive natural history collection were saved. Only for a decade or so because, after the Revolution, the mob fired the entire complex. It is now being restored with copies of original decorations. The gateway has a frieze above four Corinthian columns, with pilasters supporting the pediments. The keep looks domesticated. None of your unbreachable walls without openings but large Renaissance windows and stonework embellished at the corners purely for ornamentation. Overlooking the valley is a fine sweep of terrace to which you are directed by a notice, La Promenade Musicale. You will become aware, that even on a Sunday workmen are busy, apparently in a nearby tower that is being restored. There is a noise of drilling, there are whining sounds. These start and stop abruptly. Then you realise that the sounds bear some relation to your movements. There are no workmen. It is music you hear, controlled by electronic barriers – *musique concrète*, I take it.

The cellars have been converted into museums, one for faience (not a remarkable collection), the other, a celebration of the Pays d'Aigues – fascinating. Well laid out, the latter makes the point that the landscape has changed very little in eight hundred years. There is much about cultivation and production, and also some history. It notes that in 500BC the Celts integrated with the Ligurians and that between the Luberon and the Durance lived the Dexivates, part of a confederacy with the Salyans of Entremont, whom we shall meet shortly in the Museum at Aix. A population chart is repeated at intervals showing the steep decline from the thirteenth century to 1470 (plague, presumably, but also roving bandits), then rising to a peak in the 1860s. The figure is only now again approaching it. Relevant to this is the information that La Tour d'Aigues was a Vaudois settlement, the Protestant sect being attracted, in the early 1500s, by a seigneur who was desperate for workers. It was their undoing because when Mérindol and other towns were attacked, they, along with the hapless heretics of eighteen communities, including Lourmarin, were persecuted.

The church of La Tour d'Aigues has two apses at opposite ends of the nave, one Romanesque, the other seventeenth-century. It has also a large square bell, and a beautiful stone *pietà* in a fragile condition.

A few miles north is Grambois, perfectly shaped for a copy-book hill town, with a church housing a thirteenth-century fresco and a sixteenth-century triptych neither of which I saw because a religious ceremony was being celebrated at the time of my visit. Instead, we installed ourselves in the Hostellerie des Tilleuls at the foot of the hill, where we had an excellent three-course Sunday lunch for 78 francs (1990).

North, south, and east of Grambois you can take agreeable drives, up to Vitrolles immediately below a mountain pass, through a woodland to La Bastide-des-Jourdans and Beaumont-de-Pertuis, or direct to the Durance near Mirabeau. It is worth crossing the river to visit Peyrolles-en-Provence where the castle belonging to King René has become the town hall. It is reached from the main *place* through the archway of a clock-tower next to a typical Bar du Midi, and along winding, narrow streets, one of which goes to the decrepit church. The Château lies behind another arched gateway and across a courtyard lined with dwellings and municipal offices. Here you can obtain the key to the twelfth-century Chapelle-du-St-Sépulcre over-looking the main road from the edge of a small hill. It is in Greek-cross style, a rare layout for this part of the world, but not painted white. It is best viewed from the car park of the Place des Héros.

The main road continues to Meyrargues where the château has not become a Hôtel de Ville but one of the other sort where you can book rooms and stay in luxurious surroundings. Far below it, in a field beside a cemetery, are the two remaining arches of a Roman aqueduct.

The other purpose of this jaunt along the northern edge of the Bouches-du-Rhône is to reach the Cistercian abbey of Silvacane. It is slightly younger than Sénanque and, to my mind, in no way as impressive either in itself or in its setting (just off the road beside a meadow). It does, though, enjoy a similar serene simplicity. The cloister, a little clumsy, has a large *lavabo* at one end; in the monks' workroom is a grand Renaissance-style fireplace. It became, for a while, the parish church of La Roque-d'Anthéron, and at another period was a farmhouse. The state has restored it as a national monument and it is regularly in use for concerts. Music also plays an increasingly important rôle in the life of La Roque-d'Anthéron where the summer piano festival attracts distinguished performers.

My enthusiasm for Silvacane might be greater if I had seen it before I went to Sénanque. Others, whose judgment I trust, think highly of it.

Return to the road beside the Durance and cross the river to reach Cadenet, situated on a hillside of red sandstone. It was here that I was lounging in the sun on page nine beside a curiously shaped church of even richer red. St-Etienne contains a font made from a Roman sarcophagus decorated with scenes from the triumph of Bacchus and Ariadne. I know it and the sculptures of fabulous beasts, housed in side chapels, only from illustrations because the authorities, secular and sacred, have frustrated my attempts to gain entry to the church. At the town hall four officials, on two separate occasions, have assured me it was open. It wasn't. Nor did the curé, next door, answer his bell.

I consoled myself by ascending the hilltop where there was formerly a temple to Jupiter and a castle, little of which remains. The Rue du Château is clearly marked at the start of the climb up the steep streets, with crossing terraces, but later the name changes and you need to ask your way. If you turn left you pass along a wall below which are gardens and patios belonging to houses on the terrace beneath. A tiny Jardin Public is opposite the Rue de l'Hôpital Vieux where it joins the Rue Baroque, represented by one squat four-roomed house. Above you can see caves inhabited by ancient man; some have been recently converted into desirable residences with plate glass windows. But you should have turned right to arrive at a track where the entrance is barred with a gate labelled ZONE DANGEREUSE. You ignore this, seeing parties of schoolchildren ahead of you, and follow the path to a little grove of firs and cypresses enclosing a small clock-tower. Overhead, up a sandy cliff, is a larger grove reached by rugged path or dark tunnels. An adjoining eminence is more easily accessible, and even higher. On it, looking like a man-made cave, is a vestige of castle. Part of the hill is fortified but there is little else in the way of ruins. The whole summit makes a marvellous natural playground for the kids of Cadenet.

Down in the town, in total contrast, are an invigorating statue and a brightly walled post office. The latter, with doors so heavy to open that they might well deter customers as well as villains, has an outside mosaic mural which is a blow-up of the old ten-centimes stamp with a lady, after Delacroix, representing the spirit of France. It is good to see a minor public building decorated thus.

The statue, splendidly sited halfway up the sloping central square, is of André Estienne, a drummer boy who served with Napoléon. He is said to have beaten such a tremendous roll that the Austrian enemy supposed it to be gunfire and retreated. He is beating another as he races down the street. He would not be here but for members of the Resistance who, in 1943, knowing the Germans were melting down all available metal for munitions, stole the statue and hid it. A few days later troops occupied the town.

The essence of this route, embracing Lourmarin, Vaugines, Cucuron, Ansouis and Cadenet, lies on a perimeter measuring only 24km. These five places can be enjoyed on a quiet day out between more exacting visits to Avignon and Aix. They have magic to offer.

10   Aix-en-Provence and environs

En Route from Avignon : Bonpas : Roquefavour : Gorges du Regalon :
Environs : Entremont : Barrage-de-Bimont : Jouques : Trets :
Vauvenargues : Le Tholonet : Cassis : Aubagne : La Treille

There are those who like to compare Aix with Avignon and are outraged if you state a preference for the one they like least. I am fond of both cities which are quite different even allowing for standardisation imposed by hypermarketing, road signs, fast food bars and advertisement hoardings. Aix, 80km south-east of Avignon, has neither river, airport nor serious rail links but it is encircled by complex road systems which cannot be avoided however you approach. Try starting, just briefly, on the N7 from Avignon to the Charterhouse of Bonpas, on the right bank of the Durance. This stands close to a point where, before the twelfth-century bridge was erected, the passage over dangerous currents was by boat. There were hazards too from bandits, so it was then known as *malus passus*. The monks arrived when the bridge was built and became protective of travellers, the Carthusians taking over, in 1320, from the Knights Templar. The latters' chapel may still be visited at all times of day (even on Tuesdays) throughout the year in the grounds of what remains of the later monastery. It is extremely simple, with a high vaulted roof (the crypt is also vaulted) and joined to a medieval fortress now converted into several houses inhabited by those who care for the gardens and vineyard. There are fine turrets, ramparts and machicolated towers. A handout tells you where you may and may not go. A spacious courtyard overlooks the Durance, and up an unguarded stone staircase without handrails is a terrace with low parapets. The Charterhouse has a well-maintained entrance arch at the end of a long avenue of pines. Beside it is a garden. Adjacent are both the motorway and the N7 either of which can, on occasion, provide a modern *malus passus*.

Reject these highways and make for Caumont on D25. On a low hill to its north is a memorial to the Deportation. It shows, in stark metal, a body with two hands raised high and a chain between them. Against this silhouette is a large F. A signpost at the foot of the hill states that 230,000 Frenchmen were deported in World War Two, including 500 from the Vaucluse. Only 35,000 in all returned after the Liberation.

After Caumont, apart from the Cavaillon ring road which you

must tolerate, comes an agreeable drive along the south side of the Petit Luberon. You may feel inclined to investigate the Gorges du Regalon where the entrance is difficult, at first glance, to detect. The break on the face of the mountain is just beyond an olive grove reached after an easy walk from the car park off the D973. The gorge is extremely narrow and high. Take care when the path rises before widening by a cavern, where you can imagine ancient man enjoying security. It then continues to the ridge – familiar territory to those who walked it earlier (see Chapter 6) and a track down the northern side of the Luberon to Oppède.

This diversion will not get you to Aix so, having noted the entrance to the Gorges for another day, continue the eastward journey, by-passing Mérindol, and also Lauris, the latter on a new road from which habitations hewn out of the rock face can be seen. You then skirt Cadenet to cross the Durance and ascend to Rognes. This little town is a centre of quarrying on the north side of the Trévaresse hills which were grievously burned in the fires of 1989. Rognes' locked church has altar-pieces (15-18th centuries) much admired by altar people; the key is with the tourist office in the main square. The south side of the Trévaresse chain has pines and vines and points across the N7 to the hill town of Eguilles, overlooking the similarly-named river that rises opposite in Ventabren.

The reason for this devious approach to Aix is to see the aqueduct of Roquefavour. It lacks the glamour of the wondrous Pont du Gard but its comparative youth gives it practicality. One hundred and fifty years after its construction it still carries water by canal to Marseille. Appropriately, since the design is essentially Roman, there are excavations of Marius' encampment nearby in the Arc Valley. The barbarians marched this way to their massacre at his army's hands in 102BC. The aqueduct, a monument to nineteenth-century engineering, is 83m high and 375m long; the Pont du Gard is 49m and 275m respectively.

At Aix I would recommend staying at the Mozart, an unpretentious, attractively designed modern hotel without restaurant in a quiet situation near the university. It is just beyond the ring road but within easy walking distance of the centre.

Aix was once a Roman city but has even less than Avignon to show for it now. The remote past seems fated to oblivion here. There are remnants of the ancient tribal settlement of Entremont but they are difficult to locate. Unrewarding, moreover, when you have, because there is little to see of the Salyan city sacked by the Romans. However, much of interest has been removed to the Musée Granet where also to be found are models of

Roman Aix, which gave way to medieval, then to Renaissance Aix, most of that being replaced by the seventeenth-century city still standing. Its finest feature is the broad Cours Mirabeau with four lines of great plane trees flanked by mansions, cafés and hotels. Mirabeau was an aristocrat who, after a stormy career as womaniser and bankrupt, took the side of the revolutionaries in 1789, although still secretly advising the crown. He wrote a famous tract on Despotism but died suddenly in 1791 before he could become a victim of the Terror. He was singularly ugly so it is ironic that this most stately and beautiful of Provençal thoroughfares should bear his name. At its western end is the Place Général de Gaulle with an enormous fountain; at its eastern end the Cours separates unevenly around a handsome house decorated with bas-relief heads. In front of it is a statue of King René holding a bunch of muscat grapes. The Cours Mirabeau contrasts markedly with the narrow streets leading from it, some of which are given a Florentine appearance by their high buildings with heavily barred ground floor windows. In some cases these have been replaced by modern shopfronts let into the stonework.

This celebrated avenue is certainly first-time-round and so are some of the fountains. Also Cézanne's atelier up a steep hill with nowhere to park, and once in a lifetime will do for that shrine. Otherwise it is difficult to evaluate the numerous other attractions of Aix, a city to be appreciated more for its whole than for its parts. It has nothing as outstanding as the Pope's Palace, the Pont-St-Bénézet or the ramparts at Avignon, nothing like the arena at Arles or the theatre at Orange. You come to Aix to absorb the atmosphere of a gracious university town associated with the arts. Cézanne was born here, Zola, who became his friend, lived here as a boy. It has been beloved of generations of poets and musicians. In its name is a touch of gaiety. You approach it with a lightness of heart which ought to be dispelled by its rather sombre streets, but isn't.

Many of the mansions in Aix have become museums or banks. No.38 Cours Mirabeau (Hôtel de Maurel de Pontèves) features, below a balcony, two caryatids making little effort to support it. One appears to be suffering a severe headache; both are legless. Just inside the ringroad is the Pavillon de Vendôme which was built as a country home before the city reached out to it, in flourishes of fine houses. From the entrance, where there is a line of noble cypresses, it is first seen beyond a lawn adorned with items of topiary shaped like whirls of Chantilly cream. It resembles a royal child's dolls' house; you almost expect to be able to unhinge the façade. Two caryatids, surely related to those mentioned above, flank the simple doorway. The interior is disappointingly cramped, the furniture and decoration are unremarkable but the setting is a delight.

Aix is a prosperous city bulging with students and members of the medical profession. Many a brass plate heralds the presence of a doctor and it was here, in 1962, when Min was ill, that one refused to charge for treatment because, in England, *his* wife had been cared for gratuitously under the NHS. (Nowadays the services are reciprocal so such acts of *gentillesse* do not arise.)

The medieval town was to the north of the Cours Mirabeau and here you will find the cathedral, the Hôtel de Ville, many museums and churches, and excellent shops, some selling the celebrated almond-based confectionary known as *calissons*. They are a popular delicacy.

Unlike Aix itself the cathedral of St-Saveur is more of interest for its parts than its whole, which has nothing of the height and might of the great Gothic churches. Its three naves, Romanesque, Gothic and Baroque, huge west door with a fine tympanum on which all the figures have been restored, twelfth-century baptistery adjoining what was once a parish church, and small but superb cloister, provide architectural students, professional and amateur, with a good exercise in spotting periods and styles. The bare interior houses a famous triptych, by Froment, featuring on one panel Good King René and his treble chins.

Next door, across the spacious Place des Martyrs, is the Musée des Tapisseries in what was formerly the archbishop's palace. If I had time for only one of them I would take the cathedral as read and go for the tapestries. Most of them were collected by the princes of the church and have been displayed here since 1910. In the first room are four of the Don Quixote series of ten, of which one has been lost. They were woven at Beauvais between 1734 and 1744 to the drawings of Charles Natoire and are perfect examples of this art-cum-craft. The Don, Sancho Panza, and Dulcinella have been interpreted with total success. More of them can be found in the second room beyond which is an earlier series from Beauvais, The Grotesque (1689), rich in colour. One is called Spanish Tobacco and depicts musicians and actors; another series of four has the title, The Russian Games. The palace courtyard has a permanent stage used every July during the Aix International Music Festival.

The Rue Gaston de Saporta goes, in one direction, past the Musée du Vieil Aix which occupies the ground floor of a rather shabby seventeenth-century mansion. It is strong on *santons*, some of them contemporary, has a fine staircase, a display of equestrian items and a corsair's trunk with an intricate locking device. The pride of the poorly labelled collection is a fascinating model (1836) of the procession known as Les Jeux de la Fête Dieu. This annual celebration, fostered by King René, has now, regrettably, lapsed.

The Rue Gaston de Saporta also leads, through an imposing sixteenth-century clock-tower to the Place de l'Hôtel de Ville. Part of the tower was built with Roman stones; the belfry is a typical example of wrought iron Provençal work. The Hôtel de Ville, from which it projects, is roughly

Palladian with three stories, a fine inner courtyard, an exhibition hall and an important library. At right angles to it is the Halle aux Grains, now a post office. It has a charming pediment where a figure which I take to be Neptune is confronted by a lady, one of whose legs dangles over the parapet. This is not *trompe-l'oeil*; it really does. The sculptor was Chastel, an eighteenth-century citizen of Aix. A fountain not quite centrally placed adds to the visual charm of the square.

In the Rue Espariat is the Natural History Museum, occupying part of the former Hôtel Boyer d'Eguilles. (Old Aix is rich in former homes of the nobility which seem to have escaped the hatred of the mob.) The entrance to the museum is across a spacious courtyard where, in one corner, a dispensing chemist works in gleamingly antiseptic quarters. You ascend a stone staircase, past a statue of Michel Adanson, botanist (1722-1806), with a lovely wrought iron balustrade, and pay your entrance fee at a cash desk with a jokey bamboo roof.

The museum was founded in 1838 and arrived at its present home in 1953 when it acquired the locally discovered collection of dinosaur eggs. The exhibits include an enormous reconstruction of what resulted when one of them hatched. There are four rooms and a passage, having sections on mineralogy, petrography, palaeontology, prehistory, astronomy, the fauna and flora of Provence and regional ornithology. It would all benefit from a facelift.

Almost opposite is the Place d'Albertas which, like rather too much of Aix, looks neglected. It forms three sides of a rectangle with cobbled courtyard and pretty fountain. There are many bas-relief heads above window frames.

Eastwards through an intriguing network of streets will be found the parish church of Ste-Madeleine, a massive item of Gothic-Baroque with an interior baptistery resembling a classical temple. As you enter, it is on the right, cowering, cramped, clandestine, when it should be celebratory. Outside is another of Chastel's works, the Preacher's Fountain. Down the road, against an almost solid jam of motor vehicles, hooting and bumping each other in ever-mounting exasperation, is the monstrous Palais de Justice where the castle of the Counts of Provence once stood. It is particularly out of place because Aix does not specialise in the grandiloquent. Here, from 1501, in an earlier building the Parlement de Provence met. The scourge of Provence, it is related, was tripartite: the mistral, the Durance and the *Parlement*. The latter's influence ended at the Revolution.

To the south of the Cours Mirabeau, in the Mazarin quarter, are to be found the Musée Granet, many stately terraces, the church of St-Jean-de-Malte and an especially charming fountain, that of the four dolphins, the work of Rambot in the eighteenth century.

The museum is named after the painter François Granet whose work is exhibited in what, even after restoration, remains a partially scruffy gallery. Once an art school where Cézanne studied, two of the rooms have been deliberately left much as they looked in his day. Photographs taken in the nineteenth century record even more cluttered hanging then. I found it difficult to concentrate in this circumstance though a self-portrait by Puget lingered in the memory a while. Michael Jacobs calls the collection a storehouse of French painting of the previous century, and I am sure this assessment is fair but at least half of it is unsympathetically displayed.

In the corridors leading to the original rooms the pictures have greater appeal, whilst in the newer galleries they are hung to contemporary standards. Cézanne is represented by a portrait of his wife looking sourly

Aix-en-Provence: Place d'Albertas

131

away from the next two smaller works, one showing the painter's favourite *baigneuses*. There really should be, here of all places, examples of his many studies of the Montagne Ste-Victoire, which looms majestically over Aix. There are two Rubens – portraits of unknowns – an Ingres of the handsome, youthful Granet himself, and a perfect David, of another young man. There is also what may or may not be a Rembrandt. It is certainly 'school of' but what really matters is, does it make you linger? Granet (1775-1849) is modestly represented with a number of views of Italy and some pastoral scenes.

The most fascinating exhibits are to be found in the cellars. Here space is allotted to Roman and pre-Roman Aix, and primarily to the finds from Entremont. The Salyans rate as barbarians and indulged in decapitation as a ritual, yet for second-century BC tribesmen they were highly sophisticated. The museum exhibits excellent pottery and tools and a reconstruction of what was a thriving olive oil industry. There are a great many sculpted figures (mostly headless) and one kneeling figure with fine features (not labelled). The other part of the cellar is devoted to an assessment of Roman Aix with a model of the supposed forum, a typical mosaic and a section of pavement. At the end of the third century AD, Aix, which became a colony under Augustus, was capital of Roman Provence but gave way later to Arles.

The church of St-Jean-de-Malte, at right angles to the Granet, has a superb tower and spire but is inextricably entangled with houses, cafés and other secular edifices. It is often closed, but if you arrive when a mass is being held you can at least peep inside and see the splendid plain vaulting and a stained glass east window.

Leave by the Rue Cardinale, turning right at the dolphin fountain, to reach the Musée Bibliographique et Archéologique Paul Arbaud. Arbaud was a nineteenth-century scholar and collector who amassed thousands of books which are available to researchers. I was glad to learn this. Otherwise, what would be the point of keeping all those volumes locked in glass-fronted bookcases? A great many pictures crowd the walls, dark reproductions of Leonardo and Michel Angelo, and a few original portraits. There is a mass of pottery and porcelain, some of it hideous, to me, though a few items bear pretty motifs. I liked most a fine panelled wooden ceiling, two carved doors and some lapidary pieces in the dingy entrance hall. It is open daily in the afternoons and can be missed without guilt.

In the Rue de l'Opéra, a narrow unimpressive street on the eastern side of the town, is a grimy mansion where St.John Perse, poet, diplomat, librarian, author of *Anabase* and winner of the Nobel Prize for Literature – so you may not have heard of him – lived. His collection is on view at the Hôtel de Ville.

At first sight there is no sign of an opera house but one of lost splendour is concealed behind what looks like the entrance to a rundown cinema. Inside it is faded red plush on four levels and there are many boxes at right angles to the stage, overlooking a large orchestra pit. The director of a locally based singing academy is enthusiastic about it. He told us it is like a miniature La Scala to work in, so it should be refurbished from the profits of the annual festival. In the same street is the birthplace of Paul Cézanne.

On the western side of Aix, on the edge of lovely country and partly surrounded by pleasant, mostly domestic, architecture, is the Vasarely Foundation. This tall complex of glass warehouses, in silver and black, does not suit its environment in either shape or colour, but the interior is most striking. Vasarely, who rescued the château at Gordes, was intensely prolific. Curious about the application of architectural design, he has here assembled hundreds of drawings, tapestries and layouts adaptable to many spheres of technology and building. The major part of the permanent exhibition is devoted to huge patterns, mostly in colour. A lot are extremely pleasing, especially one which resembles a large ludo board. Seen from the first floor gallery where, as at Gordes, there are contraptions which constantly change the myriad of designs on show, it is rather like looking down from the flies of a theatre. There are 42 monumental works on display (they are called 'mural integrations') and 800 experimental studies. The complex has a conference suite, lecture halls, and sales room.

Should you feel compelled to visit the excavations at Entremont, they are to be found near a point on the D14, where the N296 has a bridge over it. There is a sign on the right (going north) by a bus stop, pointing to a dirt track up into a copse. This is one vehicle wide for two-way traffic, and thieves are said to frequent the pot-holed car park. The remains are frankly uninteresting, consisting of a number of streets marked with low walls. A notice board tells which are the older ones. There is no admission fee. The Salyans are remembered in the name Celyon, a village to the west.

The D10 out of Aix directs to Vauvenargues. Just after St-Marc-Jaumegarde is the turning to the Barrage de Bimont where there is a rec-ommended picnic spot from which to gaze upon Montagne Ste-Victoire and understand, perhaps, why Cézanne continually painted it, ever seeking to capture its changing colours and light. The barrage dams the River Infernet, was built between 1946-51 and is 87.50m high. The river connects with the Canal de Provence which nowadays has many branches and a total length of 220km, 115 of them underground. It irrigates 60,000 hectares of agricultural land and also supplies water to industry. River and canal between them complement the function of the old Verdon canal, controlling the waters of the Durance. Traffic is not allowed to cross the dam but pedestrians may walk over it to take footpaths to Le Tholonet, or up the mountain which is slightly over 1000m high. There is a chapel at the top to which an annual pilgrimage is made.

Vauvenargues, 7km on, clings to a hillside below the Montagne des Ubacs. It is famous for its château, standing on a hillock slightly below it and firmly closed. Pablo Picasso bought it in 1958 and is buried here. He is said to have painted much of its interior but few have been permitted to see it. A message on the gates reads: 'The Museum is in Paris.' A previous owner was the Marquis Luc de Clapiers who was a friend of Voltaire. He became unpopular with many of his contemporaries because of his moralising and, after a brief spell of fame, died aged 32, in solitude and rejection. The château (16-17C) escaped the Revolution.

The narrow winding road to Jouques leads over the Col du Grand Sambuc (615m) through deserted terrain with thick vegetation. For nearly 16km there is no sign of habitation. Then, suddenly, there is a large building, probably a summer school, with a football ground below it.

In 1962 I complained to the publisher of the Blue Guides because Jouques, this village on the eastern extreme of the Bouches-du-Rhône, was not included in their South of France volume. It is still only glancingly mentioned in the volume for the whole of France, and in the Michelin Green Guide it rates a reference only for its connection with the hydro-electric scheme and the Canal de Provence.

Jouques lies in a valley with most of the town facing south in terraces beside a vast meadow flanked by plane trees. It is scallop-shaped, and on a crag above it there is not a castle but a chapel which is far from ruined. Tower and belfry are intact, it has a roof and four walls. To reach it is an arduous climb indeed past a few houses in private ownership. In the slightly curving terraces many of the old dwellings have been unostentatiously refurbished; some are bright with window boxes. There are vistas in all directions and sunshine filters between the houses. The office of tourism and incorporated museum open for a few hours on most afternoons. I did not come across any plaques or statues and, on the approach roads, there are no notices proclaiming ancient buildings. It is just a village (population around 3,000) which I find very attractive.

From Jouques we pass briefly into the Var, skirting Rians to take another mountain road through oak forests to Pourrières. Sadly the oaks have been smitten with a disease which has killed thousands of them. The sight reminded me of the 200,000 Teutons said to have died hereabouts when Marius's army struck.

Pourrières today is a typical little hill town surrounded by vineyards which stretch far across the Arc valley. At nearby Trets (to rhyme with gets) you are back in the Bouches-du-Rhône. This is a fairly unremark-able

Jouques

place but with magnificient views of hills and mountains, and that is why we have come. Below the Montagne Ste-Victoire lies the Montagne du Cengle and below that a lower range, some of it resembling a man-made ridge. It is often under a light mist or heat haze and can look as though it is emerging from water. It faces the Montagne de Regagnas.

The church at Trets was never finished and lacks a top to its belfry. The best feature of the town is its great strong walls. They enclose a melancholy interior of narrow alleys and arches.

Drive through woodland on a road totally sheltered from the close-by autoroute to Le Tholonet, nowadays an important administrative centre for the Canal de Provence. The village became famous for its Cézanne connection. The painter loved to walk out from Aix with Zola and other friends along the undulating road sheltered by umbrella pines and overlooking lush meadows. However, he did not take the hard path up to his favourite mountain but preferred recording it from a distance. The village café-restaurant bears his name, so does a windmill which has become a gallery. There is a particularly fine avenue of poplars.

Another outing from either Aix or Marseille is to the entrancing small fishing village of Cassis (The s is not pronounced). From Aix it is 46km through mostly attractive country, with many hills and hairpin bends and a certain number of unavoidable towns, unless you go out of your way to join the autoroute; from Marseille it is only 23km.

Despite what has happened to much of the Mediterranean coast, Cassis has contrived to become popular whilst remaining relatively unspoilt, no doubt because it is surrounded by cliffs which fall sheer into the sea and therefore cannot be built upon. Nor do they seem to have been much colonised on top. True, in the actual creek in which the town lies, there has been some ill-considered building, notably a block above a restaurant on the western side. This should, by public order, be reduced to two levels so that those who live behind it can also command a view of the sea and cliffs. In contrast, another contemporary block to the east, rises in step-like progression up a hillside, providing a satisfactory prospect for the inhabitants and a townscape for others. The buildings on the quay have, for the most part, been left in the picturesque state in which the turn of the century painters 'discovered' them. Many, indeed most, are now restaurants or cafés but they remain human in size and management. Arriving well after two o'clock for lunch at El Sol we were served as though the table could be ours for the whole afternoon. Following lunch – surely sea food with the excellent local white wine? – it is agreeable to take the 45-minute boat trip to the *calanques*, as the high-sided creeks are called. There is much competition for your custom, so seek out the least-crowded boat. It will take you out of the little harbour, past a kind of toy lighthouse, and up the coast, in the Marseille direction, to visit three deep *calanques;* Port-Miou, Port-Pin and En-Vau. Climbers ascend the limestone sides without ropes, pine trees grow out of the rock to considerable height, there are beaches and the water is truly blue. It can also be exhilaratingly choppy because of strong currents at the entries to the creeks. (Fire devastated the area in August, 1990. Friends of ours took to the mistral-swept open sea to escape the heat.)

Close to Port-Miou are quarries where a strong white stone, used for the docks of the Suez Canal and for the Statue of Liberty, is produced. You can walk to the *calanques,* though the going is tough, and drive eastwards to La Ciotat by a road which winds high above Cap Canaille, the red mountain which overlooks Cassis bay. Close to the town end of it is the castle of Les Baux which is justifiably so-named because in the twelfth-thirteenth centuries it belonged to the lords of the more famous château in the Alpilles. Around the fortress they built here a town grew up. When they went off to pursue pleasures and villainy elsewhere the castle fell into the hands of the villagers, but gradually deteriorated. It is now very much restored and looks rather too well pointed to be true which, in large measure, it is not. It cannot be visited unless you know the owners.

Frédéric Mistral was responsible for bringing some of its popularity to Cassis because he included it in his poem, *Calendau.* But later it was artists, from Dufy to Matisse, who sang and drew its praises. Today its harbour, and also the moorings in the *calanques,* are used by weekend sailors as well as by fishermen. So far, the approach to the town is by a winding, hilly road, although a motorway is not far distant, and there is not room for much more development or parking spaces.

Ten kilometres inland is Marcel Pagnol's birthplace at Aubagne, on the edge of the Plan de l'Aigle. He is commemorated at the Syndicat d'Initiative, a circular building in a pretty garden, by a permanent exhibition. Le Petit Monde de Marcel Pagnol displays souvenirs of his plays, books and films, facing a centrepiece which is a reconstruction of the *garrigue* hills of the neighbourhood dominated by the majestic Garbalan rock, an outcrop of the Etoile Massif. On two sides of them are model villages, based on Aubagne and La Treille and peopled with Pagnol characters. The exhibit was made in the *santon* workshops of the town, a dozen or more of which are open to visitors. In the winter a panoramic Christmas crib is provided from the same source.

La Treille is a village in the hills near the house where the Pagnol family spent holidays and weekends. Michael Jacobs wrote that it has been swallowed up by modern Marseille, but I did not find it so. It is still very much a village aloof from the awful conurbation, on the slopes of a steep hill between two valleys. In the surrounding countryside some villas have been built but apart from one flat-topped block on a ridge (it looks like a sanatorium) there is nothing offensive. We drove in at the munching hour and found a space on a terrace below the church. There we had a tranquil picnic. But we should have toiled up the hill on foot, like the Pagnol family on their way to the Bastide Neuve. Their house still stands on the edge of almost totally unspoiled countryside, and so does the one where Marcel's friend Lili lived. If you have read the autobiographies and seen the films based on them you will not, I think, be disappointed by a visit to La Treille.

Since 1862 Aubagne has been the home of the French Foreign Legion, founded in 1831 by Louis Philippe. Its deeds are celebrated in a museum on the very edge of the town, just off the D2 to Marseille. It is not easy to locate. So best stop at the guarded gates of an army camp and enquire. The museum lies at its rear behind a row of palm trees, up a lane. Admission is free to a collection so meticulously tidy that I think its maintenance must come under the jurisdiction of a sergeant-major determined that each artefact shall conform to rules laid down in regimental standing orders. On the ground floor is a hall containing little more than an enormous table with four upright chairs. Off it is a chapel where all legionnaires killed in battle are remembered individually. Elsewhere are cases of uniforms, weapons, battle trophies, photographs, commands; but most impressive are the paintings, depicting the chaotic horror of battle, and a series of pencil drawings of individual soldiers. Souvenirs of this unique army, which has French officers but other ranks from all countries, are on sale – from ties and ashtrays to CDs and books.

The old town of Aubagne has excellent shops, many of them in pedestrianised alleys reaching up to a much restored church. On the plain around it there are numerous hôtels; at Gémenos there is also an open air theatre. This neat town has smart municipal features in the Hôtel de Ville (once the 17C château) facing down gardens with fountains, to a landscaped roundabout on which olive trees grow beside hillocks.

The limestone hills enclosing the plain are especially memorable when they shimmer in a heat haze. Pagnol's Provence does not let you down.

11   Marseille

It is unlikely that many summer visitors to Provence will wish to spend part of their precious holiday time in France's second largest city, even though it is beside the sea, so Marseille is for visiting in the spring or autumn.

The city is proud of its heritage and there is no more obvious indication of this than at the Jardin des Vestiges where a compromise has been reached between the claims of archaeology and modern commerce. In 1967, during building operations for a new business centre, Graeco-Roman and medieval remains were unearthed. Some of the earliest have been incorporated into a public garden where walls, and a cistern from the first century BC are preserved amongst the greenery. At one end, forming the lower two floors of a shopping complex is the Musée d'Histoire de Marseille, and it is here that your visit to the city should commence. When you leave the railway station (*don't* bring your car) take a taxi or travel two stops on the metro to the Vieux Port.

The museum is clearly laid out with films, diagrams, models and briefly worded notices used to introduce the visitor effortlessly to the story of Marseille which, as recorded in Chapter 1, began when a boatload of Phocaeans put ashore in about 600BC. They arrived at the very moment when Gyptis, daughter of a Ligurian chieftain, Nann, was about to select a husband. She chose Protis, the Phocaean leader, and thus was founded the Greek colony which became part of Roman Provence. (The source for this story is Justin's abridgement of a lost history of the world written by a native of Gaul six hundred years after the event.)

Prior to this romantic occurrence some sort of trading post had already been established by the Phocaeans but, following the nuptials, Massalia became an important Mediterranean port and also a republic. The Greeks traded with other settlements inland and along the coast, founded a university and became allies of the Romans, whose help they called upon when they were threatened by tribes of Franks from the north. Later Massilia, as it became, unwisely backed Pompey against Caesar. The latter, as punishment, diverted much of its trade to Arles but it maintained a level of prosperity which continued even after the fall of the Empire. The Crusades boosted commercial activity which grew, despite periods of plague and attacks from the sea. Marseille enjoyed independent status for short and long periods but was, after 1481, nominally, at least, a part of France. It supported the Revo-lution – though La Marseillaise was actually composed at Strasburg by an Alsatian. The battle hymn was adopted by the volunteers of Marseille who are said to have sung it at every stopping place on the march to Paris. In the nineteenth century the city fluctuated between support for the crown and for the republic and has, ever since, displayed a fiercely individual character in all national disputes.

To return to the museum, the most exciting discovery – partly destroyed by a mechanical digger – was the hull of a merchant ship of the third century AD that had sunk in the ancient harbour. The timbers are now being preserved by a method known as freeze-drying and may be observed, behind glass, in the position where they were found. (The harbour spread further eastwards at that time.) Elsewhere in the museum is a reconstruction of a similar vessel, showing how it was made.

There is a model of Greek Massalia in the third and second centuries BC; maps showing the extent of explorations from the port by the intrepid Pytheas and other voyagers, who sailed down the African coast and northwards to Iceland, Britain and the Baltic; a plaster case of a large pottery kiln (first or second century AD) illustrating in sectional form how it functioned; amphorae, sliced vertically in half to show what was stored in them; and a visual aid demonstrating how the Greeks, using enormous tongs, built with massive blocks of stone.

Part of the museum is used for temporary exhibitions about other aspects of Marseille's history. There is a library of 4,000 books about Provence, and a lecture theatre. Courses of study are arranged for the young, and guided tours of the garden and museum are part of a regular schedule.

The Vieux Port no longer stretches this far but ends at the Quai des Belges where a fish market is held every morning. Nowadays it is used only by pleasure craft and excursion boats which are moored here in thousands, making a forest of masts.

New docks were built in the nineteenth century a little to the north. They were destroyed by the retreating Germans in 1944 but swiftly reconstructed, since when the trading fortunes of Marseille have ebbed and flowed. By 1989 it could accommodate the largest tonnage afloat and, in Europe, was second only to Rotterdam, but it has recently suffered from recession and labour troubles.

The ancient city lay on the northern side of the Vieux Port where there are three more museums, two cathedrals, several churches, fortifications and the town hall, in an area widely dynamited by the Germans in 1943. The Hôtel de Ville, which survived, is a perfectly symmetrical late seventeenth-century building on three stories of diminishing height. There is a central balcony below an elaborate coat of arms in stone. It is the work of Pierre Puget, a Marseillais much represented in his home town. Behind it and its more modern extension lies the Maison Diamantée, a Renaissance house which is now the Musée du Vieux Marseille. This concentrates on times more recent than featured in exhibits at the Musée d'Histoire. The ground floor has much eighteenth-century furniture including one of those slatted wooden bread bins fixed to a wall, of which we shall see other examples at Arles and Maillane. In the lobby is a large narrative painting of corn being unloaded from a sailing barge. The artist, Alphonse Moutte (1840-1913), depicted well-known resident merchants.

You are encouraged to start your visit on the second floor, reached up fine stone stairways carved on their undersides. Here you will find a room devoted to photographs and captions of the outrageous destruction of 1943 when the inhabitants were given only twenty-four hours to leave their homes and told to provide themselves with two days' provisions. Many of them were deported to the camps of central Europe. Fourteen hectares (nearly 35,000 acres) of streets were systematically blown up on the excuse that they were harbouring criminals and spies in a formerly fashionable district which had become notoriously seedy. What it looked like can be seen from the harrowing photographs, but also from the present state of some streets which escaped.

Another room on this floor is more tranquil in character. It has displays of playing cards, the manufacture of which was a local industry practised, for instance, at the Salle Camoin (1760-1906) whose frontage is placed against a wall.

The first floor has a fine model of old Marseille and a *santon* museum. Pride of place in the latter goes to Homage à la Provence, a spectacular creation of 1981 by Georges Prost, illustrating traditional dances and occupations. There is homage also to Jean-Louis Lagnel (1764-1822) who was the first to make clay *santons*. They became popular when the Revolution closed the churches, as symbols of a belief still held by many a favourite subject was, and is, the crèche. (A regular market in *santons* is held in the Allés de Meilhan in the winter.)

In one of the rooms is a print of Marseille as it was in 1574, showing the walls and gates on the north side of the port but with the south barren of buildings apart from a church high on the hill where Notre-Dame-de-la-Garde now stands, and a hospital. On the quay where the nineteenth-century cathedral was built, overlooking the modern docks, were windmills.

Around the corner from the Diamantée is the smaller Musée des

141

Docks Romains, created in 1963 by the archaeologist Fernand Benoit who excavated the site of a warehouse in use in the first century AD. A faintly engraved plaque by the entrance refers to the Docks Romains du Lacydon, the name of the creek which became the Vieux Port. Here Benoit found huge clay storage vessels and uncovered wells. These can be viewed *in situ*. Around the walls are cases containing amphorae of smaller dimensions and a mosaic, from the third century AD, showing a lady taking a bath. Nearby is the ruined hull of a boat, said to be Caesar's galley, but not all attributions should be taken at face value.

Most of this area has been rebuilt with drab apartment blocks some of which hem in the attractive little church, on a mound, of St-Laurent. This is twelfth-century with a much later belfry but the site is hallowed indeed, having housed temples and an earlier church. From a viewing point on its south side you can observe the old port and the forts which guarded it. Round a bend, past another dull block of flats, you are overwhelmed by an immense neo-Byzantine pile known as La Cathédrale de la Major. Beside it, dwarfed, dirty, but not as uncared for as it recently was, and no longer unsafe to visit, is what is left of the Old Major (Ancienne Cathédrale de la Major), a Romanesque church which was partly gobbled up by the equivalent of a nineteenth-century mechanical digger. The structure of the dome over the crossing is of particular architectural interest (as at Avignon). Morning visitors should note that both cathedrals close for an early lunch at 11.30.

Marseille: The Old Port

Marseille: The New Major and the Old

The New Major is not at all a bad building once one's indignation about what has been allowed to decay in its shadow, is overcome. Its proportions are splendid, its roofscape of domes, turrets and terraced balcony, though not as lively as that at Perigueux, is imaginative, and the main south-facing doorway has intricate ornamentation. Inside the decoration is restrained, but the size of the nave can take what there is, and at the crossing there are excellently sculpted figures of apostles by one Botinelly (1937). The altar is a beast; there is a gaudy golden Mary in a side chapel facing an enclosed glass office complete with desk, phone and knitted lampshade – and somewhere about, but I missed it, is an ivory reliquary from a church six hundred years older. The vast, gloomy ambulatory is broken by a spacious, unfurnished chapel in the apse. This enormous edifice stands high above an esplanade where shops face the new docks.

A short walk away is La Vieille Charité, an example of chaste seventeenth-century building with a chapel by Puget more restrained than anything else of his in Marseille. The former hospice is now a cultural centre to which collections from the Château Borély are being removed. By mid-1992 the Egyptian, African, American and Oceanic had been installed in galleries off the first level balconies. The Egyptian is entered through an unlit, unsigned doorway (just go on trying until you find the right one). A dark vestibule leads in to what you could easily imagine to be the interior of a pyramidal tomb. There are narrow chambers with cases of mummified animals, amulets and inscribed stones, and an open sarcophagus revealing the skeletal, partly embalmed body within.

The other collections are equally off-putting when it comes to making access but the effort is worth it. In the American and Oceanic Gallery are shields, spears and shrunken human heads, all impeccably displayed and documented. Note the Solomon Islander with an early make of underwater goggles. The African gallery with its exquisitely carved reliquary figures is no less impressive. When the remaining sections from the Château Borély – Greek, Roman, Etruscan etc – have been moved here, the Vieille Charité will be a major museum.

Make your way back to the old port, through narrow thorough-fares, to take lunch at one of the numerous restaurants offering the famous *bouillabaisse* (fish stew). Some, but not all, are tourist rip-offs; La Sirène, on the south side, has reasonably priced menus and the pleasantest of service. I avoid establishments on the Quai des Belges but if the French find they have a palate for American convenience foods that is their business and, to be fair, one of the restaurants there is listed in Michelin.

On the south side of the port, on ground said to be the dowry Protis had on behalf of Gyptis, are two churches demanding obligatory visits, one for itself, the other because of its site.

The Basilica St-Victor, the remains of a fortified abbey, seen from the harbour looks toy-like with its forlorn twin towers, one raised slightly higher than the other. The approach to it is also uninspiring, through grimy streets (where the dogs do not respond to the drawings on the pavements directing them to the gutters) but, once inside, the journey proves worth while. The church takes over from the fortress, and then the crypt from the church. Decoration is minimal in the high Romanesque nave and vaulted apse, though in a chapel with a baptismal font there is a 1975 tapestry of the Apocalypse by S. Lorimy-Delarozière. The new Jerusalem is depicted centrally in a heraldic lozenge surrounded by highly animated panels in modern-primitive styles. Another contemporary item is the simple bronze altar (1966) which fits well into the 700-year-old surroundings. It stands on two legs with decorated capitals of knights and saints. Nearby are cases of relics, saintly bones allegedly.

The abbey served by the church was founded in the fifth century and is now present only in the highly complicated crypt which should not be missed. It is spacious and dry, with ramifications including catacombs having tombs and altars of their own. The sarcophagi are elaborately carved and some have pagan motifs, notably that of St-Mauront which is decorated with centaurs and scenes of Bacchus. It was fashionable to be buried here and local sculptors thrived on the business; they also produced impeccable work. There are minor parts of the crypt leading off the main area where columns with curiously carved figures can be found; there are large burial chambers and small ones, and particularly there is an apparently man-made cave for St.Victor, after whom the church is named, with a sculpted mural (Puget again) above an altar. The whole crypt, from which the base of the towers may be entered, makes for a strange and eerie experience, also encapsulating the history of Marseille. It is, too, very much a working church associated with fishermen because Victor was the patron saint of sailors.

Far above on the summit of the hill, reached by bus or taxi, is the more immediately impressive Notre-Dame-de-la-Garde which is the first sight of Marseille for most of those arriving by air, sea or train. Its Baroque tower is surmounted by a temple which is a pedestal that itself bears an enormous golden Mary. The whole gross edifice illustrates the church of Rome at its most suave and businesslike. It occupies the best site in town and glorifies it with no expense spared. The design is good of its kind, the materials used are of the very best, there is hardly a speck of the usual dust on the glitter. It has a lift, a spacious cafeteria and a shop which takes credit cards. It must make a good return on capital. The faithful have adorned its walls with ex-voto offerings which also hang in the nave, shaped as boats. It is one of the most visited of all buildings in Provence. If you come for the views they are unparalleled but they do unfortunately reveal how Marseille, like so many other cities, has been severely blemished by tower blocks and urban sprawl, the one having failed to stem the tide of the other. The most famous skyscraper in these parts is Le Corbusier's Cité Radieuse where he proposed that people should not only live but also shop and meet communally at 'high rise' level. If you visit it to see how it is weathering you go via the President J.F.Kennedy Corniche that literally overhangs a number of fishing villages lying in the creeks below.

A bus will also take you along the Corniche to the Château Borély, a late eighteenth-century mansion beside a park in a low-lying region of outer Marseille. Its treasures, as noted, are being removed to La Vieille Charité.

Others, from the Musée Cantini, are to be housed here but when is uncertain. These matters are not rushed in France. Beside the château is a path past a clearing where a statue of Pierre Puget stands with an inscription which translates as 'Marble Crumbles Before Me.' This leads to the Botanical Gardens which include beds of plants grouped in categories for nervous diseases, skin complaints and other maladies. There is also a hot-house for exotic blooms where, one February, we saw a sumptuous display of orchids.

The most famous street in Marseille is La Canebière which runs eastwards from the Vieux Port culminating in an overbearing but banal church, St-Vincent-de-Paul. From here another boulevard leads to the Palais Longchamp, a ludicrously pretentious construction reminiscent of the even more appalling Vittoriano in Rome. It comprises two solid wings of enormous chambers joined by a vast colonnade broken in the centre by a *pavillon* with an absurd fountain featuring men (or maybe, gods) and cows. It was built (1860) by Henri Espérandieu who bears responsibility also for Notre-Dame-de-la-Garde. (Ironically his name is perpetuated in a rather drab, cramped street nearby.) In one wing is the Musée des Beaux Arts; in the other, the Musée d'Histoire Naturelle. In the Beaux Arts one 'ground'-floor gallery is devoted to sculptures and paintings by Puget, a second has figurines by Jean-Barrabe Amy (1839-1907) and more Puget and across a spacious hall, amongst other works badly in need of cleaning and better lighting, is a Rubens canvas churning with activity. On the floor above, past a mural representing Marseille when colonised by the Greeks, nonsensically implying that the settlers erected ruins, is a room of sculptured nudes. They are well displayed against a backing, through windows, of Notre-Dame-de-la-Garde. Between the windows are two bas-reliefs by Barthelemy Chardigny (1757-1813). The theme of one is olive gathering, featuring a lady in classical robes topped by what looks like a military tin helmet of World War Two.

In the main gallery at this level are a murky Millet and a dirty Courbet, two pleasant Corots, a Canova bust of Benjamin Franklin and a painting 'in Caravaggio style' by Théodoule Ribot (1823-91) of a young chef. There are many good portraits by little-known artists, such as Françoise Duparc (1726-78) who painted ordinary people. Provençal painting is well represented: I liked Guigou's fine *Collines d'Allauch* and Loubon's *Vue des Aygalades,* showing cattle being driven towards Marseille. There is a bronze statuette by Daumier (*Le Ratapoil*) and a partly completed study of Eve by Rodin.

The exhibits in the Natural History Museum are, for the most part, traditionally displayed in glass-fronted or -topped cabinets so that the dead hand of regimentation prevails. Yet how else are thousands of beetles, shells, butterflies, flints, sponges and stones to be presented? And, indeed, once one has become absorbed by the intricate and highly colourful patterns on the tiny wings of the butterflies, does it matter? On one floor there are dozens of stuffed animals standing about, which lessens the monotony, whilst the beak count of embalmed birds is prodigious, proving that the French don't eat all that they capture or kill. Amongst them are species of vulture either extinct or in danger of becoming so, due to hunting, or to the lack of carcasses for them to feed upon now that sheep farming has declined. Represented, too, is the lovely bartavelle, a reminder of Marcel Pagnol's *La Gloire de Mon Père*.

In one chamber the curators have achieved a more dynamic method of display. As you enter you are confronted by the model of a mauve dinosaur. No one, explains the attendant, knows what colour they were and mauve appeals to children. You then see road signs indicating APT, GARGAS etc. This is to tell you where the exhibits to which they point were found. There is also a cut-out of a workman, in blue dungarees, putting the finishing touches to walls of greatly varying height. These symbolise the time span of particular epochs of pre-history. It is something of a surrealist approach but most engaging once the message has penetrated. I particularly enjoyed an artist's impression of a cave in which Homo Erectus is shown having a jolly lunch.

If you can face more steps, there is an aquarium in the basement but that means you must remount them before descending two tiers to the street. Across the way lies a less exacting experience.

This is the Maison Grobet-Labadié, also of the nineteenth century but it could hardly be in greater contrast to the Longchamp. It was built for a merchant named Labadié whose daughter married a violinist and painter named Grobet, and bequeathed by that lady to the city in 1919 as a permanent museum of domestic life at one level. In fact it is more, because there is an interesting collection of musical instruments and a small gallery of paintings. The walls are hung with Aubusson tapestries. In the lovely Louis XVI room there are richly upholstered chairs and sofas and on the first-floor landing stands a carved door, adorned with cherubs, from a mansion in Aix. Its brass handle has a fierce tiger's head. There are bedrooms and sitting-rooms furnished as they were for the family but the ground-floor front drawing-room now has rows of chairs for recitals given at a piano and a clavichord. In the hall beyond are cabinets of faience. The second-floor gallery has a great many paintings indifferently hung which is no more than most of them deserve. However, they include a Corot and a Constable.

The pictures at the Musée Cantini may well stimulate you more but that depends on what, from the permanent collection of contemporary art, happens to be on show. The gallery is also used for visiting exhibitions such as the Edward Hopper we saw here in 1989.

Another small museum is housed in the Bourse et Chambre de Commerce, at the western end of La Canebière. It has models and paintings of ships, including two impressive canvases by Alfred Casile, and such objects as a heavy metal diving suit and curious cylindrical containers decorated with oriental ceramics. The latter are to do with the conditioning of silk. The actual Bourse, nineteenth-century, neo-Classical-cum-Baroque, has a huge hall, once the exchange. It is in red brick, rising to a ceiling on which richly carved panels illustrate, yet again, the history of Marseille. Medallions of the trading nations are now mounted here because the Bourse has moved into new premises close to the History Museum complex.

On the most famous of the offshore islands is the Château d'If, built by François I as an extension of the city defences and notorious for the prison it became. The *if* is a yew tree but the island is not named after it and there is nothing green about this grim place which Alexandre Dumas immortalised in *The Count of Monte-Cristo*. A visit is more or less obligatory, but I would not repeat it. Boats leave from the old port, at the Quai des Belges, and the short trip is agreeable, offering good views of the protective forts at the harbour entrance and of the Château de Pharo, with its park, where the Empress Eugénie, Napoléon III's wife, had a second home.

There is an utterly basic landing stage at the Château d'If and from it an unruly path, designed to twist ankles, leads up through the walls to a barren area of loose stone in front of the drawbridge. The château has two round towers on either side of the bare frontage and another taller one set obliquely at the rear. There is an inner courtyard off which are the cells at two levels. They are labelled with emotive names – The Man in the Iron Mask, Mirabeau, Abbé Faria, and suchlike. You can see where Edmond Dantès, 'the Count of Monte-Cristo', made his escape. More truthfully on a wall there is a plaque commemorating the 3,500 Protestants who were imprisoned whilst awaiting their turn on the galleys. There is a lot of graffiti – the work of desperate men. The whole place strikes a chill, so it is better to turn your back on it and take in the view of Marseille, perhaps imagining its appearance to the early adventurers, to the Greeks who came to trade, the Romans to conquer, the Saracens to raid and the soldiers and sailors of 1944, to liberate.

The excursion continues to the nearby islands of Ratonneau and Pommègues, now joined by a causeway forming the harbour of Frioul, favoured by weekend yachtsmen. On Ratonneau are the ruins of a fever hospital and a spruce-looking temple. If you wish you may disembark and wait for the next boat back, or you can return at once and enjoy a drink on the quayside of the old port.

For a stay in Marseille I recommend the Grand Hôtel Genève in a street beside the old Bourse. The prices are not at all grand, the service is friendly, the position central and it is as quiet as anywhere can be in a city.

I have searched in vain for the Hôtel Splendide where I spent my first night in France in 1946. This provided a motive for wandering the streets and helped to an understanding of the city. Marseille has a reputation for vice but Min and I felt ourselves unmenaced as we trod its paving stones which, after the vicissitudes of so many hill towns in the Luberon and the Dentelles, felt comfortably firm. Perhaps our liking for it was increased when a taxi driver spoke enthusiastically of his only visit to London where he found the citizens 'charmants'. There was another cabman who, when we hailed him outside the Gare St-Charles said, on hearing where we wanted to go, that it would be quicker to walk. There was also a bus driver who gave us a free ride because we had only a 100 franc note, and a passenger on the same vehicle, so concerned lest an inspector should board it and find us out, that she offered to pay our fares. Yes, we had reason to like the Marseillais.

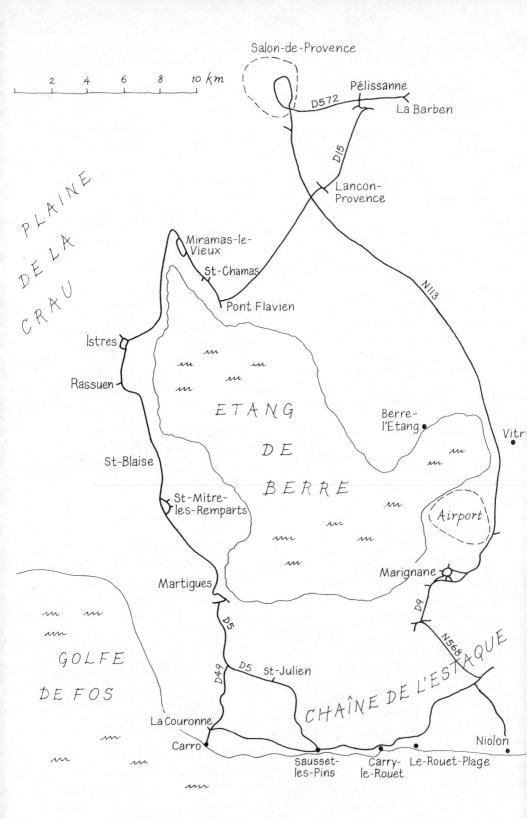

Salon-de-Provence

Pélissanne

La Barben

D572

2   4   6   8   10 km

D15

Lancon-
Provence

PLAINE
DE LA
CRAU

Miramas-le-
Vieux

St-Chamas

Pont Flavien

N113

Istres

Rassuen

ETANG
DE
BERRE

Berre-
l'Etang

Vitr

St-Blaise

St-Mitre-
les-Remparts

Airport

Marignane

Martigues

D9

D5

N568

D49   D5   St-Julien

CHAÎNE DE L'ESTAQUE

GOLFE
DE FOS

La Couronne

Niolon

Carro

Sausset-
les-Pins

Carry-
le-Rouet

Le-Rouet-Plage

12   Berre and Crau

Salon-de-Provence : La Barben : Pont Flavien : St-Chamas :
Miramas-le-Vieux : St- Blaise : Martigues : Etang de Berre :
Chaîne de l'Estaque

The area between Marseille and Arles though heavily industrialised has pockets for the tourist and even some stretches of unalloyed natural
beauty. Much of it is covered by a large lake, L'Etang de Berre, and as much
again by the Plaine de la Crau which was formerly stony and desolate from
the deposits washed down upon it from the Rhône and the Durance. Around
the Golfe de Fos is a complex of ports which is, confusingly, regarded as
being part of Marseille; at the south-east end of the Etang is Marignane
international airport. The Crau, like the Camargue on the west side of the
Rhône, is flat; the Etang de Berre is surrounded by low limestone hills which,
on the southern edge, become the Chaîne de l'Estaque. On the Mediterranean
side are some partly unspoilt fishing villages. Unless you stay at one of these
it is not a part of Provence in which you are likely to linger. There is much of
archaeological interest, especially on a hill between Fos-sur-Mer and the
inland sea, where Ligurian and Greek traders were active even before
Marseille was colonised, and all sites are within easy reach of Salon-de-
Provence, the capital of the Crau.

On our first visit to Salon the mistral blew fiercely. We took our
picnic to a small park where the wind drove icy spray over us from a fountain.
Bread and pâté were dashed from our plates, our tumblers of wine were
whirled into the dust. An observer sympathised, but half-derisively. He was
a Parisian who had come south in search of sun and blue skies. Now he
couldn't wait to return. 'The wind drives everyone mad. All the Provençal
people are terribly unhappy. You will see.' It was not to be our experience.
We find almost all people helpful, friendly and invariably polite. A few have
an alarmingly explosive manner of speaking but eruptions are usually
followed by smiles. Mind you, we have not lived in Salon which, a few
months after this encounter, returned a national front candidate to parliament; folk could be different there.

Salon stands on a low hill dominated by a well-restored castle
and is associated with Nostradamus (1503-66) who practised as a doctor
before taking to prediction. He acquired fame thanks to his extraordinarily

successful preventive medicine for plague in Toulouse, Bordeaux and Aix. When he went to Lyon to offer his remedy there he was denounced by defenders of medical orthodoxy and in retaliation he refused to reveal his treatment. So Nostradamus, who was born at St-Rémy, returned to Provence and took up astrology, publishing rhymed prophecies which appealed to Catherine de Medicis and the boy king, her son, Charles IX. Catherine visited him in Salon where he lived from 1547 in a house close to St-Michel's church. Nostradamus was buried in another church on the edge of town, St-Laurent, where his tomb is in a side chapel beneath a portrait of him by his son. Even if it were not in dire need of cleaning it would be difficult to see because of the inadequate lighting. Nearby is a more interesting item, a finely carved *pietà* standing above the monument to the five hundred men of Salon who perished in World War One.

The astrologer was not buried in St-Michel because it was thought less prestigious than the other church, yet it has two stone belfries, one with five bells, and a well-carved tympanum above the west door. Round a corner is a twentieth-century development with a wall featuring a giant image of Nostradamus. This area was badly affected by an earthquake which shook the region from Salon to Aix in 1909.

The town's other celebrity was Adam de Craponne (1527-76) an engineer whose statue stands near the Hôtel de Ville close to St-Michel. He built canals that are still part of the overall irrigation system of Greater Provence. One of them, bearing his name, goes from the Durance to the Etang de Berre.

Salon was a fortified town belonging to Arles in its early days and had to resist invasion by Saracens and Normans. The castle is known as L'Empéri because the next overlords were rulers of the Holy Roman Empire. It was started well over one thousand years ago and has been rebuilt and altered continually. Although parts of its battlements and some of its towers have gone it is still one of the largest in the region – but less imposing than another to follow. It was damaged in the earthquake, probably suffering no more than it had during the Wars of Religion and the Revolution. The main street runs fairly gently around its walls and visitors are directed to a car park with 570 spaces. This lies within boiling-pitch range of the castle which is reached up steep flights of steps. Much of it is occupied by a celebrated museum of militaria featuring all the awful paraphernalia of war arranged in tableaux. Here are pistols, bayonets, swords and gun carriages, uniforms, medals, saddles and drums, ten thousand items in all. There are life-sized models of soldiers, commissioned and lowly ranked, also of the women who followed them into battle with food and drink; there are books, letters, commands, portraits, orders of battle, maps and drawings. There is even a statue of the fourteenth Louis draped, it seems, in a similar quantity of duvets.

The museum is a must for all those fascinated by the memorabilia of war and for film-makers and novelists researching historical detail.

Across a courtyard, in a crypt, is a separate permanent exhibition concerned solely with the first great carnage of this century and with the defence of Verdun in particular. The scarlet uniforms of the past, with their spurious glamour, have turned to khaki. It is yet another monument to the futility of those terrible years.

A knowledge of the costumes you have seen is not unhelpful when you emerge and seek to interpret the visual aids on the loo doors.

Salon is noted for its jazz festival (annually in late July), as a centre of the olive oil industry and as the home of the Ecole de l'Air, where officers of the French air force have been trained since the 'thirties. Their presence is marked by all too frequent sorties when aircraft which look to me alarmingly close together swoop and dive over the countryside trailing brightly coloured exhaust fumes.

The Salon and Crau Museum is only worth visiting if you are desperate for diversion on a wet day, or are a student of the soap industry. It also features innumerable stuffed birds of the region, paintings of sheep farming and many portraits of ex-mayors of whose worthy lives you may know nothing and care less.

The museum lies on the road to Pélissanne leading to the fine castle of La Barben situated on a great eminence over the river Touloubre, and above a garden laid out by Le Nôtre. On the hill opposite is an associated zoo, a modern attraction, which was not present during the five hundred years when the Forbins were in residence. The family was granted the castle by King René, but long before his time the owners were the monks of St-Victor at Marseille. The Forbins converted part of the heavily fortified building into tolerable and in some cases, exquisite, living quarters. You enter up a triple-flighted Henri IV stairway which opens on to a terrace overlooking the woods and fields of the valley. A somewhat crumbling double staircase goes from the terrace to a balcony in front of the splendid drawing- and dining-rooms, sumptuously hung with Aubusson tapestries. One room is painted in deep red which is unfortunate considering the meagre light from small windows, and another, much larger, has leather-clad walls. Best of all is the enchanting suite once occupied by Napoléon's sister, Pauline Borghese. A delightful corridor leads to a boudoir and dressing-room all cheerfully papered and painted, one with a four seasons motif.

The kitchen is full of fascinating culinary objects and also has a grandfather clock of the Louis XIII period when the face had hour hands only. Below, in the very depths of the thousand-year-old fortress, is the baking oven, the well, and all manner of strange passages over rough terrain.

153

Pont Flavien

By one of them you are returned to the foot of the Henri IV staircase.

The castle, one tower of which was rebuilt after the earthquake, is still privately owned by someone to whom the guide refers guardedly as 'un monsieur'. The Forbin family sold it in 1933.

Take a cross-country route from La Barben to reach the Etang de Berre just south of St-Chamas. You go by minor roads back through Pélissanne, where I saw on the kerbside market rows of grandfather clocks with two hands (an odd object for a casual purchase in the street), and Lançon-Provence (up 48 steps to viewing table with panorama). Skirt Cornillon-Confoux (a *village perché*) and stop just south of St-Chamas at a triumphal Roman bridge erected by one Flavian across the river Touloubre. For a single span to be glorified by triumphal arches at both ends makes it sound pretentious; Flavian's bridge gets away with it. The pillars have sculpted lions ready to spring but only one of them is an original. You may walk across and look at the inscriptions.

St-Chamas is a small port with a large power station attached. The town is dominated by a high aqueduct with three arches and a clock-tower (1902). At one end is a hill, inhabited long before the Greeks arrived, and riddled with caves and fortifications, some of which can be seen in the yellow limestone cliff facing the lagoon. A long flight of steps points the way to a museum which I confess I have not visited, nor have I been in the seventeenth-century church to admire the altar.

Just north of St-Chamas is the old town of Miramas, standing too high and too close to the lake to be served by the railway when it was laid down in the last century. So a station was placed on the lonely Crau a few kilometres away. It has now become a junction with sprawling sidings and is surrounded by the modern town – population over 20,000.

Miramas-le-Vieux is a jewel of a hill town built in the local limestone and commanding a view of the whole Etang which, from the car park, resembles a loch or fjord except that, in Scotland and Norway, the incidence of olive groves is so low as to go unremarked. There is a ruined castle with two heavily mullioned but low doorways which seem to be lacking signs stating HOMMES and DAMES. A great segment of wall survives independently and there is one extant archway of the ramparts. The church has a two-bell tower and leans heavily on the house across the impasse. Beside it is a viewing terrace looking down towards St-Chamas. Miramas is less dramatically situated than Les Baux but walking its streets recalls that more famous place (see Chapter 14). It is obviously popular from the number of cafés and restaurants but does not seem to have been invaded, to any large extent, by the *brocante* industry.

On leaving, drive towards new Miramas before turning on to a charming road beside the Etang, rising and falling, always with new vistas.

Miramar-le-Vieux

From it the great lake sparkles. It does not look polluted but, regrettably, it is. Istres, a village with ancient sites to north and south of it has become a modern industrial town contributing to this factor. It lies south of Miramas and is surrounded by dual carriageways and roundabouts. It has a museum, referred to in respected publications, but at the time of my visit it was closed for restoration. So I concentrated on finding the correct exit from the thirty-second roundabout in order to arrive on a minor road in the direction of dreaded Fos, but from which I could deviate to reach St-Blaise. This is the antique site referred to earlier where Ligurians, and Greeks from Rhodes came to trade, and where large prosperous townships flourished, with breaks, from the seventh century BC, until the 1300s.

Outer Istres is not at all unpleasant apart from the advertisement hoardings on stilts in the gardens of private dwellings. Don't be distracted by these. The place name to look for as you drive through is Rassuen. This lies off the N569 to Fos, and from there you can make your way through scrubby country and lagoons until you arrive at a clearing between the Etangs de Lavalduc and Le Citis. Park here and climb up the track to St-Blaise, enjoying sight of Lavalduc and contrasting it with the distant view of belching chimneys at Fos. On your right is a medieval wall, on your left a pine grove overshadowing a small Romanesque chapel with attached seventeenth-century hermitage.

Archaeology aside, it is a tranquil place to be, whether you pay to pass into the area where you can hardly see the ruins for the trees, or wander along paths at several levels around it. Long before there were Christian saints, the settlement went by the name of Mastramella and such it was when the first wall was built about 700BC, and when the Graeco-Roman one of, say, 300BC, was erected. By the time the paleo-Christian defences of 500AD went up the name had changed to Ugium. Remains of all three can be seen in close proximity. Mastramella declined in importance because of Marius who, whilst waiting to trap the barbarian hordes, had his army dig canals making for easier and safer passage across the lagoons from Marseille to Arles. Trade was thus diverted to Fos which takes its name from this operation – the Fosses Mariennes. More tribal incursions from the north sacked the later city of Ugium and although the bishops of Arles attempted to revive it the site was abandoned and lay undiscovered until recently. It is still something of a mystery to archaeologists which may account for the scant labelling. Much remains to be dug and unravelled but despite the intensity of commercial activity in the neighbourhood it is likely that they will be left to pursue their work. However, it is worth remembering that those who were at St-Blaise, long before Marius' army, were occupied in trading just as much as are the present commercial enterprises around the Golfe de Fos. We shall not be civilised until we are able to reconcile the claims of environmentalists

– a worthy and necessary breed – with business. For man cannot live only by resplendent views and the ruins of the past.

From St-Blaise to St-Mitre-les-Remparts, a walled town not greatly memorable. From the balcony of the church there is a view over yet another étang. Inside you may enjoy the series of pop art stained glass windows and note the unusual shape of both nave and apse which are slightly curved to fit the ramparts.

Continue to Martigues, the fishing port at the end of the canal joining the Etang de Berre to the sea. It is now a town of nearly 50,000 inhabitants living under the shadow of the impressive Viaduc Autoroutier de Caronte, constructed in 1972 to take road traffic between Fos and Marseille. The bridge is 300m long and 50m high. It is a triumph of engineering but aesthetically unappealing. If it survives for a thousand years will it become as emotive as the Pont du Gard is to us?

Martigues is an amalgamation of three villages, one of which is an island, on the edge of the Etang. They became officially linked in 1581. It is a place which has enjoyed much popularity with artists in the past but has more nowadays with those who like 'messing about in boats.' Hundreds of craft are moored here, some in the famed Birds' Looking Glass, a small quay with a charming row of little houses behind gaily coloured shutters. Near one end a brute of a church stands on the Ile Brescon, the central village. The other two are Jonquières and Ferrières.

Among the painters attracted here was Félix Ziem (1821-1911), a Burgundian whose widow left the town twenty-six of his canvases to form the basis of the local museum. Now in a new location, this is named after him and exemplifies all that is best about modern collections. Ziem drew inspiration from the local townscape/landscape and Venice was another favoured subject; approached in Turneresque style. Other Provençal artists are represented and well hung.

The museum has numerous archaeological items laid out with the aid of effective charts. They have drawn on excavations made in the neighbourhood and include a model of a neolithic farmhouse with one circular chamber and one rectangular, divided by a curtain. There are photographs, too, of the Gallo-Roman villa, St-Julien, discovered in the 1970s on the road to Sausset, south of Martigues. St-Pierre, another ancient site, is close to it.

At the south end of the village of St-Julien, on a road leading to the cemetery, stands a chapel, secluded on the edge of a wooded hill. On one wall it has a rare item of Gallo-Roman art, a simple funeral group from the first century AD.

The road to Sausset-les-Pins leads also to La Couronne and Carro, fishing villages with a rising popularity as seaside resorts. To cater for tourists the D9 to Marignane is dual carriageway which, out of season, has a sombre emptiness. There, cut through the arid rock, are four lanes and a central barrier but scarcely any traffic. The people of these villages, who once made their living from the sea, are entitled to bid for their share of western prosperity by attracting summer visitors, but I question the long-term wisdom of lining yet another section of coast with more hôtels, chalets, restaurants and other adjuncts of tourism. Carro, so far, has suffered least. Its small harbour is surrounded by slightly shabby, comfortable looking dwellings and a few shops. La Couronne, with a lighthouse on its Cap, and view of Marseille, is more infected. At Sausset, whole new suburbs have grown to west and east of the harbour, while at Carry-le-Rouet a skyscraper has been erected ruining the proportions of the overall settlement. Carro also has a casino, but the beauty of the low cliffs, with umbrella pines silhouetted on their crest, remains despite much building. To the east are Le Rouet Plage, Niolon and L'Estaque, the latter now joined to Marseille but once a village beloved by Dufy, Cézanne and other painters. They were attracted to the coast here by the combination of deeply coloured blue sea, bright green trees and white limestone cliffs. Today they would surely prefer Niolon which is still isolated round a tiny *calanque* at the foot of a low gorge. The road to it runs through exquisite folds of rock and small meadows of wild flowers.

Much of the Chaîne de l'Estaque is inhospitable rock familiar to air travellers who use Marignane, a town which has grown rapidly since it was chosen to host Marseille's airport. From quieter days when only birds, angels and witches were airborne it has retained its thirteenth-century chapel with a gilded high altar. At Berre-l'Etang, across the Etang de Berre, there is a church which has as its prize treasure a Roman crystal vase said once to have held a strand of the Virgin's hair.

If you are intent on the total experience of Provence you will doggedly visit these places, plus Vitrolles (seventeenth-century chapel, eleventh-century tower built for defence against the Saracens) and also steel yourself for a trip, westerly from Martigues, to Fos and Port St-Louis-du-Rhône. Fos, like everywhere else, has castle ruins and ramparts and Port St-Louis is named after the tower built in the eighteenth century to fortify the mouth of the river. Another, a little younger, is still to be seen at Port-de-Bouc, struggling to maintain its identity in the industrial complex.

You may, however, accept philosophically that you cannot have a total experience in a limited visit, and leave much of the Etang de Berre and its environs for another occasion. Or even for the one after that. But don't miss Miramas-le-Vieux, St-Blaise or the Ziem museum before you head across the Crau to Arles.

13   Arles

To me, Arles means Julius Caesar and Van Gogh, marvellous classical remains, a superb cloister beneath an exceptionally graceful tower and a strange avenue of tombs. It also means mosquitoes and sheep.

On our first visit in 1962 Min and I stayed at an hôtel in the Place Lamartine close to where the little yellow café painted by Van Gogh had stood. We retired to bed one night having anointed the bloated insect bites sustained during the previous twenty-four hours. It was June and extremely hot. The mosquitoes were evidently employed on a piecework basis. I tried all the usual rituals for inducing sleep when I became aware from an incessant bleating in the square that there were actual sheep to count. The Place Lamartine was crammed with them. It was transhumance time. They were being marshalled by a towering shepherd and his dogs to be taken by rail to their summer pastures in the Jura.

Today the *place*, once a car park (when not in use as an open-sided sheep pen) and once, in August 1944, the scene of a pitched battle for the liberation of Arles, has become a roundabout with lawns and shrubs. This makes the immediate approach to the old city attractive, in striking contrast to the road from Avignon which is one long avenue of hoardings. At the south side of the roundabout, opposite the Hôtel Terminus et Van Gogh, is what remains of an ancient gateway.

Arles is as different from Avignon and Aix as they are from each other. Except for the Boulevard des Lices it has nothing of the elegance of the latter, nor any single natural feature as dominating as the Rocher des Doms, but the Roman presence is much, much greater than in the other cities. It looks older, whether or not it is (for who is to say which of these ancient places was the first to be inhabited, and by whom?), because of its splendid arena, its theatre, its necropolis, its baths. It was known to the Phocaeans who founded Marseille. They came trading to the rocky plateau in the marshlands of the lower Rhône and colonised a Ligurian settlement, but it was the Romans who put it on the map some centuries later. It became a crossroads where the Via Domitia, connecting Spain and Italy, met the roads from the north and the canal from Fos.

Following Pompey's defeat in 49BC Marseille, having sided with him, was in disgrace. Caesar transferred its authority and much of its wealth to Arles which had formerly been dependent on the seaport. He domiciled his Sixth Legion here. Arles' fame and prosperity were assured for several centuries during which it also became an early bastion of Christianity. Long before the Romans departed the first cathedral of St-Trophime was built. There was a conclave of bishops in 314AD and Augustine's appointment to the new diocese of England was confirmed there in 597. Almost two centuries previously Constantine had considered making Arles the capital of his empire but that honour went to a city far to the east. Arles, however, became the administrative centre of Roman Gaul which also included Spain. Then, following the strife of the next few centuries when it was fought over by various invaders (whilst retaining its standing as a bishopric) it emerged in its own right as a kingdom with territory in other parts of Provence, and also in Burgundy. It fell later to the Visigoths, then to the Counts of Provence, before being officially incorporated into France in 1486 with most of the region. Only the papal possessions remained independent of the King.

After Arles ceased to be a kingdom in its own right and Aix became the first city of Provence, it never regained its early superiority, although, because of its position on the waterways, it continued until the nineteenth century to be an important trading centre. The coming of the railway temporarily ended that but later brought industry, encouraged by the poet-politician, Alphonse de Lamartine. In this century it has become a market place again thanks to reclamation of land in the Camargue, to which Caesar referred as 'the granary of Gaul'.

The amphitheatre, larger than any other surviving in France, became a town in itself during the middle ages, with churches and two hundred houses enclosed within its thick walls. For the citizens it was a natural fortress with watchtowers, three of which remain. Dismantlement of the town, built partly with stone from the now missing top tier of the arena, began in 1825. Today the amphitheatre is used for bull fighting, in which the animals are not always deliberately fought to the death, and other spectacles. It becomes humanised when made the setting for dancing and you may find a rehearsal taking place during your visit. It is reached through mean streets typical of much of Arles. Close-by are the evocative ruins of the Roman theatre with just two pillars and part of a lintel standing silhouetted against a background of cypresses and the lovely tower of St-Trophime. This is one of the most moving sights of Provence. A modern platform has been erected where the Roman stage once stood and one tier of the auditorium provides seating for contemporary performances. Originally there were three, as in modern theatres, and room to seat 12,000.

Arles: Les Alyscamps

A combined ticket for visiting nine sites and museums can be purchased. In 1992 this cost 40f whereas admission to each of them separately came to 106f. Make time to tramp across the Boulevard des Lices and down to the Alyscamps on the south side of the city. Pass the modern Hôtel de Police with heavily barred windows, cross a single track railway not, I think, in use and a road which most certainly is, then enter the gates of the shady burial ground lined with stone tombs, some having lids as large as the coffins they cover. At the end of this tranquil avenue of the dead is the church of St-Honorat, familiar from Van Gogh's paintings. Parts of its are Carolingian, more are Romanesque. Only an attached funerary chapel may be entered because the interior is otherwise unsafe.

The Alyscamps are but a fraction of their former size. Much of the land over which they once spread was absorbed when the city was industrialised. The beneficial effects of this, in terms of higher employment, were already evident when Vincent Van Gogh arrived in the freezing winter of 1888.

The other principal Roman site to be seen on your overall ticket is the Baths of Constantine standing close to the Rhône at the junction of two busy streets. Unfortunately it resembles, even on a bright day, an inexpertly taken black-and-white photograph taken on a dull one; it is strictly for

161

scholars. In the Place du Forum, and visually more interesting to this layman, are two pillars and a pediment now part of the wall of a modern hôtel. They belonged to a temple. The actual Roman forum was slightly to the south of this engaging square, where a statue of Mistral overlooks the tables occupying the greater part of the surface. It is a perfect venue for lunch. There is plenty of shade from the eight great plane trees and, if you are in luck, a free-range

Arles: Place du Forum

musician may be playing trad jazz. Around here there are signposts to Le Grenier à Sel which is on a corner site of the road by the river. It would not make a worthwhile detour except for the opportunity it affords of walking through some of the ordinary by-ways of Arles.

Of the museums the one most likely to be visited first time round is the Arlaten, founded by Mistral in 1896 to house a collection of all things Provençal. And I do mean *all* things. There are even four native peach stones, and a conker, lovingly preserved. The collection rambles on through room after room, on floor above floor, of the Hôtel Laval-Castellane, on two sides of a courtyard where there are excavations relating to the Roman forum. It is thinly and eccentrically labelled with many of the captions in faded ink. One, surprisingly, is in English beneath a regional bread bin such as we saw at La Barben. There are dresses, clocks, portraits, models of the monster La Tarasque, furniture, life-size tableaux and *santons* galore. On an upper staircase there is a map of Arles in 1660 showing the bridge of boats crossing the Rhône to the suburb of Trinquetaille. For long this was the only way of getting from one side to the other on foot; Mistral describes using it as a boy when he went to the gypsy festival at Stes-Maries-de-la-Mer. In a room on the top floor are instructive paintings showing the antique theatre at different stages of excavation. In another, devoted to the *Félibrige,* there is a useful case of photographs of the seven founders with their dates. Mistral, of course, as their leader, gets two portraits. They were: Théodore Aubanel (1829-86), Jean Brunet, (1823-94), Paul Giera, (1816-61), Anselme Mathieu, (1828-95), Frédéric Mistral, (1830-1914), Joseph Roumanille, (1818-91), Alphonse Tavan, (1833-1905). Close by is a king-sized canvas of Mistral being acclaimed in a crowded arena. This is reasonable homage; his generosity founded the museum. (Many streets in Provence bear the name of a *félibre.*)

A recent extension indicates that the management is well aware of modern methods of display and lighting. Various objects, mostly to do with work on land and at sea, are exhibited sparingly; but the Arlaten as a whole is still badly in need of drastic editing.

Step out into the pedestrianised street, avoid being knocked down by a passing cyclist, and round the corner in a narrow alley is the massive façade of a former Jesuit church now housing the early Christian section of the Musée Lapidaire. It is said to be a very fine frontage but to appreciate it you would need to hover in a helicopter at roof level. If you are fortunate enough to enter the museum when it is not occupied by rowdy hordes of bored schoolkids, or a group being loudly lectured, you will be faced by several magnificently preserved carved sarcophagi. On the left are others, on your right, yet more. In the side chapels, there they are again. They come from the Alyscamps and from a burial ground at Trinquetaille. The sculpture is refined and, in many cases, intact. On some, where parts of the original are missing, there are engraved reconstructions of what was thought to be there. The centrepiece is a three-tier coffin in which a husband and wife were buried together. Their images are highlighted in a circular panel surrounded by biblical scenes. They were presumably of high rank to aspire to so splendid a tomb although others nearby are only slightly less extravagantly treated. I particularly like the one decorated with naked figures picking olives. You may well have time to appreciate it as you wait to examine the centrepiece in detail. And it can be a long wait if a tour leader is in full spiel, commenting on each and every sculpted figure. (In my experience the late afternoon is the best time of day for avoiding parties.)

A quite different experience is to be had down several flights of steps to an eerie cellar of vast proportions lying far below the church. It is called the Cryptoporticus and was probably a Roman granary. There are three long galleries in a square bottomed U, vaulted, chill and bare, but dry. Such lighting as there is comes through old air channels. Little can be seen but the gloom does not deter tour leaders whom I have heard droning on incessantly in the murky depths. (In fact, in these circumstances their presence is not unwelcome.)

The other lapidary museum, in the Place de la République opposite the great west door of St-Trophime, is devoted to pagan art. This also is in a disused church, less grand than the Jesuits', and where the altar once stood is a statue of the emperor Augustus from the theatre. Behind him, around the apse, are many pre-Christian heads. In a side chapel is a copy of the lovely Venus, also from the theatre. The original, unfairly, is in the Louvre; It ought to be here. In another chapel is a gem depicting a lady and her freedman, sculpted in confidential conversation. There are large mosaics from Trinquetaille featuring Jupiter astride a bull, and Orpheus enchanting animals with his lyre. The tombs are fewer and none is as fine as those in the early Christian collection. The labelling is disgraceful and the entire interior is both musty and dusty, but don't overlook it.

The Place de la République is the centre of Arles. At one end is the extremely handsome late seventeenth-century Hôtel de Ville with rustication up and around the four ground-floor windows. A simple balcony on the first floor has twin columns either side of the central window, and above the top story are balustrades and *pots à feu*. Then, as if to mitigate so much fearful symmetry, the clock-tower surmounted by a classical temple is set on one far corner. In fact the tower is one hundred years older and this may have been the only way of incorporating it in the design. On the ground floor there is a splendid vaulted hall.

Apart from St-Trophime, which is to one side of the town hall, the architecture of the *place* is ordinary. I have mentioned the cathedral tower and cloister; its third glory is the exquisitely carved west door which, as I write, is undergoing lengthy treatment to save the stone from disintegrating. The interior of the cathedral, now officially demoted in status to 'church', is simple and dim. Its predecessor was erected in the fifth century but there was another on the site even earlier. The present building dates from the tenth century and its tower from the twelfth. The latter is a perfect example of Romanesque, plain and square with a pyramidal spire; it belongs to one's first glimpse of Arles from many directions. The cloister is entered by a gateway beside the church and across a courtyard. It is partly twelfth- partly fourteenth-century but the styles blend and, unusually, the whole may be admired from an open gallery above. At one end stand three cypresses. The columns are richly adorned with saints and episodes from the gospels; the corner ones on the north side are especially fine. Thereby hangs a tale told by Provençal shepherds during the traditional transhumance trek. This alleges that the figures are real people turned to stone by wizardry but, before he could complete the cloister, the sculptor's black magic was revealed to the bishop, who despatched him to the galleys. (See Michael de Larrabeiti's *The Provençal Tales*.)

Perhaps the least visited of Arles' museums is the Réattu, close to the Roman baths. Reaching it may prove trying because traffic in this town of narrow streets, many without even a pretence of pavements, is amongst the worst in Provence. But it is worth perseverance, not only for the pleasure of the courtyard where you are protected from motor cars and bikes, but for what there is to see above. As you mount the stairs, on one small landing there is a red portrait medallion by Jacques Réattu (1760-1833), the minor painter who came to live in this robust early seventeenth-century demi-mansion built for the Knights of Malta. It is easy to be snooty about Réattu who was certainly not in the front rank of old masterdom, but pause before a pleasing portrait of one of his sons, and again at a family grouped around a beautiful young girl. In the next chamber there are some of his interiors and Italian landscapes, agreeable but unremarkable, and also – not by Réattu – three unusual Flemish tapestries from an earlier century, of the ancient wonders of the world – the Colossus at Rhodes, the Colosseum, and Diana's Temple at Ephesus. What happened to the other four is not related but these make a refreshing change from the pastoral and allegorical scenes hanging on so many walls.

Rousseau can usually be taken to mean the customs official whose amazing imagination is preserved in primitive nightmarish paintings featuring powerful animals and hostile vegetation. At the Réattu it denotes one Henri, an unrelated Rousseau (1885-1933) who drew and painted – mostly in watercolour – the Camargue and Arles. He has a room to himself and richly deserves it. His studies of horses and *gardians*, of landscapes and skyscapes, of Aigues-Mortes and Stes-Maries-de-la-Mer, are enchanting.

After him come the modern galleries, the first two of which are devoted to Provençal painters of this century who still belong to a representational tradition. They are colourful, striking, worth returning to. Then comes the experimental section which on one occasion displayed pieces of wood lying against a wall – ASSEMBLAGES – and a crunched car engine – COMPRESSION. In order not to spoil the mood engendered by Rousseau I looked out of the window at the Rhône flowing by. That provoked me to wonder

Arles: Espace Van Gogh

how long it would be before someone arranged troughs of water by the skirting boards and labelled them – IRRIGATION. Never mind; pass on to the Picassos before you get cross.

Pablo Picasso, who veered between getting the best prices he could and performing acts of generosity, came to Arles in 1971 and, with his immense energy and creativity, quickly threw off about seventy caricatures which now belong to the Réattu, having been presented either by him or by his widow. They are fun. Some, perhaps, are more. All are vividly alive but you will see only a selection because they have not stood up well to exposure. A nicely produced booklet of them is on sale; this contains the fine, traditional portrait in oil of the artist's mother, also hanging here.

The museum has, in another Renaissance building opposite, a gallery of contemporary photography.

After one visit to the Réattu, seated at an open air café in the Place Voltaire, we were looking at a postcard of André Marchand's *Arlèsienne* (1949). The waitress delayed serving our order whilst she commented enthusiastically and knowledgeably about the picture. Van Gogh did not receive such acclamation from the locals a century ago, but Arles has now honoured him by transforming the old hospital, to which he was admitted after attacking Gauguin and mutilating himself, into a cultural centre. The balconies and garden of the Espace Van Gogh have been painted and planted to match the colours the artist put on to canvas in 1889. Even on a grey winter's day, they dazzle. Part of the building is now a gallery, another is La Médiathèque d'Arles where the municipal archives are stored and where young and old may study and select books, tapes and pictures to borrow. The shell of the original building has been retained but inside it is now all cat walks and girders. A veritable forest of steel rods supports the roof. Large flat paper dolls decorate one wall. It is very hi-tech and rather jolly.

The Espace also houses a College of Literary Translations. What it lacks is a permanent collection of the great Dutchman's work.

Arles is situated on a slight hill rising from the Rhône. Part of the ancient wall is intact on the eastern side where the aqueduct from the Alpilles brought water to the city. Lying below it is a simple memorial to the Resistance, of three Moore-like figures. There is an opening through which you can reach a little frequented quarter of the town with terraces of houses and a convent. A road leads to the lovely gardens bordering the Boulevard des Lices. The Jardin d'Eté is a suitable place at which to end a long perambulation but even here there are things to see – a statue of poor, savage-looking Vincent, by William Earl Singer (1969), and a fountain of Niobe weeping over her children within a circle of stone seats where, in the heat of summer afternoons, elderly Arlèsiennes sit knitting and chatting. Opposite is the four-star Michelin hôtel, the Jules César, where one of my friends once stayed – but he was a publisher. I have no recommendation to make because I have not spent a night at Arles since that confrontation with the trans-humance in 1962. However, a daughter and son-in-law, who are not wealthy, found Le Clôitre (also in the Red Guide) agreeable. And the mosquito count, in 1990, was negligible.

14   Alpilles and Montagnette

Eygalières : Barbegal : Montmajour : Tarascon : Beaucaire :
St-Andiol : Noves : Boulbon : Barbentane : St-Michel-de-Frigolet :
Maillane : St-Rémy-de-Provence : Glanum : Les Baux

The area between Avignon and Arles is bounded by the Rhône, the Durance and the Chaîne des Alpilles, a range of low limestone peaks. These rise to nearly 400m at their highest which is scarcely mountainous, but their bare, jagged summits make them appear so. On a clear day they provide one of the most striking views in the region. In their midst is the small plateau

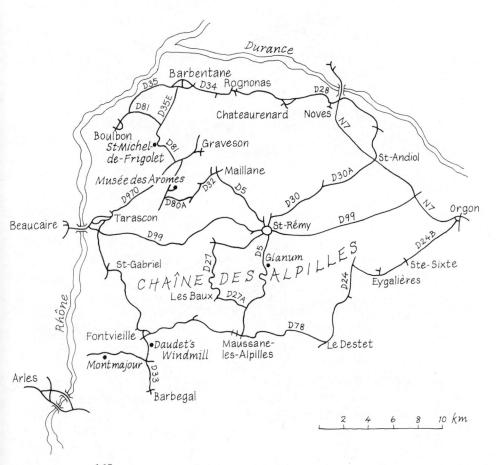

St-Rémy-de-Provence: Musée des Alpilles (see p 184)

on which the castle of Les Baux was built. Midway, on the northern side, at the foot of a winding pass through uninhabited scrubland, lies St-Rémy-de-Provence, successor to Greek and Roman Glanum, now its southern suburb. Les Baux, Glanum and Daudet's windmill, close to Arles, come high on every tour operator's list of attractions; St-Rémy and all the territory to the north embracing the Montagnette, do not.

St-Rémy is the obvious centre for exploring this region and a day commencing with a stroll around its compact older part would be a day well begun. But it should not be isolated from Glanum so leave it until the more specifically next-time-round places have been covered.

Go by D99 in the Cavaillon direction, following the road probably trodden by the doomed Teuton hordes massacred by Marius' army, although there were then no long, long avenues of plane trees to shelter them from the sun and wind. Alas, there are gaps in the rows now because some of the 300-year-old trees have been removed to allow access to a bypass constructed to alleviate the traffic jams in St-Rémy. This is a shame because the hold-ups were not that chronic and the rape of the countryside to provide yet more roads should cease.

The D99 runs roughly parallel with the Alpilles and from it there are various turnings to Eygalières. But to reach that village we will approach it from Orgon where Napoléon, on his way to exile in Elba, was detained by a mob who forced him to watch his own effigy being burned. The mayor intervened and he was sent on his way to Aix, to a better fate than awaited the wretched Teutons. Orgon is not remarkable but it stands beneath a formidable outcrop of the Alpilles known as Les Plaines, and on the cliff above is the large, thistle-domed chapel of Notre-Dame-de-Beauregard. Not a distinguished building, but a useful landmark for travellers. The N7 bends to avoid Orgon and off it is the D24b which offers a more tranquil experience, although one should never assume that any road in France is necessarily a slow one. This minor road makes a lovely way of approaching the Alpilles again. Near a junction close to Eygalières stands the ancient chapel of Ste-Sixte, a stolid, much admired example of Romanesque built on a rocky rise. Isolated amongst orchards and vineyards, it is frankly woebegone, with flaking plaster and uncared for surrounds; but who is to look after all these historic monuments? It has an unusually large porch which must have sheltered many a vagrant, hiker, or worker from the fields. To see the interior you must obtain the key from the presbytery at Eygalières. This village stands on what was once marshland (*eyg, aigues* and *palud* are always an indication of water) and from here the Romans built an aqueduct to take water to Arles. On a knobby hill where early man found sanctuary are the ruins of a castle, a well-preserved bell-tower and two chapels, one with a white marble madonna quite out of harmony with the rugged setting. A Penitents' chapel, now a museum, is open during the afternoons except in winter. The hillside is wooded, slippery, and irresistible if you enjoy looking not only at the jagged hills but also down on the pink and cream of roofs and houses. Eygalières is popular with artists and writers and even supports a small bookshop.

Leave by D24 through the middle of the Alpilles, first past vineyards with many signboards to *caves*, then through a sprawling pine wood, and past olive groves, by a very wiggly road. Next comes wild, uncultivated country, followed by farming land with an occasional dwelling until the hamlet of Le Destet, overlooked by a great chunk of limestone, is reached. After that are further undulations with evidence of sheep and cereal farming until Maussane. (Another road runs east to Eyguières through equally uninhabited terrain made more haunting latterly because of the fires which have destroyed so much of the pine forest.)

On the south side of the Alpilles centres of population grow larger again but the going is still mostly rural. Don't leave the hills until you have passed Fontvieille and made (or not made) a ritual halt at Daudet's windmill – which I regard as the foremost non-event of the Provençal tourist itinerary. It did not belong to the writer but to a farmer friend of his, and none of his famous letters was penned from it. However, it was a source of inspiration for his highly esteemed works which include *Tartarin de Tarascon* and the play *L'Arlésienne* – incidental music by Bizet. It stands back from the road, an endearing little structure, and if you haven't realised before what

Eygalières

all those small, stubby edifices dotted around the countryside were for, you will now that you see one with sails attached.

Drive on to a crossroads at the foot of the hillside and turn left for the remains of the Barbegal aqueduct which not only conveyed water to Roman Arles but provided a much larger mill with the earliest known instance of hydraulic power. Walk beside the ruins until what was the conduit passes through a short canyon. At the end, where the aqueduct took off high above fields, look down upon the ruins of the mill which were discovered by the archaeologist and humanist, Fernand Benoit (1892-1969). He is a familiar name for those who have been to the Roman Docks Museum at Marseille. To inspect the mill more closely take a footpath from the D33.

It is easy to miss Barbegal and go bowling along a road back towards Maussane. What there is of the aqueduct lies low on the ground.

The same crossroads indicate to the abbey of Montmajour which

is lucky to still be there. After the Revolution it was sold as scrap to a woman who began systematically to tear it apart and dispose of its treasures in order to meet the commitments of her purchase price. She soon defaulted on payments and the property passed to an estate agent who, more realistically (because it is a formidable edifice, not a simple demolition job) rented parts of it as living accommodation. Later in the nineteenth century the citizens of Arles, displaying greater feeling for the past, began its restoration; now, for the seond time, it has been nationalised.

Montmajour is a different experience from Sénanque. Originally a Benedictine abbey built upon a rock surrounded by marshes, it is enormous, part-castle, part-church, part-eighteenth-century palace. You enter by the crypt which slopes according to the lie of the rock. You can imagine beaching on it; perhaps the first monks did. The crypt has an ambulatory and is, like most of the church, unadorned. Take a ramp to steps leading up to the great wide nave which was intended to be twice as long, but the extension was never realised. It has side chapels, and a great bowl of an apse. There is some vaulting and a few columns are delicately decorated around their capitals. (Signs in French, English and German explain all parts of the building.)

The cloister is superb and frames marvellous views of the château and the keep. Its decorations are fascinating and macabre with monstrous beasts eating people whole or spewing them forth.

A partly covered way leads from the church into a courtyard beside the gaunt ruins of a Renaissance palace with high gaping windows. Round the corner from it is a keep, or abbey tower, of 1369. It was built for defence at a time when brigands marauded the countryside. There are forty-four steps rising to a first-floor chamber of immense height. Stone supports halfway up the walls show it was once divided into two stories. Higher still, up many more steps, is a platform from which there are even grander views. Below the abbey, in an adjoining field, is a chapel, Ste-Croix, tiny in Greek-cross style. It was used for funerals. To the south is Mont de Cordes which, like Montmajour, was once an island. Within it is a stone age burial chamber which can be seen on application to the owner.

Return to Fontvieille, famous for its quarries as well as its wind-mill, and make for the exquisite chapel of St-Gabriel, perched at the foot of a wooded hill on a little terrace. The carvings over the door, on pediments and tympanum, are delicately done and show Roman influence. The village the chapel once served has disappeared, its primary purpose having gone with the draining of the surrounding marshland. The boatmen who transported traders and travellers on their way to Arles, Tarascon, Avignon, lost their living. Now the chapel alone survives, dignified but unused, between two quarries and below a ruined château. Its proportions are perfect. Spare time to walk around it and rejoice in the stone and the carvings.

At the junction where once the boatmen rowed travellers is a roundabout. Take the exit to Beaucaire and Tarascon; the distance to both is shown as the same although the wide Rhône separates them.

Whatever rivalries may persist among their citizenry, Beaucaire on the right bank, Tarascon on the left, are as one to the uninitiated despite the natural water barrier. Historically both were Roman, then one belonged to France, the other to Provence. Now one is officially in the Languedoc and the other still in Provence, though both for long have been part of L'Hexagone, as Metropolitan France is now often called. Each was, and is, an important trading centre. Beaucaire has had a famous fair since medieval times; Tarascon was an outpost for Greek Massalia. Beaucaire's once massive castle, high above the river, is a magnificent ruin; Tarascon's, at water level, is in a state of fine preservation without the helping hand of Viollet-le-Duc. Both towns have seventeenth-century town halls worthy of better settings. Tarascon has a church which bears its proximity to the castle without looking at all diminished; Beaucaire has one of much later date which is almost lost amongst the jumble of narrow streets. Each town is a joy to wander in.

Tarascon felt the impact of Christianity early in the first century when Martha, one of the passengers in that boat which came ashore at Stes-Maries-de-la-Mer around 45AD (see next chapter), arrived here carrying a cross, the sight of which tamed a ferocious monster. This creature, part lion, part crocodile, emerged from the Rhône at every mealtime to devour any passing Tarasconnais. Martha quelled the beast and tethered it but the people, reasonably, were not taking any chances and, doubting its long-term conversion, slaughtered it. At the same time they were grateful to Martha who was, in due course, canonised. Her remains were unearthed by eager zealots in the twelfth century and are now held in the crypt of the church named after her. This exuberant item of ecclesiastical architecture, with its splendid roofscape, all pinnacles, lanterns and gargoyles, is basically four-teenth-century but was consecrated in 1197.

King René played a part in establishing the festival of Martha still celebrated today when a 'monster' is conducted about Tarascon by a girl acting the rôle of the saint. The townsfolk have fun and do not permit the dread Tarasque to become as docile as the original after Martha had dowsed it with holy water. Its modern counterpart frisks a tail or two and sends the youth of Tarascon scampering for safety. The fête takes place annually on July 29.

Tarascon is famous for its monster and also for the character Tartarin, created by Alphonse Daudet. This poked fun at the locals but whatever offence may have been taken at the time, the descendants of those whom Daudet mocked have been forgiving. There is now a House of Tartarin where the deeds of this fictional personage are commemorated on two floors and in the garden. Tarascon has accepted fantasy as fact, which seems to be Daudet's fate hereabouts.

Good King René's father, Louis II of Anjou, rebuilt the castle on a Roman site about 1400, when it had been restored to his family following annexation by Raymond of Turenne. Raymond gave it back and honour was thus satisfied on both sides. René, in due course, furnished it sumptuously, entertained in lavish style and made it his favourite residence.

Nowadays it is singularly bare. When I first visited it a guided tour was compulsory; now, at least out of season, one may wander at will and I found doing so a desolating experience. The great chambers are empty but, except for the treads on part of the spiral staircase, everything is in marvellous repair. To what end? I was permitted to view the interior of a great medieval castle which is nothing more than a husk. If only it were filled with furniture, tapestries, armour, portraits, sculpture, all the impedimenta of its heritage. What is the point of standing in the Court of Honour when there is nothing in sight to suggest the vivacity of medieval high life at its best? You are at the bottom of a great well of yellow stone, hemmed in by walls of skyscraper height. I found it extremely depressing and could not too quickly return across the drawbridge to appreciate this great building from outside.

For a long while it housed the governor, having ceased to be a royal seat, and later became a prison where British sailors of the eighteenth century were incarcerated.

It is remarkable that Tarascon's castle survived when many buildings seemingly as impregnable suffered demolition during the Wars of Religion, the Revolution and World War Two.

Parking is little problem in Tarascon, or in Beaucaire where, as the road divides to lead drivers to spaces on a quay beside the Canal du Rhône à Sète, there is a small garden. In it is a statue (recreated from one destroyed in 1943) commemorating the Bull of the Camargue. This much esteemed breed is now suffering the same diminishment as the famous fair which, even in the nineteenth century, still brought a hundred thousand visitors from all parts of Europe and the Mediterranean. It was held on a vast site beside the Rhône where a smaller version still functions around pavilions resembling theatres. Some streets are named after the products associated with it. Beaucaire was also the setting for the romance of Aucassin and Nicolette, a thirteenth-century tale of love first thwarted, then triumphant, the music to which has survived.

The castle does not live up to the image projected of it across the Rhône, or down on the Champs de Foire beneath its walls. It has a hollow interior, approached up steps and garden paths. But the donjon can be climbed and a chapel has become the town museum, exhibiting documents concerned with the fair and items of lapidary interest.

What it has lost as a great trading centre Beaucaire may have gained by its involvement in hydro-electric schemes. It is proud of its power station to which visitors are welcomed if they give a fortnight's notice. The attractions of Provence are indeed varied.

There is no shortage of accommodation in St-Rémy. If you are feeling self-indulgent you may favour the Château de Roussan, conveniently situated on the road back from Tarascon, up an enticing avenue of plane trees. Here, in an eighteenth-century country house is a privately owned hôtel handy for the start of the second day's itinerary which skirts St-Rémy and makes off in the direction of Noves. First there is a deviation to St-Andiol, a village lying mostly off the busy N7. On it is a house with a plaque to Jean Moulin who passed his boyhood holidays here with his grandparents. On another wall is a map of the Chemin de la Liberté, La Route Jean Moulin, which goes from St-Andiol, through Mollèges, Eygalières, Orgon and Senas before ending at his memorial near Salon. It takes this indirect way because Jean and his sister Laure bought a house at Eygalières where they spent holidays together before the second world war. In early 1939 he became prefect of L'Eure-et-Loir with headquarters at Chartres, remaining at his post after the German occupation until, as first President of the Comité National de la Résistance, he returned to Provence. The plaque on the family house records that he died in 1943, the 'victim of Nazi barbarity'.

The old village of St-Andiol is well within rumbling distance of the heavy lorry traffic, by no means all of which makes use of the adjacent autoroute, yet it has a peaceful air. There are houses with wisteria and roses round windows and doorways, a park with fine chases, a large meadow and a formal, slightly forbidding, seventeenth-century château. This faces, behind railings, a church fortified against the mercenaries who ravaged much of France during the reign of the scholarly Charles V (1364-80). From the outside the church looks as though it may have been sliced in half at some tempestuous moment in history, but inside the twelfth-century proportions are perfect. The apse, walled with carved, unpainted wood, is balanced by a charming semi-circular balcony over the west door. Above it is a sombre painting on more wood which is also the material used for the pulpit. This has an entrance staircase, literally inside a big, square, stone pillar. The side chapels, added in the nineteenth century, contribute for once to a harmonious whole.

There is a choice of the fast N7, or minor roads through the village of Cabannes to reach Noves, possibly the birthplace of Petrarch's beloved Laura. Her association is not exploited and the attraction is the church of St-

Baudile.

Nothing remains of the Celtic, Gallic or Roman settlements (apart from the horrendous sculpture known as the Tarasque of Noves, now in the lapidary museum of Avignon), nor is there any longer a castle on the hill beside the small market town. A high long segment of fourteenth-century wall and two gateways survive, however, protecting the remarkably shaped church. Visible above is the handsome belfry which was used as a look-out point. It is at the culmination of an interestingly busy stone roof which was adapted for use by sentries. The fifteenth-century staircase is more military than ecclesiastic and was added in the latter part of the Hundred Years' War. The belfry obscures the dome which is better appreciated from inside once your eyes have become used to the gloom. Enter through metal doors carved with angels. Whichever way you turn there is an altar. I counted at least eleven, but there may have been more in the farther, darker, recesses. The building dates, as you will have guessed, from the twelfth century but seems to have been left untouched after the Gothic attentions it received in the fifteenth.

While you are at Noves you may wish to cross the Durance and visit the Charterhouse of Bonpas which is described earlier (see page 125) but keep a cool head as you negotiate the various filter roads to and from the N7, or you may find yourself speeding into Greater Avignon. Otherwise, it is but five kilometres to Châteaurenard from where vast quantities of fruit and vegetables are exported daily to other parts of France and Europe. Vines are grown in this part of the Bouches-du-Rhône, but even more ground is devoted to market gardening. This does not always enhance the appearance of the countryside as much of it is done under cover of plastic, domed tents. On a hill above the town are the ruins of a castle built for the Counts of Provence. Most of it was demolished at the Revolution but two stark towers stand, sentinel-like, as a reminder of times past. There is no need, in my opinion, to climb close to them to observe their quality.

On through Rognonas and Barbentane to Boulbon, a small town on the side of the Montagnette which was strategically important in earlier times. It overlooks the road from Avignon to Tarascon, so the Counts of Provence ran up another fortress, more of which is extant than at Château-renard. Various alleys off the Grand' Rue (a quaint little street of un-pretentious two-decker terraced houses) appear to lead to it. They have names such as Rue du Fort, du Tour, and so forth, but I got the uncomfortable impression that I was trespassing as I passed close to cottage windows. At least there were no snarling canines but I opted, as at the previous stop, to enjoy the castle from below. In the Grand' Rue is a sculpture of a man with an angel clambering about his head and shoulders. He is St.Christophe and not, as I first assumed, St.Marcellin who is remembered in the name of a pretty little chapel that is the best feature in an otherwise hideous cemetery defacing the hillside. It is the setting for an annual blessing of the vines each first of June. This is – for the present, anyhow – a totally male celebration.

Return to Barbentane to see its château and old town hall, known as the Maison des Chevaliers, with colonnaded gallery at first-floor level, over an open-fronted courtyard, with two wide arches. High above is the Tour Anglica, a survivor from the fourteenth-century bishop's castle, reached up steep streets through medieval gateways. There is a perfect view of the tower from the exquisitely proportioned seventeenth-century château at the foot of the town. This has been the home of the Barbentane family for over three hundred years. Previously the domain here belonged, in the ninth century, to King Boson, who gave it to the Archbishop of Arles. It later passed to another prince of the church in Avignon and has prospered quietly through the centuries, as can be appreciated from the existence of large houses from various periods and sedate contemporary suburbs.

The château, which came unscathed through the Revolution, is on two main floors plus attic and basement. It faces the town across a formal garden. At the rear are several terraces with wide steps leading down to parkland and a pool. There is a guided tour of about half-a-dozen rooms, a small chapel (tucked into the side of the elegant staircase) and a spacious entrance hall. The salons have ceilings vaulted in a vice-like way, using a stone-cutting technique by which individual parts hold each other together through the precision of the carving. There are many marble floors, some with worrying *trompe-l'oeil* patterns in apparent cubes. The dining-room, formerly a bedroom, has two small corner pavilions with sloping roofs, once used for ablutions and for dressing. Later they screened a quick way to the kitchens. A small sitting-room has been decorated in Chinese style with eighteenth-century hand-painted paper. In a larger one there are listed Louis XV sofas and a fountain with taps. Much of the furnishing was the responsibility of a Barbentane who was ambassador to Tuscany in the eighteenth century. Thus, all the fireplaces came from Florence. A more intimate note is struck with a simple, round, polished Chippendale table.

Barbentane is at the northern end of the Montagnette where a ruddy escarpment rises sheer from the valley beside the Petite Crau, the area between it and the Alpilles. Unlike the Grande Crau to the south, this was always a fertile part. The road to the monastery of St-Michel-de-Frigolet is one of the most delightful in Provence, gently climbing and descending through pine forest and grassland. There are numerous picnic tables beneath the trees and a large choice of footpaths. Immediately before the monastery, on the left, is a spacious field with shade at both ends. You may park here or in a smaller, rockier enclosure beyond St-Michel.

It is thought that monks from Montmajour founded a Benedictine abbey here in the tenth century. Despite the fierce mistral, whose effect can be perceived in the fir trees permanently bent to an angle of 45°, they were wise to choose this high ground. It offers peace and solitude. Present-day brothers, in ivory coloured robes, have their quarters, including cloister and garden, between two churches. They work on the land, in the library and at a distillery where they produce their own liqueur. This is sold in a shop also well-stocked with books, pottery and souvenirs, sacred and secular. The churches and the monastery are part of an extensive complex including a hôtel, restaurant, dormitories for hikers, rooms for group meetings, a workshop where candles are made and a concert hall. After the Revolution St-Michel became a school which Frédéric Mistral, a pupil, described disparagingly in his memoirs. Following the return of the monks it was variously choir school, orphanage, centre for classical studies, then secondary school. There is also Friar Xavier's Hall, named after a monk who enjoyed meetings with Mistral when the poet returned to St-Michel as an adult. Xavier subsequently went to Storrington, in Sussex, to a priory founded by Frigolet.

Of the two churches, the smaller Romanesque one has unadorned walls and simple modern stained glass windows. The façade is nineteenth-century but the roof and bell-tower are original. The other, highly decorated neo-Gothic of about 130 years ago, has an interior brightly painted with abstract mosque-style motifs except on the lower pillars where saints predominate garishly. Incorporated into the building is the twelfth-century chapel of Notre-Dame-du-Bon-Remède which is also lavishly ornamented. Why was so large a church thought necessary for a small community? Its ostentation does not accord with the monastic life.

A monk guides visitors to the cloister and surrounds. It is not as impressive as many others we have seen but the garden in the centre is lovingly tended. In the chapter room is the finest exhibit in the complex, a modern nativity scene carved in olive wood by a contemporary sculptor. The grouping is arresting. The three wise men, the shepherds, the donkeys, Joseph and Mary, are arranged as for a theatrical tableau, with the stances of the various characters leaning gracefully, reverently, towards the central figure which, unfortunately, has not been so happily realised. The infant Christ, looking too old and too large for his cradle, seems almost to be by another hand.

It is a shame that on the stretch of green heath above the monastery the authorities have permitted the installation of a container truck selling *Boissons de Provence*. It is the one jarring note. Surely visitors could bring their own drinks or use the restaurant?

The walks from here are not as easy to undertake as they at first appear. The going is mostly over hard shingle but the rewards are great. The top of the Montagnette is all small peaks, ravines, folds of hill and scrubland bright or scented with wild flowers and herbs. There are paths in all directions and it is possible to walk for hours without finding any habitation, although you are never far from an eminence from which the monastery buildings can be glimpsed. St-Michel provides space enough for everyone's enjoyment – for walking, playing games (click-clack of *boules* is strangely comforting when one is far above the pitch, battling against the wind on a rough track), reading, dozing, comtemplating. I rate this visit highly for the very next time round.

The road down to the D970 starts dramatically with a number of hairpin bends overlooked at intervals by great pottery vessels on walls that are part of the monastery. When you reach the main highway take the Avignon direction until signed to Graveson, a small town deserving a visit for the sake of its church with an oven-vaulted apse. Mistral wrote, 'Our mothers never failed to take us in our childhood to the church at Graveson, there to show us St-Anthime and Beluget, a Jack of the Clock who struck the hours in the belfry'. In times of drought St-Anthime would be taken to St-Michel-de-Frigolet to induce rain. If this failed the statue was dipped in a brook three times. The poet did not relate what other steps were taken if the rains still did not come.

Off the road from Graveson to Arles there is a lane 1,200m long leading through cultivated countryside to the Musée des Aromes et du Parfum, occupying a converted barn. At the door stand three gleaming copper alembics. Inside more are on display. Hidden from visitors are others still in use for distilling and purifying processes. It is unlikely that many readers will have been here first-time-round because the museum wasn't opened until 1989 when two doctors practising holistic medicine founded it. One of them, Dr Nelly Grosjean, prescribes twelve *frictions* for aromatherapy, herbal potions blended to relieve respiratory, glandular, skin, digestive and other complaints. These, with perfume, soap, etc, are on sale. They are not inexpensive, but this is explained on a poster noting that it takes three tonnes of rose petals to make one litre of essential oil. The plants producing them require three hectares of land, grow for five months, are picked with care and distilled each day. (Nostradamus's successful treatment of plague was based on a kind of aromatherapy.)

At the museum you are back to monastic calm. You also feel yourself surrounded by deep countryside although a busy road is not far off. Here is a piece of Provence which has not been sold to developers, that is not made unsightly with large, luridly coloured hoardings, yet is quietly industrial and commercial. And not all the aromas are bottled; some, along with serene music, delicately pervade the air you walk in.

When you emerge on to the highway take the Arles direction until Maillane is signed to the left. This quiet little town would not be too un-familiar today to its most famous son who died at a ripe age during World

War One. Frédéric Mistral was born in a house on the way to St-Rémy but spent much of his unmarried, and all of his married, life in Maillane. He was responsible for the movement that revived the Provençal language, which can be sampled by every road user on the approach to every town and village in the region, where the Provençal name is juxtaposed on signs with the French.

Such is the influence of the *Félibrige* movement more than a century after its inception. Its leader's name is perpetuated everywhere in Provence in street names especially, and here, in Maillane, in a brand new Centre Frédéric Mistral. Yet there is irony in the latter's freshly tarmacked car park lying within leaping distance of the overgrown garden of Mistral's house, a building which, if not actually crumbling, is in a state of serious deterioration. It receives about 5,000 visitors each year, at 6f per head, quite insufficient for its maintenance. The French state provides, rightly, for national institutions such as the new Bibliothèque de France but apparently withholds grants from many small museums. So I cannot help wondering if some of the money spent on all that dual signposting might not have been better used on subsidising Mistral's house. It is still open, however, and visitors can hardly fail to take away a vivid impression of the man. The walls are covered with photographs of Mistral, the rooms display busts and likenesses of Mistral, and the garden is almost bissected by a hugh stone carving of Mistral placed against a hunk of rock. It is all, apart from the statue, we are told, precisely as it was on the day the poet died. So we must assume that he favoured having all those representations of himself on show. Or, since he was an extremely good-looking man, was it his much younger wife who insisted? The custodian's explanation is that Mistral would have thought it discourteous to the fans who sent him pictures of himself not to have displayed them. (Or did they expect to get them back, signed?)

There are photos of other *félibres* and of the poet's eminent admirers such as President Theodore Roosevelt who signed his own portrait and sent it with a message of warm praise. Souvenirs of fellow authors are also displayed – Lamartine, Daudet, among others – and of composers, notably Gounod, who made an opera from the most famous of the poems, *Mireille*.

It is a comfortless interior. The living-room has a customary Provençal tiled floor but the effect is sombre where no sunlight penetrates. The study has a big, ugly, glass-fronted bookcase containing volumes long without readers; the flooring is wooden. The *salle à manger*, with every utensil necessary for producing good Provençal cuisine, has yet another picture of Mistral, seated at table wearing his hat. (Note the traditional bread bin on the wall, as seen at the museum in Arles.)

The custom of leaving, so far as is possible, the homes of the great in the condition in which they last knew them, may not be the kindest or most effective way of attempting to keep their memory fresh. The Mistral house at Maillane is a museum in the worst sense. It is dowdy. Justice is not done to a remarkable man – because it is too reverent.

Mistral is remembered for having led the cultural revival of Provence. He spent his Nobel Prize money endowing the Musée Arlaten (see page 163); his Memoirs suggest a sensitive man who cared passionately about his heritage and origins; his greatest work was the Dictionary of the Provencal Language, *le Trésor de Félibrige*. He dedicated his life to a movement which was regional without being separatist. And what he and his colleagues achieved, remember, was done without bloodshed.

As we left the house I pondered aloud how much it matters that Provençal is kept alive as a literary language when it is no longer a vital spoken one. My wife had no doubts. To her it is a kind of linguistic archaeology, quite as worth-while as digging for Glanum.

Close to the sad shrine is a restaurant, the Maiane, which is how Mistral would have liked us to spell the name of his town. On your way back to St-Rémy, you will pass the farmhouse where the poet was born, le Mas du Juge. No Provençal alternative is given. It is not open to the public.

There are hôtels conveniently situated on the road from St-Rémy to Glanum within walking distance of both the town centre and the ancient site.

It is necessary to appreciate that, until this century, little of Glanum had been excavated and that the road to Les Baux ran across part of what are now the uncovered ruins. After its destruction in the third century AD the remains became hidden beneath alluvial deposits washed down from the Alpilles. The only evidence of a former city lay in the two massive structures a few hundred metres away, a triumphal arch and a tall mausoleum with a cupola. These, known as 'Les Antiques', stand nobly in a paddock beside the main road, and until comparatively recently they were all that visitors saw of the city founded well over two thousand years ago beside a spring whose source can now again be seen. As archaeology became a preoccupation of scholars and others, evidence of the city was collected and today the site is being cared for as well as limited funds allow. It is beginning to rank in importance with Vaison and Arles, but the chief treasures it has yielded are safely housed in the Centre Archéologique at the Hôtel de Sade, a Renaissance mansion in St-Rémy. A visit is essential, preferably before going to Glanum itself. (Tickets are available for both and for other museums, making for a worth-while overall saving.)

Several gateways to medieval St-Rémy are extant. The best way to explore the old town is to plunge into it through one of them and turn this way and that as the whim takes you. You are unlikely to get lost and are bound to see everything of interest. There are two principal squares in one of which is the Hôtel de Ville. The weekly market penetrates here from the Place de la République which lies outside the walls. The other is smaller but more distinguished and on one side of it is the Hôtel Mistral de Mondragon dating from the sixteenth century. This is now the Musée des Alpilles Pierre-et-Brun, also known as the Musée des Beaux Arts. It has a delightful inner courtyard with seats from which can be observed the irregular walls of a rounded tower, stone balconies and blind windows. The tower staircase leads to galleries with rooms named after the *félibres* Roumanille and Giera. There are paintings, costumes, documents, relating to Nostradamus (born in St-Rémy, 1503), farming implements, spinning wheels, items of geological interest. There is one haunting, unsigned, un-named painting (dated, I think, 1940) of a ragged column of men wearing long cloaks that are blowing in the mistral. They are being searched by an armed soldier. The cypresses above them are also windswept. A stone registers: 7km, St.Rémy. Who painted it, and of what?

Adjoining the museum is another palace, the Hôtel de Meyran de Lagoy, which mounts temporary exhibitions. Opposite is the Hôtel de Sade where, on the ground floor, is a courtyard opening on to the ruins of a baptistery of the fifth century and baths of a slightly earlier time. Under cover are imposing finds from Glanum, funerary stellars, an acroterion detached from its pediment and remarkably well-preserved because it was carved from a single piece of limestone, columns representative of the main classical orders, various fragments of cornices, and a number of tombs. Some of the monuments were first erected by the Gauls but are inscribed with Greek phonetics because that tribe did not have a written language. The French guide points out with a nice partisanship that this did not make them feel inferior; they were proud of their oral tradition. There is much evidence of cultural mix in the votive offerings of all periods. Perhaps the single most splendid exhibit is a head of Poseidon which had been a fountain.

On the first floor are numbers of outstanding treasures including an impressive acroterion honouring the goddess Valetudo, a small panel of Mercury and Fortuna, and statues of a Gallic prisoner and of Hercules. (An acroterion is a plinth and the carving it supports at the end or point of a pediment.) By the second floor it is allowable to feel sated. The guide has much information to impart and although he is both personable and erudite, enough is enough, and the show cases crammed with everyday items found on the site do not make for interesting narrative. However, for anyone wishing to check the precise nature of tools, household utensils, jewellery, lamps and other objects used by the citizens of Glanum, there are numerous examples. But a reconstructed interior would be an aid to the imagination.

In the Rue Estrine is another fine building of the eighteenth century, now called Le Centre d'Art Présence Van Gogh. This is a slightly misleading name because although there is an audio-visual room with reproductions of paintings associated with St-Rémy, most of the interior is devoted to temporary exhibitions of works by other artists.

You will probably notice a much less handsome house with a battered door. This is the birthplace of Nostradamus. In front of it is a more agreeable relic in the shape of a fountain surmounted by a bust of the astrologer. You will certainly not overlook the church of St-Martin which is of boastful proportions, having a portico facing the Place de la Républicque with four dominant neo-classical columns at odds with the original fourteenth-century tower. The entrance for ordinary mortals is not by the door beneath this grandiose frontage but up slightly broken steps on the south side. Immediately inside, on the right, is a kitsch grotto with a gaudy virgin rising from it. Everything within sight is large and vulgar. Very dark paintings hang from very tall pillars. The side aisles have painted ceilings. It is a building lacking conviction; the town deserves better and, as if to affirm this, the shops nearby have bright frontages and sell attractive Provençal goods. Three opposite the drab south door of the church are named La Boutigo, Cecilo, and Soleiado. On market days their entrances are partly blocked by stalls, some specialising in headily aromatic herbs and spices. All the streets in the town are signed in French and Provençal, with blue for the former, yellow for the other. So the Rue Hoche is in blue above Carriero di Barri de l'Espito in yellow. The latter, for good measure, has a crest. (At least the Provençal names do not change, as often happens to the French ones.)

On the way up to Glanum is a deconsecrated fifteenth-century chapel, Notre-Dame-de-la-Pitié, now dedicated to the memory of a twentieth-century painter and writer, Mario Prassinos, who lived in nearby Eygalières. This church has suffered various alterations and additions in its five hundred yeas; it now has to endure a totally glass fronted west door inside a charming old stone porch. You may judge from the reproductions in a side entrance whether or not you wish to pay to examine the works of Prassinos which now adorn the nave.

In the garden on the south side is a statue of Gounod.

Before you reach Glanum there is a turning to the left to St-Paul-de-Mausolé. Beside it is the hospital where Van Gogh was a patient for a year from May 1889. This is still a psychiatric clinic, not open to visitors; although the chapel and cloister, so familiar to the artist, are. In the driveway to the latter is a plinth, sadly now lacking the Zadkine bust of Van Gogh which stood there until thieves removed it in early 1989. In the cloister, as some sort of recompense, is a stone cornucopia carved on a wall. Most of the fruit has been ousted by sunflowers, which seems not inappropriate. Van

Gogh painted more than 150 pictures during his year here. He was looked after by the nuns who helped care for patients when the monastery, established before 982AD, was disbanded at the Revolution. The church tower – twelfth-century – is very fine indeed, a superb example of local Romanesque, with a pyramidal roof above the decorated square belfry. It is a shame that the lower parts are obscured by the domestic buildings. The gardens, lovingly described by Pope-Hennessy in 1952, are not open to the public but on land beside them a Van Gogh trail leads to the quarry and the hillside which he painted.

The excavations can be seen from the gateway to St-Paul and so can 'Les Antiques', the mausoleum and arch. (Close to them is the start of a three-hour walk up and down the Alpilles to Les Baux.) The arch was erected to celebrate Caesar's victories over the Gauls and deserves close inspection for the well-preserved detail of the carving. The mausoleum, which it has been discovered is not a tomb, but a cenotaph, has statues of the two it commemorates, who were grandsons of Augustus. It is even richer in carving than the arch, with wholly preserved panels and complete Corinthian columns supporting the temple. Some of what you see belongs to the foundations of the monument because the level of the earth has been lowered. It is astonishing that these marvellous structures have survived the ravages of time and war and equally surprising that no one thought of digging for Glanum until 1921.

There is a small car park on the track (once the road) leading to a pavilion on a slight hill. Inside are models of the ancient town, at two different periods, and paintings recreating various buildings. A particularly instructive visual aid shows a decorated interior of a house, the colours and patterns of which are known thanks to surviving fragments of wall displayed beside them. From here you enter Glanum which, it is reasonable to suppose, covered more ground to the north and west and already, below the pavilion, a further dig is taking place, whilst work also goes on in the forum and elsewhere. Glanum is a complicated site because there were three distinct towns during the Graeco-Roman era and, earlier, there was a Ligurian settlement around the spring. Some mosaic floors are preserved under cover but most of the ruins are unadorned, so it is well to recall what was seen at the Musée de Sade, and to bear in mind the models in the pavilion. The curia, or meeting place, with a high apse, stands beside a covered canal which was essential to the drainage system. The ground plans of two patrician's houses are easily recognisable; so are those of temples and baths. At the south end, against one hillside, were fortified walls to protect encroachments from the mountain top, and on the eastern side the position of the theatre has recently been determined. It is always worth returning to Glanum to see what is 'new'.

The site was important strategically and commercially for many centuries. Marius based his troops here whilst planning how to defeat the Teuton bordes. He encouraged the enemy to pass by Glanum unharmed and it is said that the Roman soldiers who were jeered at had to be restrained from going into the attack. But the Teutons were unaware that they were walking into a trap from which few escaped alive. Four hundred years later it was the turn of the Romans to suffer defeat; the town was destroyed by Germanic invaders about 270AD.

The pass over the Alpilles immediately above Glanum is through mostly wooded terrain with constantly changing views as the road cork-screws before reaching a cultivated area given over to the grape. Turn right for Les Baux, which is very much first-time-round and has scars of tourism. But if you have to go in midsummer, or at Easter, it can still be memorable. As you emerge on to the plateau there is a sense of infinite space. At one end are the remains of the castle whose lords were often the scourge of the surrounding countryside. There were, though, times when their influence was more benign; during the thirteenth century when the courts of love prevailed and two hundred years later under King René who gave the entire place, lock, stock and plateau, to Jeanne, his second wife. In 1632 it was destroyed by order of Louis XIII. Thus ended a long period during which Les Baux had either dominated, or been a vassal of, Provence.

When the troubadour cult was at its height Les Baux was one of its many centres in western Europe. It was prestigious for all great lords to patronise its exponents and to encourage their presence at the courts of love. The language in which the troubadours wrote and sang was Occitan, more popularly known as Provençal, wherever they were performing, even as far away as northern Italy. They were the inventors and masters of western lyric poetry and their subject matter was by no means confined to the artificial paeons of love addressed to high-born ladies as a matter of court etiquette. Biographical records of many of the poets survive, as does a mass of their work, some with music, some without. They were innovators who prided themselves on their prowess, deriding those whom they considered lesser poets. Many were deeply, some spuriously, religious; others showed intimate knowledge of natural history in their work, or referred to contemporary events and society. And their audiences must have been as familiar with Provençal as they were with Latin from which it was derived.

Much imagination is needed today to conjure up the presence of troubadours amid the ruins of the escarpment where the medieval castle was erected. It is easier to visualise the appalling Raymond of Touraine, overlord in the fourteenth century, one of whose viler practices was to screech with laughter when prisoners were hurled, at his command, from the windows of his fortress on to the rocks far below.

To reach the plateau and castle you enter a small lapidary

museum containing examples of bauxite, an ore of aluminium discovered here in 1821 by Berthier. As you come out on to the plateau, on your left is the fourteenth-century chapel of St-Blaise displaying two showcases of soap and olive oil products. Ahead of you is a bust of Charloun Rieu (1846-1924) who sang the praises of this territory. Turn back and climb a slope to the château, entered through a 'Saracen Tower' so if you missed the one at Vitrolles you will now be compensated. Enough survives of the castle to emphasise its enormous size. Staircases have been equipped with railings and you can climb to dizzy heights, but the views from the other end of the plateau are equally spectacular.

The town itself has fine Renaissance houses of sufficient intrinsic dignity to rise above their contemporary use as shops, restaurants and galleries, so do not heed those who talk sneeringly of Les Baux as a tourist trap. On the irregularly shaped Place St-Vincent, a visual delight in itself, are the ancient parish church, the chapel of the White Penitents and the Hôtel des Porcelets. The church is built into the rock and is only marginally wider than it is deep. One part of the nave is tenth- another twelfth- a third fifteenth-century. The furnishings include small stained-glass windows, the gift of Prince Rainier III of Monaco to Les Baux. The White Penitents' Chapel is less appealing inside because of the brash murals by Yves Brayer. This artist, who died in 1990, identified with Provence. He had a second home here and the former Museum of Contemporary Art in the Hôtel des Porcelets has been re-named after him. It is hung with his vivid post-Impressionistic canvases. There are 68 of them on three floors and they demonstrate forcefully that he should not be judged by his work in the chapel which, it is said, he undertook reluctantly, late in life. Another old mansion, in the main street, is the town hall, once accommodated in the house forming part of the ramparts and now a museum of tastefully displayed *santons*.

In winter, a picnic in the car park can be a joy. It will be almost deserted so it is an ideal opportunity for studying the surrounding hills and giving rein to your fancy. The limestone crags and rock formations do not change as clouds do but the light on them does. There is one rock with the face of an amiable philosopher, and another whose resident savant has a familiar in the shape of a sharp-nosed rodent clinging to his scalp. Yet another resembles a madonna with bowed head.

Les Baux is like an enormous irregularly constructed barge moor-ed into an impregnable position. On its west side it looks down on to a mostly modern village where there is a large *gendarmerie*, several smart restaurants and hôtels, and Queen Jeanne's *pavillon*. The latter attracted the *félibres* and Mistral so admired it that he ordered a copy for his tomb at Maillane. From here you can walk to the Val d'Enfer through weirdly formed rocks, which are chillingly bizarre, haunting, daunting, comical, according to how you see them. On D27 back to St-Rémy are the bauxite quarries where a photographer, the late Albert Plécy, created a Cathédrale d'Images, 'a huge practical research laboratory for pictures used as a wordless language like music'. That is part of the message greeting visitors to a strange audio-visual presentation. It is certainly something completely different. In Provence you never know what the next museum will have on offer.

15   The Camargue

Méjanes : Etang de Vaccarès : Mas du Pont de Rousty :
Salin-de-Giraud : Albaron : Parc Ornithologique :
Stes-Maries-de-la-Mer : Aigues-Mortes : Port Camargue

When you feel surfeited with views, start on a tour of the
Camargue where there aren't any; there is only horizon.

Many parts of Provence are different but this one is more different
than others. It excites not so much affection as a devotion which can verge on
the mystical. Voices quaver, eyes mist over, cheeks glow when people tell
you how they feel about the Camargue. It is the light, they say, the strange-
ness, the solitude, the space. Then come ecstatic references to the wild white
horses, to egrets and flamingoes, and some go so far as to name it the most

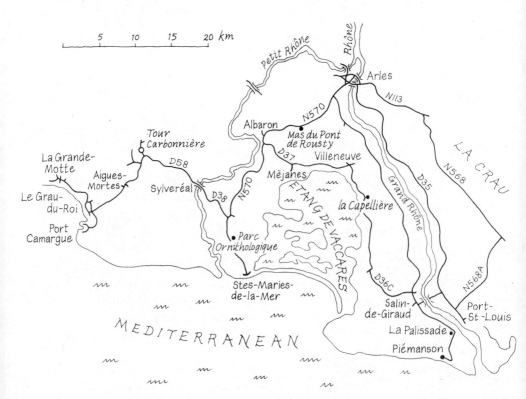

beautiful region in all France, let alone Provence. On our first visit in 1962 I, particularly, did not fall under its spell. I didn't like the flatness, I thought the horses looked dirty, I failed to identify an egret and we had a foul meal at Aigues-Mortes which struck me as being a squalid little town festering behind its ancient walls. Familiarity has changed my attitude and now I have at least some appreciation of the variety to be found in the Camargue, ranging from the market gardening districts close to Arles, to the salt flats by the mouth of the Rhône, to the heavily-reeded marshy terrain around the Etang de Vaccarès. It is different, even in itself.

The actual outline of the Camargue has changed much over the centuries as the sea has receded here or reclaimed ground there. It is of primary importance as a breeding and nesting region for birds of many species, and for that reason it was declared an area of conservation by the Council of Europe in 1965. Nearly forty years earlier a reserve had been formed by the Société Nationale d'Acclimatation de France. It is organised so that tourists, although prevented from going wherever may take their fancy, can see the black bulls, white horses and pink flamingoes without disturbing the animals and birds. The Camargue receives over 900,000 visitors annually so it is essential, if the wild life is to be protected, that they should be chan-nelled into the parts where they can do least harm. The majority make for the sea coast and the new townships and harbours built for them and their boats, but many like to hire horses and be led on gentle treks by *gardians*, the cowboys who don traditional costumes to add local colour. Bull fights are staged, some in makeshift corrals, others in the ring provided at Méjanes by the Pastis king, M. Ricard. Here he has set up stables, a restaurant, a hôtel and also a miniature railway which, on Sundays and holidays from 13 April to 30 June, goes for nearly five kilometres along the shores of the Etang de Vaccarès. In May the trip is made memorable by the sight of great clumps of yellow irises.

Start your visit at the Musée Camarguais, housed in a long barn, once a part of the Mas du Pont de Rousty. Inside is a well-planned display, at first difficult to see because the lighting is very much a 40-watt enterprise. There are self-operated slides of life in the Camargue and a version of Mistral's *Mireille* in quaint sepia postcards. At one end are farm buildings in miniature which light up in sections as a spoken commentary plays. There is a model of the church at Stes-Maries-de-la-Mer and cabinets displaying every imaginable aspect of local activity. The car parking is ample and there are picnic tables. The farmhouse cannot be visited because it is private property in use as a meteorological station. The museum is open all year round and, in the high season, even on Tuesdays.

From the Rousty take the first of two walks which will impress upon you the tranquillity of the Camargue. Begin on what was a Ligurian

191

Mas du-Pont-de-Rousty: Le Musée Camarguais

track used in tribal times for bringing iron here. It became a path for trans-humance, the annual migration of the sheep and cattle to the mountains for fresh pasture during the hot months. They now go by road, in lorries.

The walk is well signposted and takes the shape of a right-angled letter 'p' – unless you choose to prolong it by venturing into the marshes. One notice board tells you what to look for at which season, another indicates the drainage canal of 1543 that is crossed, without meeting it, by the irrigation channel of 1627. Another, strong in visual aids, shows a small flat-bottomed barge equipped with fishing nets to catch carp, mullet, eel and other creatures called *sandre* and *gambusie,* in the ditch below. At the top of the 'p' turn right into the *roselière,* a long path between tall reeds, beside which ducks nest and there are frogs and other inhabitants of the watery world. At the end is one of those three-part barriers designed to inhibit bicycling. They might well have the same effect on some paunches I have observed locally.

When you next turn right, at last all is not flat. Beyond Arles the Alpilles can be discerned, but they are too far away to break the spell and might be dismissed as a mirage. You now walk beside grazing ground netted against your possible invasion. Animal footprints are shown on a notice, so beasts must forage amongst the heather. On the opposite side is the drollest 'museum' yet. It simply proclaims an area where generations of *mas* families have thrown all their rubbish. The actual items are not labelled. At the next change of direction stands one of those gleamingly whitewashed small cabins made of reeds, wood and local vegetation, the traditional abode of a *gardian*, though in fact they were not necessarily lived in by romantic cowboys who roamed the marsh flats, but were used by all workers.

If you have time visit Salin-de-Giraud which has salt flats and tips, more widespread and higher than those near Aigues-Mortes. There is an observation platform beyond the southern end of the town where the presentation is most helpful, explaining in detail the scene around you, noting how the salt water is let in through a barrier in the sea wall, well to the west, at Beauduc. It then flows through various *étangs* and across the Petit Rhône to the flats where it evaporates and the salt is collected. After processing it is stored close to the railway behind the viewing point. The road continues to the Plage du Piémanson across thin strands of lagoon. On the way is La Palissade which belongs to the Academy of Coastal Areas and Lakesides but the atmosphere is informal. For a modest fee you can see a herbarium, an aquarium in brackish water, and take guided tours beside the river which here is the Grand Rhône. Alternatively you can picnic under the pine trees and look across to Port St-Louis, noting the toy-like eighteenth-century fort built to deter invaders.

The old part of Salin-de-Giraud is like an open prison, with blocks of barracks constructed by the owners of chemical factories for their workforce. The new town has hôtels and evidence of growing tourism; both can be reached by ferry across the Rhône.

Take a minor road signed to Vaccarès from which you can deviate to the sea dyke. Leave the car at the start of a trail stretching for 20km; you are not permitted to walk on the dunes. If you remain on the Vaccarès road you will pass many a private *mas*, one of which, Tour de Valat, is owned by Luc Hoffman, who rings an average of 20,000 birds every year. Another is at the entrance to the National Park of the Camargue from which hikers, picnickers, campers and most forms of two-legged and four-wheeled traffic are forbidden. But you can obtain tickets for three observation points, open before 10.00 and after 16.00. These are available at La Capellière, an information centre further along the road. Once there you may settle for the trail which begins on the spot, has two observatories (fitted with powerful binoculars) and winds for 1.5km through marshy territory named Sentier des Rannettes (Way of the Frogs). I was impressed at the care taken by the authorities to ensure an enjoyable experience for the visitor at the same time as fully protecting the wild life.

Beyond La Capellière is Villeneuve, scarcely even a hamlet now, but it was well-known to Romans who had villas in the north of the Camargue. Then all you see, apart from the lagoon, are reeds, reeds, reeds until, at last, a few trees arise beside isolated dwellings. The approach to Méjanes brings large buildings; M. Ricard's enterprise must be a mixed blessing. At Albaron, an important centre for desalination, there is a much admired and well-preserved church but little else. The road from there meanders back towards the coast for twenty kilometres or so past many hôtels, *gîtes* and points of hire for horses, to the destination of another walk, the Parc Ornithologique.

Once again, there is ample space for parking and picnics. Seated there, before taking the long or short walk around the Parc, you will appreciate again that the horizon, for all 360°, is almost at field level. To the north, vision is blocked by reeds and bushes, though if you stand you wil see people taking the long walk and also a few umbrella pines in the distance, beside a *mas;* to the west are more, low, deciduous trees, a few fields, a distant row of poplars; to the south is the irregularly shaped information centre, the taller part leaning, like a recumbent Thurber figure, on the lower circular building, and a hôtel beyond; to the east are great expanses of marsh and *étang.* Above it all is the light blue sky, as much light as blue.

At first the Parc repelled me because of its many cages. Admittedly they are tall and wide with room for the smaller birds to fly without perhaps feeling too imprisoned, but I did not enjoy watching a buzzard flapping its wings at the netting, surely in frustraion. I had supposed that a bird park in the Camargue would be entirely natural, with the creatures left to fly in and out at will. Beyond the caged area they can, over an expanse of marshland where you may walk for hours. The official time given for the Red Route, the longest, is one-and-a-half hours but there are seats, there is the ground to lie upon and there is no sense of urgency whatever. You will probably see flamingoes in their most northerly breeding place. They spend half of the year here. There may be a lark ascending.

The Parc is close to the Stes-Maries-de-la-Mer, the once tiny fishing village on the shores of the Mediterranean where the boat carrying the Marys, Martha, a black maid called Sarah, and other hangers-on, beached very early AD. Do not be surprised that, frail though the craft was, it had come all the way from Judaea, apparently without mishap. This was the age of miracles. Missionary work began at once, which was how Provence came so early to Christianity. Martha went north to Tarascon to tame the monster; others went to Ste-Baume and Marseille. The Marys were enshrined here where the myths and legends surrounding them have become associated with Gypsies. A place of pilgrimage was established when the bodies, alleged to be of the Marys, were discovered in the fiteenth century. The maid Sarah was already revered by the Gypsies who took over homage to the Marys as well. Now it is the most famous of Romany meeting places, with Gypsies from all parts of the world gathering there on 24 and 25 May to take part in the ceremony and also to meet each other, rather as world statesmen take the opportunity of a head-of-state funeral to hold informal conferences. The *gardians* join in the proceedings when the shrines from the church are paraded around the streets before being taken into the sea. Sarah, who lies in the crypt for 364 days of the year, is brought out for an airing. She is also present when the Gypsies elect their queen, which they do here every few years. It is all extremely colourful with displays of horsemanship, bull fighting and revelry by night. Mistral, in his Memoirs, describes a visit on foot from Maillane in the mid-nineteenth-century. Mary Jacobé is honoured at the May celebration. In October when there is another pilgrimage it is Mary Salomé's turn.

The church is ancient and rather dismal. It has a gloomy low-ceilinged crypt where there is a model of the famous boat with two simple, upright figures in it. This is surrounded by votive offerings in marble and card. In the upper chapel are the shrines of the Marys. The church is fortified and it is possible to climb to the ramparts around the tower. Below it runs a path for sentries. In the vicinity is the Museé Baroncelli occupying a charming little wedge-shaped building, once the town hall. Tucked into the ground floor, in poky rooms and a passage, are glass cases of stuffed flamingoes, herons, kingfishers and birds of prey displayed against their natural habitat. On the first floor are costumes and furniture of the region, and a portrait of Baron Folco de Baroncelli-Javon who dedicated his life to the revival and preservation of old customs of the Camargue. He was a *félibre* and made his home in a *mas* where he reared bulls. What would he make of present-day Stes-Maries, especially in the summer months when it becomes an over-crowded holiday resort?

On one wall of the museum you can see a notice for the Antique Confrérie des Gardians founded, it says, in Arles in 1512. A few kilometres north is the Musée de Cire (waxworks) with a Galérie Ornithologique, a 'Salle du Fou Rire' and exhibits of rural life and and folklore. It is but one of many now that the Camargue has become popular. A hôtel is not enough, it must be an entertainments complex as well, although there are still some simple, whitewashed auberges offering accommodation.

There is a statue to Baroncelli at a landing stage just on the western edge of Stes-Maries, where a 75-minute boat trip starts and ends. It goes up the Petit Rhône by one bank and back by the other. I found it dull, the high point being reached when the boat bumps the river bank so that a crew member can throw bales of straw to horses and bulls in an enclosure. Otherwise there is less to see than on the roads and paths, and much of what would be visible is hidden by endless clumps of reeds. (The horses, incidentally, change colour as they age, from black, through grey, to white.)

Back on the road, cross the Petit Rhône at Sylvéreal, and go through somewhat monotonous terrain until Aigues-Mortes, the other major town, almost certainly first-time round, is reached.

Louis IX of France, known as St.Louis, because of his tendency to wage war on those whom he thought infidels, bought Aigues-Mortes from the Abbot of Psalmody to provide himself with a port from which to crusade. He already had rights over Marseille, because he had married Margaret of Provence, but deemed it circumspect to have a harbour of his own. It was his son, Philip III, who fortified the port with walls which still enclose it today. From the eighth century Aigues-Mortes had been a salt-producing centre which was what first attracted saintly Louis to it. A canal was constructed to convey the precious commodity to Beaucaire.

The well-preserved walls can be walked for their entire length

Port Camargue

starting at the simple, circular Constance Tower at the north-west extremity of the old town. There are other towers and gateways, in one of which the dead bodies of the besieged were kept in salt to protect the defenders from disease until there was an opportunity to bury them. That was in the thirteenth century. Four hundred years later Marie Durand, a prisoner for nearly four decades, whose crime was being a Protestant, gained her freedom in advance of the general edict of tolerance.

Aigues-Mortes has lost its port because, at times of flood, the deposits from the Rhône reclaimed the land from the sea, now a few miles distant at Le Grau-du-Roi and Port-Camargue. The Etang de la Ville brings water closer to the ramparts but not sufficiently to detract from the forlorn appearance they now present, guarding a flat area of rubble and rough grass where once lay the moat. Nevertheless, it is a perfect example of a medieval walled town built on the grid system, and I am glad to have revised my first impression of it. Within the walls, although many of the shops sell little but souvenirs, there is evidence of a living town. At its heart is the basically thirteenth-century church where the *chevaliers* of St.Louis are commemorated. Just off centre is the restaurant La Goulue with a shady courtyard in which waiters wearing shirts of extravagant design will serve you. Try the local Vin Listel, the rosé version of which is named Gris.

Beyond Aigues-Mortes, on the road to Le Grau-du-Roi, are the salt flats and tips. The latter was once a fishing village but is now like any seaside resort anywhere. To its west is the more stylish La Grande-Motte, invented for tourists after more than £7m had been spent in ridding that part of the coast of mosquitoes. Lovers of the wildness and solitude of the Camargue must be appalled by what has occurred on the shores here, and it will certainly be regrettable if there is any more development. Unfortunately there is evidence that more is to come on the eastern side of Le Grau.

That said, I confess to admiring the design of that other new resort, Port-Camargue. The blocks of apartments, hôtels and studios do not conform to anything approaching the conventional. Curves are preferred to angles and the buildings are functional for sun worshippers, with balconies laid back above each other to give maximum solar infiltration. The town encloses a harbour where thousands of small vessels are moored; the roads are wide and lined with newly-planted conifers. Visit Port-Camargue out of season and enjoy its architecture which provides an antidote to an overdose of twelfth-century churches, fifteenth-century altars, ruined castles of all ages, and classical remains.

Then, after leaving Aigues-Mortes along the causeway beside the canal, you will approach the Tour Carbonnière, a fourteenth-century fort, restored in 1858, standing beside an *étang* in an attitude of 'They Shall Not Pass.'

That is how it was. Now it is hidden by a motorway bridge. Neither views nor horizons matter to those who construct autoroutes to disturb the calm of the Camargue.

La Tour Carbonnière

16   Nîmes and the Pont du Gard

Tavel : Châteauneuf-du-Pape

In Nîmes it is not as easy, as at Arles and Avignon, to visualise the city of the past. At Avignon the papal palace and cathedral rising above the almost intact walls aid the imagination; at Arles, the central hillock overlooking the Rhône defines the ancient settlement. But the urban sprawl of modern Nîmes merges with the older parts so that I find it difficult to comprehend the limits of the Roman and medieval cities, though I have enjoyed trying to unravel its layout, especially on warm, early spring days.

Nîmes, in the department of the Gard, is not part of modern Provence but was a major city of Roman Narbonensis, both before and after 284AD when that territory was divided for administrative reasons. The part to the west of the Rhône retained the old name, that to the east, including Arles, became Viennoise.

Like Arles, Nîmes (Nemausus to the Romans) lay on the Via Domitia, with cross-roads to the Cévennes and the Camargue. Augustus, grand-nephew of Julius Caesar, favoured this city and gave land in and around it to his legionaries who had defeated Antony on the Nile. From this derives an item in the city's heraldry: a crocodile in chains symbolising Egypt. In 1535 this was incorporated in the coat of arms, by permission of François I. By then Nîmes, with the rest of the Languedoc, had been part of France for nearly three hundred years, after its support of the Albigensian heresy. Although it surrendered to the appalling Simon de Montfort (father of the founder of the English House of Commons) it maintained a heavy bias towards Protestantism and became a Huguenot stronghold in which massacres of Catholics occurred. Despite this, and perhaps hoping to placate the inhabitants, Louis XIV honoured them by giving their Academy equal footing with the national Académie Française. Modern Nîmes takes pride in this – and also in its world-wide fame as a centre of the textile industry whose home-spun denim spawned blue jeans. In 1990 an exhibition was mounted at the Musée du Vieux Nîmes, illustrating the history of the most popular garment ever. Examples decorated the rooms and staircases of the seventeenth-century former episcopal palace. I thought this was going too far; the entire world is a daily exhibition of blue jeans.

The pride of Nemausus was its amphitheatre, the best pre-served of all to be found in France, and only slightly smaller than the arena at Arles. To the untrained eye they are identical, much as all classical temples look alike to some of us. However, more of the top tier of arches remains than in the other city, and in it have survived the apertures used by the ancients to slot the mechanism for moving canvas of some sort (though not denim) over the entire structure, to protect audience and performers from the excesses of the weather. Knowledge of this is probably what led the present authorities to fit a moveable winter roof in 1989.

There is something ironic in the Romans taking such pains to shield spectators from the heavy rain and blazing sun considering what was permitted in performance. Men and beasts fought one another – man against man, beast against beast, beast against man – often to the bloodiest of deaths, as part of a highly organised entertainments industry.

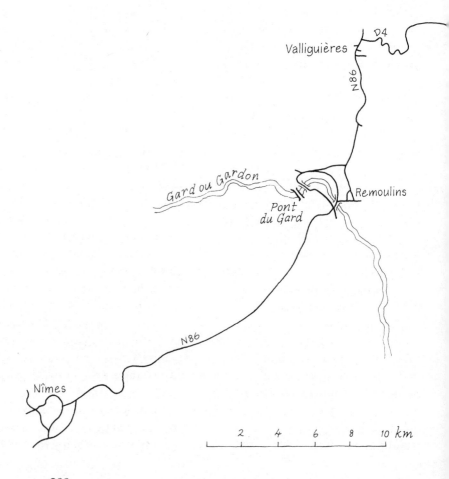

The arena, like that of Arles, has survived for two thousand years despite a chequered history. The Visigoths occupied it, turning it into a fortress and erecting defensive towers which, unlike Arles', were removed at the time of restoration. Later it became a town centre in itself with 700 inhabitants, terraced private houses and two chapels. It was lived in as late as the eighteenth century and cleared only in the next when official bull fights (*feria*) were inaugurated. It is now a more perfect example of Roman archi-

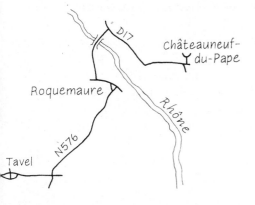

tecture than its larger counterpart across the Rhône. It also appears more formidable perhaps because it can be seen unimpeded by other buildings. On one 'side' is a wide road and, diagonally, it faces a public garden, so it is possible to stand back and appreciate its immensity, as you cannot at Arles.

The other first-time-round Roman monument is the Maison Carrée which has come through two millennia virtually unscathed. A Greek-style temple, built in the reign of Augustus, it stands severe, and a little ungainly, on a rectangular plinth reached up fifteen harsh steps. It faces, with its fine pediment and Corinthian pillars, the site of the forum of which no trace remains; like the arena it endured various uses before being restored in the early eighteenth century. A museum is now housed in it.

Lesser remains include the ruins of the temple of Diana in the Jardin de la Fontaine. This is less classically severe than the Maison Carrée and, thanks to the decay of most of the roof and many of the walls, it can be viewed as though it were a cross-section drawing. Erected in the early part of the second century AD it was taken over by Benedictine nuns and converted into a church. This was later mostly destroyed in some religious fracas.

The Tour Magne, on Mont Cavalier, is pre-Roman in origin and was incorporated into the city walls by Augustus. At the top of the 140 steps of an interior stairway there is the finest view of Nîmes. Another remnant of the wall is a gateway close to the church of St-Baudile and a further vestige of the Roman occupation lies below the seventeenth-century castle, now a prison. This is a tower into which water flowed from Uzès, via the Pont du Gard, before supplying all parts of the town through ten lead ducts.

The permanent exhibits in the museums of Nîmes sometimes get cast aside in favour of temporary attractions, such as the celebration of blue jeans already mentioned at the Musée du Vieux Nîmes. Here, you should be able to see pottery, plate, painted cupboards and whole interiors restored to resemble their appearance in earlier centuries. At the Musée des Beaux Arts it would be difficult to store away a magnificent Roman mosaic which covers almost the whole of the main ground floor chamber, but once I was unable to view the paintings kept here without paying for another exhibition which did not attract me. On another occasion I was allowed to roam freely, in both senses, and saw the permanent collection which is strong on portraits and narrative paintings. At the museums of archaeology and natural history the

Nîmes: La Tour Magne

exhibits are what you might expect. For me, they do not compare favourably with others in the region.

To see the museums and antiquities entails much plodding about a busy modern city centre, so make sure you leave Diana´s temple to the last. Then you can relax in the Jardin de la Fontaine where, at weekends, the whole of Nîmes seems to congregate. There is room for all, either at ground level where there are well-shaded concourses and seats beside sunken fountains, or on the balustraded paths and terraces below the Tour Magne. The spring, sacred to the tribes who preceded the Greeks and Romans, is in the garden. There was good reason in a land where rainfall can be low to cherish it, although beneath Nîmes is a whole system of waterways which can still lead to dangerous flooding after torrential storms. The last instance was in the autumn of 1988 when cars were washed away and some drivers drowned.

Leading to the gardens is the wide Avénue Jean-Jaurès, Nîmes' most splendid highway. It has ample space between the lanes of traffic to accommodate a fair. Great efforts have been made to keep vehicles on the main thoroughfares, which are better able to cope with the flow than at Arles, and there are spacious underground car parks. The narrow, twisting alleys of the old town are fairly free from traffic, and in them are to be found shops many and varied. One of them, offering sportswear, is called JEFF and has on its fascia the figure of a cricketer padded up to bat. In a lane nearby on the shutters of a bookshop is a quotation from the writer Jack Alain Léger, encouraging children to read:

> 'Reading is like going down a river in unknown territory, let yourself be carried along by the words, don't fight against the current, don't try to know in advance where the author will take you.'

This author will certainly lead you into unknown territory in old Nîmes so perhaps you should follow the route recommended on the free brochure obtainable from the Office of Tourism in the street facing the Maison Carrée. Or maybe you should just wander. There are dozens of cafés and restaurants and several charming little squares, such as the Place du Marché where there is a fountain incorporating the chained crocodile. It was sculpted by V. and S. Tongiani in 1987. The *place* is the site of the old corn market. Somewhere close by is the Place de l'Horloge with a tall, thin, free-standing clock-tower. Down another lane you will chance upon the cathedral which merges into the maze of streets. Its lineage is long but itself is almost entirely nineteenth-century when the original 800-year-old church was rebuilt. It was well done. The interior is an excellent replica of Provençal Romanesque.

Nothing could be more first-time-round than the Pont du Gard but it is unthinkable that it should not be revisited as often as one is in Provence. It is the most famous of Roman marvels in the region although it is difficult to explain to anyone who has not seen it why a three-tiered aqueduct crossing the valley of a minor river should so rank. Once experienced, it is unforgettable for its simplicity, majesty and setting. Nearly 300m long and 50m high, it spans the river Gard (or Gardon) between thickly wooded hills which drop to a beach on the left bank and to rocks on the right. It is built of blocks of masonry, some weighing up to six tons. They were quarried nearby and are soft golden yellow and grey in colour. They have weathered for almost two thousand years.

The function of this wonder of ancient engineering, constructed on the order of Agrippa, son-in-law to Augustus, was to carry water from Uzès to Nîmes. It is estimated that nearly 180 million litres flowed daily on the 50-kilometre journey. It was maintained until the fourth century, fell into total disuse in the ninth and was restored by order of Napoléon III in the nineteenth, although not for the purpose for which it was erected. By then a bridge had been added, in 1743, for road traffic at the level of the top of the first tier of arches.

The building of the aqueduct involved the use of a human tread-mill and of the block and tackle system. The water channel was on the top tier where there are over thirty small arches. It is possible to walk along the murky tunnel and to poke your head out, where the roofing has been re-moved. You may also, if you have a head for heights, walk along the un-guarded top but be warned that wind has blown some intrepid persons off. Nevertheless, it is common to see figures moving boldly from one end to the other.

The Pont du Gard is a major tourist attraction which has necessi-tated the laying out of car parks on both banks. From the one on the left you can walk to the aqueduct, past some rocky ground on which, in 1988, three ancient olive trees were replanted. They came – at vast expense – from an arid valley in Spain where they had lived since 905AD, so they are more than half as old as the bridge (c.19 BC). A protection society concerned about plans for developing surrounding hectares to attract more tourists, thus spoiling the natural setting, has enquired, reasonably, why some of the millions of Provençal olive trees could not have been used.

You reach the beach by steps down from a wood where trees from all over the world grow, and it is from here that you get the finest view of the aqueduct because the road bridge is hidden, although not the traffic which is still, at times, allowed to pass over it. Take your fill of this incomparable sight. Absorb its simple beauty.

One summer's night, in the church at Goult, we heard the

Schubert string quintet superbly played. We left as the audience thundered with rhythmic clapping for an encore, but how could any other music have topped it at that moment?

With what do you follow the Pont du Gard?

When you can tear yourself away, make for the N86, going north. Just beyond Valliguières turn right into the Forest of Malmont, which is linked to the Forest of Tavel, neither of which is a forest in the fairy-tale sense of thick, high trees ranging over hectares of dark, eerie woodland, but rather expanses of densely vegetated *garrigue* with stunted oaks. Through them the road winds to a high point, where there is an isolated power station, before descending to fields and fields of vines from which the local *rosé* is made. Tavel proclaims itself immodestly, but surely with justification, as the Premier Vin Rosé Cité de la France and what you see of the bustling little town, with many hôtels, suggests it is no idle boast. It is also a reminder that the premier Vin Rouge of the Rhône comes from even larger stretches of stony earth not far away – at Châteauneuf-du-Pape.

Here it was that the Avignon popes had a summer palace (they had another, since vanished, at Bédarrides five kilometres away) on a hill above the now prosperous little terraced town which has more points of *dégustation* than it has *boulangeries*. Châteauneuf-du-Pape is not only the most

Châteauneuf-du-Pape: Le Verger des Papes

famed of Rhône wines, it was the first in all France to receive an *appéllation contrôlée*, giving its producers 'copyright' in their vintage. We will wait to taste it until we have taken the Orange road, off which lies a turning through vineyards to the château. Little of it is left apart from a tower under reconstruction and two walls joined at right angles. It was already partly destroyed (the work of des Adrets) when the Germans, who stored explosives in it, blew it up in 1944. Its site commands a view of so much of what you have seen – the Rhône, the towers of Avignon, the start of the *garrigue*, the Alpilles, Dentelles, Luberon and Plateau, the vineyards, orchards and market gardens of the plain and, of course, Mont Ventoux. At the restaurant-bar Le Verger des Papes, a few steps down, you can have a light lunch (Aioli Provençal always served on Fridays), sample the prestigious local wine and sit on a terrace, savouring it all.

It is more than half-an-hour since the Pont du Gard. You will be ready for this last wonderful experience of Provence.

Index of People and Places

Places are shown in upper case.
Monarchs, popes, rivers and most geographical features are in groups.
Bold numbers indicate main entry.

Bibliography

The literature about Provence is vast and increasing all the time. This is a short list of volumes which I have found particularly helpful. I also derived much information from the dozens of pamphlets and brochures available, at source, from the various galleries, museums, châteaux, churches, abbeys, archaeological sites, gardens, *Offices de tourisme*, etc, which I visited.

Bailly, Robert, *Dictionnaire Des Communes Vaucluse*, Barthélemy, Avignon, 1985.
Bonner, A, *Songs of the Troubadours*, Allen & Unwin, London, 1973.
Clebert, Jean-Paul, *Guide de la Provence mysterieuse*, Tchou, 1986.
Cook, Theodore A, *Old Provence*, Rivington, London, 1905.
Dix, Carol, *The Camargue*, Gollancz, London, 1975.
Hamilton, Ronald, *A Holiday History of France*, Hogarth, London, 1985.
Jacobs, Michael, *A Guide to Provence*, Viking, London, 1988.
James, Henry, *A Little Tour in France*, Sidgwick & Jackson, London, 1987.
Mackendrick, Paul, *Roman France*, Bell, London, 1971.
Mehling, Marianne, (ed) *Provence and the Côte d'Azur*, Phaidon, London, 1986.
Michelin, *Tourist Guide: Provence*, Michelin, Paris & London, 1989.
Mistral, Frederic, *Memoirs*, Arnold, London, 1907.
Paire, Alain & Sarramon, Christian, *Villages de Provence*, Rivages, Marseille, 1984.
Pezet, Maurice, *Les Belles Heures du Pays d'Arles*, Lafitte, Marseille, 1982.
Pope-Hennessy, James, *Aspects of Provence*, Longman, London, 1952.
White, Freda, *West of the Rhône*, Faber, London, 1964.
Wylie, Laurence, *A Village in the Vaucluse* , Harvard UP, 1977.

In addition, as background reading, I much enjoyed Marcel Pagnol's memoirs and stories; M F K Fisher's eccentric account of Aix and Marseille, *Two Towns in Provence,* and Peter Mayle's highly entertaining and completely relaxing, *A Year in Provence.*

About the Author

Ian Norrie, born Southborough, Kent, in 1927 was a journalist in Eastbourne before becoming a bookseller. From 1956-88 his main occupation was as manager, then proprietor, of Hampstead's High Hill Bookshop but he also wrote and edited many books, contributed reviews and articles to various newspapers and magazines, and dabbled in publishing. He was secretary, and later, chairman, of the Society of Bookmen and served on the executive council of the National Book League (now Book Trust) for thirteen years, and on the Management Committee of the Booker Prize for three. He and Mavis, his wife, who have two daughters and three grandchildren, live for most of the year in Hadley Wood, Herts, and for part of it in the Vaucluse.

Michael Floyd, born Somerset, 1923, is an architect who qualified in 1950 after war service with Bomber Command had interrupted his studies. He was in private practice for thirty years and is a member of the Society of Architect Artists with whom he has exhibited at the RIBA. He contributed appreciations of the architecture of Hampstead, The City and Westminster to symposiums published by the High Hill Press during the 1960s. He lives in London, is married and has four children and nine grandchildren.

Notes on the Second Impression

February 1995

St-Saturnin-lès-Apt
p. 58   The extensive remains on the plateau include those of an early town as well as a castle.

Roussillon
p. 77   The walk among the ochre cliffs has been made less hazardous and is accessible in any footwear, but the sand still stains.
   The correct translation of the Aiguilles du Val des Fées is 'The Fairies' Valley'.

L'Isle-sur-la-Sorgue
p. 87   The town's image as an antiques centre has been sharpened. There is much less junk than formerly and there are many new, smart outlets, some in shop premises vacated by traders who have moved to out-of-town shopping complexes. Unfortunately the municipality has not provided the urgently needed extra parking space and the town is choked by traffic, especially on Sundays.

Avignon
p. 102   Flooding up to the ramparts recurred in 1994.
p. 104   There is still no reopening date for the Musée Calvet.

Arles
p. 161   The combined ticket for nine sites now costs 44f.
p. 167   The Picasso booklet is now out of print.

Les Baux
p. 187   There is evidence that the plateau may be converted into a theme park.

General
The author regrets that certain words in his text, such as 'miraculous' (p. 79) and 'revolution' (p. 140), are printed with hyphens in their midst. These errors are entirely due to the computer typesetter. If they had occurred in the days of hot metal, they could have been corrected cheaply. Now thanks to the prevailing revo-lutionary and miracu-lous technology the cost is prohibitive.

A companion volume

NEXT TIME ROUND IN THE DORDOGNE

also by IAN NORRIE
with drawings by Michael Floyd

will be published early in 1996